# CAT

**PRACTICE & REVISION KI**

Level C Paper 1

# Drafting Financial Statements

---

BPP is the **official provider** of training materials for the ACCA's CAT qualification. This Practice & Revision Kit forms part of a suite of learning tools, which also includes CD-ROMs for tuition and computer based assessment, and the innovative, internet-based 'virtual campus'.

**In this February 2003 edition**

- **DO YOU KNOW**? Checklists to test your knowledge and understanding of **Drafting Financial Statements** topics

- **QUESTIONS WITH HELP** and questions with **HELPING HANDS**

- Feedback on examiner's comments in **WHAT THE EXAMINER SAID** and an **EXAMINER'S MARKING SCHEME** at the end of each past examination question

- **TWO MOCK EXAMS** - the June 2002 and December 2002 examinations

**FOR JUNE AND DECEMBER 2003 EXAMS**

---

BPP Professional Education
*February 2003*

*First edition 1998*
*Sixth edition February 2003*

*ISBN 0 7517 1079 2 (Previous edition 0 7517 5207 X)*

**British Library Cataloguing-in-Publication Data**
*A catalogue record for this book*
*is available from the British Library*


*Published by*

*BPP Professional Education*
*Aldine House, Aldine Place*
*London W12 8AW*

*www.bpp.com*

*Printed in Great Britain by W M Print*
*45-47 Frederick Street*
*Walsall, West Midlands*
*WS2 9NE*

*All our rights reserved. No part of this publication may be reproduced, stored in a retrieval system or transmitted, in any form or by any means, electronic, mechanical, photocopying, recording or otherwise, without the prior written permission of BPP Professional Education.*

*We are grateful to the Association of Chartered Certified Accountants for permission to reproduce the syllabus, the pilot paper and past examination questions of which the Association holds the copyright. The answers have been prepared by BPP Professional Education.*

©

*BPP Professional Education*
*2003*

## Contents

|  | Page |
|---|---|
| **INDEX TO QUESTIONS AND ANSWERS** | (iv) |
| **INTRODUCTION** | |
| How to use this Practice & Revision Kit | (vi) |
| Syllabus | (vii) |
| The examination paper | (viii) |
| **QUESTIONS AND ANSWERS** | 3 |
| **MOCK EXAM 1** | |
| June 2002 examination: questions | 221 |
| June 2002 examination: answers | 227 |
| **MOCK EXAM 2** | |
| December 2002 examination: questions | 241 |
| December 2002 examination: answers | 247 |
| **TOPIC INDEX** | 259 |
| **REVIEW FORM & FREE PRIZE DRAW** | |
| **ORDER FORM** | |

## Index to questions and answers

|  |  | Page reference | Done |
|---|---|---|---|
| **PART A: INTRODUCTION TO FINANCIAL REPORTING** | | | |
| 1 | Question with help: Accounts preparation | 5 | ☐ |
| 2 | Limited company issues (6/00) | 9 | ☐ |
| 3 | Concepts (6/98) | 13 | ☐ |
| 4 | Interested parties (6/99) | 17 | ☐ |
| 5 | Lecture notes (12/99) | 21 | ☐ |
| **PART B: PREPARATION OF FINAL ACCOUNTS** | | | |
| 6 | Question with help: Income and expenditure accounts | 27 | ☐ |
| 7 | Happy Tickers | 31 | ☐ |
| 8 | Rackets | 37 | ☐ |
| 9 | K Guy (6/01) | 41 | ☐ |
| 10 | R Thomas (6/99) | 47 | ☐ |
| 11 | Mr Bends | 53 | ☐ |
| 12 | Opening balance sheet | 57 | ☐ |
| 13 | Smith, Jones and Matthews (12/98) | 61 | ☐ |
| 14 | Smith and Jones (Pilot Paper) | 67 | ☐ |
| 15 | Cain and Abel (12/00) | 71 | ☐ |
| 16 | Green, Brown and Gray | 77 | ☐ |
| 17 | G Padgett (12/01) | 81 | ☐ |
| 18 | Cheapstake (Pilot Paper, amended) | 85 | ☐ |
| 19 | Muggeridge (6/00) | 91 | ☐ |
| 20 | Arnfield (12/99) | 97 | ☐ |
| 21 | Pollard (12/01) | 103 | ☐ |
| **PART C: REGULATORY AND CONCEPTUAL FRAMEWORK** | | | |
| 22 | Question with help: Regulatory framework | 111 | ☐ |
| 23 | Conceptual framework (12/00) | 115 | ☐ |
| 24 | Regulators | 119 | ☐ |
| **PART D: ACCOUNTING STANDARDS** | | | |
| 25 | Question with help: Miscellaneous accounting standards | 125 | ☐ |
| 26 | New colleague (12/98) | 129 | ☐ |
| 27 | Goodwill | 133 | ☐ |
| **PART E: INTERPRETATION OF ACCOUNTS** | | | |
| 28 | Question with help: Emma | 139 | ☐ |
| 29 | Rene | 145 | ☐ |
| 30 | Newton (6/00) | 149 | ☐ |
| 31 | Evans (12/01) | 153 | ☐ |
| 32 | Dawson (6/01) | 157 | ☐ |
| 33 | Paper (6/00) | 163 | ☐ |
| 34 | Peanut (12/98) | 169 | ☐ |
| 35 | Hester (6/99) | 173 | ☐ |
| 36 | Lewis and Gordon (6/01) | 177 | ☐ |
| 37 | Gilson and Wardner (12/99) | 181 | ☐ |

## PART F: SIMPLE CONSOLIDATED ACCOUNTS

| | | |
|---|---|---|
| 38 | Question with help: Boo and Goose | 187 |
| 39 | Consolidated financial statements | 191 |
| 40 | Shark and Minnow (12/00) | 195 |
| 41 | Oak (12/98) | 201 |
| 42 | Bamber (12/99) | 205 |
| 43 | Addley (6/01) | 211 |
| 44 | Sand (12/01) | 215 |

*How to use this practice & revision kit*

# HOW TO USE THIS PRACTICE & REVISION KIT

### Aim of this Practice & Revision Kit

> To provide the practice to help you succeed in the examination for C1 *Drafting Financial Statements*.

To pass the examination you need a thorough understanding in all areas covered by the syllabus and teaching guide.

## Recommended approach

- Make sure you are able to answer questions on **everything** specified by the syllabus and teaching guide.

- Learning is an **active** process. Use the **DO YOU KNOW**? Checklists to test your knowledge and understanding of the topics covered in C1 *Drafting Financial Statements* by filling in the blank spaces. Then check your answers against the **DID YOU KNOW**? Checklists. Do not attempt any questions if you are unable to fill in any of the blanks - go back to your **BPP Interactive Text** and revise first.

- When you are revising a topic, think about the mistakes that you know that you should avoid by writing down **POSSIBLE PITFALLS** at the end of each **DO YOU KNOW**? Checklist.

- Once you have completed the checklists successfully, you should attempt all of the questions in this Practice & Revision Kit. Each section has one **QUESTION WITH HELP**, and one question without any help or guidance. All of the other questions have **HELPING HANDS** which you should use in order to help you answer the question in the best way.

- Once you have completed all of the questions in the body of this Practice & Revision Kit, you should attempt the **MOCK EXAMS** under examination conditions. Check your answers against our suggested solutions.

This approach is only a suggestion. You or your college may well adapt it to suit your needs.

# SYLLABUS

## DRAFTING FINANCIAL STATEMENTS - INDUSTRY AND COMMERCE

### AIM

To develop knowledge and understanding of the application of techniques to prepare year end financial statements from a trial balance and the interpretation of financial statements for a range of organisational forms.

### OBJECTIVES

At the completion of this module candidates should be able to:

1. describe the role and function of external financial reports
2. identify the users of external financial reports
3. explain the accounting concepts and conventions present in generally accepted accounting principles
4. draft limited company, sole trader and partnership year end financial statements
5. compare and contrast the form and content of financial statements for differing organisational types
6. use appropriate ratios to analyse financial statements for performance, position and adaptability

### CONTENT

(a) Financial statements: uses of and users, balance sheet, profit and loss account/income statement, cash flow statement and notes to the accounts: function, form and method of preparation for limited companies, partnerships and sole traders.

(b) General legal framework of limited companies, partnerships and sole traders; obligations of directors, partners and sole traders in respect of the accounts; forms of capital and capital structures.

(c) Generally accepted accounting principles and concepts: application of accounting standards and legislation to the preparation and presentation of financial statements.

(d) Taxation in accounts.

(e) Key features, including the capital structure, of financial statements of a wider range of organisations; standard classification/chart of accounts; general principles of consolidation.

(f) Interpretation of accounting information for different types of organisation to assess performance, liquidity and vulnerability; use of accounting ratios, trend analysis, performance indicators.

*The examination paper*

# THE EXAMINATION PAPER

## Assessment methods and format of the paper

Questions based on demonstrating that the candidates have acquired the required skills with all questions to be answered.

| | *Number of marks* |
|---|---|
| Four compulsory questions | 100 |

Time allowed: 3 hours

## Prerequisite knowledge

Successful completion of Levels A and B.

## Development of Paper C1

This paper builds on the knowledge acquired in Paper A1 and Paper B1 enabling students to draft year end financial statements and interpret financial statements for a range of organisations.

It should be noted that a detailed knowledge of UK accounting standards and the UK regulatory environment is not required. However students should be familiar with the principles expressed in these documents and be able to apply them in general terms when drafting financial statements.

*December 2002* *Marks*

| | | |
|---|---|---|
| 1 | Accounts from incomplete records | 40 |
| 2 | Cash flow statement; usefulness of statements | 30 |
| 3 | Consolidated profit and loss account | 15 |
| 4 | Profitability and liquidity ratios: calculation and commentary | 15 |

*June 2002*

| | | |
|---|---|---|
| 1 | Partnership accounts from trial balance | 40 |
| 2 | Consolidated P & L and balance sheet; definition of associate | 30 |
| 3 | Analysis of company's performance using ratios | 15 |
| 4 | Financial statements: objective; useful characteristics | 15 |

> **What the examiner said**
> The candidates sitting this paper achieved a similar pass rate in this examination to the June 2001 sitting. As in previous examinations, candidates tended to be better prepared for computational aspects of questions rather than those parts requiring written answers.

*December 2001* *Marks*

| | | |
|---|---|---|
| 1 | Limited liability accounts from trial balance | 40 |
| 2 | Cash flow statement; usefulness of statements | 30 |
| 3 | Consolidated balance sheet | 15 |
| 4 | Preparation of profit and loss account from ratios | 15 |

# The examination paper

> **What the examiner said**
>
> Candidates sitting this paper achieved a similar pass rate in this examination to previous sittings. On this occasion no particular question stood out as being very well answered. Typically, candidates did moderately well in all questions to secure a good pass.

## June 2001

| | | |
|---|---|---|
| 1 | Preparation of accounts from incomplete records | 40 |
| 2 | Cash flow statement: preparation and discussion | 30 |
| 3 | Consolidated profit and loss account | 15 |
| 4 | Analysis of company's performance using ratios | 15 |

> **What the examiner said**
>
> The pass rate for this examination was similar to the pass rate for the December 2000 sitting. Candidates did well on both the computational questions as well as those questions requiring written answers.

## December 2000

| | | |
|---|---|---|
| 1 | Partnership: P&L, current accounts and balance sheet | 40 |
| 2 | Consolidated balance sheet; intercompany adjustments | 30 |
| 3 | Ratio analysis | 15 |
| 4 | Conceptual framework; accounting concepts | 15 |

> **What the examiner said**
>
> The pass rate for this examination has slightly improved from the June 2000 sitting. Once again candidates tended to do better on the computational questions rather than the questions requiring written answers.
>
> The paper was designed to test not only a candidate's ability to draft financial statements, but also whether they were able to analyse financial information and understand the accounting conceptual framework that underpins financial reporting. The examination paper consisted of four compulsory questions and most candidates.

## June 2000

| | | Marks |
|---|---|---|
| 1 | Limited company accounts from trial balance | 40 |
| 2 | Cash flow statement: preparation and discussion | 30 |
| 3 | Ratio analysis; limitations of ratio analysis | 15 |
| 4 | Types of share and loan capital | 15 |

> **What the examiner said**
>
> The pass rate for this examination was similar to that achieved in December 1999. As in previous examinations, candidates tended to do better on the computational questions than on the narrative questions.

## The examination paper

*December 1999* — *Marks*

1. Preparation of limited company accounts from trial balance — 40
2. Consolidated financial statements — 30
3. Ratio analysis — 15
4. Limitations of and alternatives to historic cost accounting — 15

> **What the examiner said**
> The pass rate for this examination was slightly lower than for previous papers, with candidates performing better on computational than narrative questions.

*June 1999* — *Marks*

1. Accounts from incomplete records — 40
2. Cash flow statement and commentary — 30
3. Financial trends; calculation of selected ratios — 15
4. Objectives, qualitative characteristics and users of financial statements — 15

> **What the examiner said**
> The majority of candidates were well prepared for this examination with some candidates producing exceptionally good answers. In general candidates tended to be stronger on the computational aspects rather than the written evaluation elements.

*December 1998* — *Marks*

1. Partnership: P&L, current accounts and balance sheet — 40
2. Consolidated balance sheet; intercompany trading transactions — 30
3. Calculation of and discussion of ratios — 15
4. SSAP 17, forerunner of FRS 12 — 15

> **What the examiner said**
> The pass rate for this examination was again high, with candidates demonstrating a sound knowledge of the techniques, required in drafting financial statements, together with good computational skills.

*June 1998* — *Marks*

1. Preparation of limited company accounts from list of balances — 40
2. Cash flow statement: preparation and discussion — 30
3. Ratio analysis — 15
4. Discussion of accounting concepts — 15

**What the examiner said**

The standard of answers for this (the first) sitting was very pleasing. Candidates were particularly good at drafting the financial statements but weaker on the accounting concepts. Presentation was very good – candidates took the time to prepare neat working papers that were cross-referenced to appropriate parts of their answer.

## Pilot Paper

| | | |
|---|---|---|
| 1 | Preparation of limited company accounts from trial balance; forerunner of FRS 12 | 40 |
| 2 | Consolidated balance sheet; criteria for consolidation of subsidiary | 30 |
| 3 | Report on company performance with ratio analysis | 15 |
| 4 | Amalgamation of two sole traders to form partnership | 15 |

## The examination paper

### Examiner's approach to the level C examinations

**Approach to the paper**

Paper C1 seeks to build on the skills and techniques acquired in papers A1 and B1. The objectives of this paper are to test a candidate's ability to prepare and interpret year end financial statements for a range of organisations. For a candidate to be successful they will need a thorough knowledge and understanding of the application of the accounting techniques involved.

**Interpretation of syllabus**

The syllabus is wide ranging and therefore it is impossible to test every subject area in a single exam. Questions will therefore tend to be focused on specific areas. However, a question which requires the preparation of a financial statement may also be used to test other aspects of a candidate's understanding of accounting principles.

It would be unusual for a C1 examination paper not to include the preparation of a profit and loss account and balance sheet for either a sole trader, partnership or company. Another fundamental area of the syllabus is the analysis of an organisation's financial performance. Candidates should not only be able to calculate accounting ratios, but also be able to interpret them within the context of the information they have been given.

**Examination format**

The examination paper consists of four compulsory questions. Questions 1 and 2 are worth 40 marks and 30 marks respectively. Questions 3 and 4 are worth 15 marks each. It would be unusual for the examination paper not to include the preparation of a profit and loss account and balance sheet for either a sole trader, partnership or a company. Another fundamental area of the syllabus is the analysis of an organisation's financial performance. Candidates should not only know how to calculate accounting ratios, but also be able to interpret them within the context of the information they nave been given.

The style and presentation of an answer is important. When drafting final account statements UK candidates will be expected to apply appropriate UK accounting standards and conventions in their answers. Overseas candidates should prepare statements in accordance with international or local accounting standards. Written answers may also require a particular format to be adopted, for example: a report, a briefing note, a memorandum or just personal notes. In all cases it should be clear to the examiner that you have used the format requested in the question.

# Questions and answers

# DO YOU KNOW? - INTRODUCTION TO FINANCIAL REPORTING

- *Check that you can fill in the blanks in the statements below before you attempt any questions. If in doubt, you should go back to your BPP Interactive Text and revise first.*

- The accounting equation is as follows

  ..................................................

- The two main financial statements of a business are the ..................... and the ..................... .

- You should be able to identify the qualities of good accounting information, which are:

  o .....................        o .....................

  o .....................        o .....................

  o .....................        o .....................

  o .....................

  TRY QUESTION 2

- An ..................... is something a business ..................... . A ..................... is something a business ..................... .

- Stocks are valued at the lower of ..................... and ..................... (SSAP 9).

- To calculate cost of goods sold, the formula is:

  ..................................................

  TRY QUESTION 1

- The four fundamental accounting concepts are ....................., ....................., ..................... and ..................... .

  o ..................... - an enterprise will carry on in existence for the foreseeable future.

  o ..................... - revenues and expenses should be taken into account in the period to which they relate.

  o ..................... - like items should be accounting for in the same way, even though they arise in different periods.

  o ..................... - costs should be charged, and liabilities accounted for, as soon as they are recognised; income should be taken into account when its receipt is reasonably certain.

- A number of other concepts may be regarded as fundamental, and you should make sure that you understand them.

  o The entity concept        o .....................

  o The separate valuation principle        o .....................

  o The historical cost convention        o The stable monetary unit

  o .....................        o The realisation concept

  o Duality

  TRY QUESTION 3

- *Possible pitfalls*

  Write down the mistakes you know you should avoid.

## Questions and answers

### DID YOU KNOW? - INTRODUCTION TO FINANCIAL REPORTING

- *Could you fill in the blanks? The answers are in bold. Use this page for revision purposes as you approach the exam.*
- The accounting equation is as follows

    **Capital + liabilities = assets**

- The two main financial statements of a business are the **balance sheet** and the **profit and loss account**.
- You should be able to identify the qualities of good accounting information, which are:

    - **Relevance**
    - **Reliability**
    - **Objectivity**
    - **Comparability**
    - **Comprehensibility**
    - **Completeness**
    - **Timeliness**

    TRY QUESTION 2

- An **asset** is something a business **owns**. A **liability** is something a business **owes**.
- Stocks are valued at the lower of **cost** and **net realisable value** (SSAP 9).
- To calculate cost of goods sold, the formula is:

    **Opening stock + purchases – closing stock**

    TRY QUESTION 1

- The four fundamental accounting concepts are **the going concern concept, the accruals (or matching) concept, the consistency concept and the prudence concept**.
    - **Going concern** - an enterprise will carry on in existence for the foreseeable future.
    - **Accruals** - revenues and expenses should be taken into account in the period to which they relate.
    - **Consistency** - like items should be accounted for in the same way, even though they arise in different periods.
    - **Prudence** - costs should be charged, and liabilities accounted for, as soon as they are recognised; income should be taken into account when its receipt is reasonably certain.
- A number of other concepts may be regarded as fundamental, and you should make sure that you understand them.

    - The entity concept
    - The separate valuation principle
    - The historical cost convention
    - **Objectivity**
    - Duality
    - **The money measurement concept**
    - **The materiality concept**
    - The stable monetary unit
    - The realisation concept

    TRY QUESTION 3

- *Possible pitfalls*
    - **Not applying concepts and definitions in the context of the question**
    - **Mistakes in double entry**
    - **Not presenting workings clearly so the examiner cannot follow your answer.**

# Questions and answers

## 1 QUESTION WITH HELP: ACCOUNTS PREPARATION

The following trial balance has been extracted from the ledger of Mr Yousef, a sole trader.

TRIAL BALANCE AS AT 31 MAY 20X6

|  | Dr £ | Cr £ |
|---|---|---|
| Sales |  | 138,078 |
| Purchases | 82,350 |  |
| Carriage | 5,144 |  |
| Drawings | 7,800 |  |
| Rent, rates and insurance | 6,622 |  |
| Postage and stationery | 3,001 |  |
| Advertising | 1,330 |  |
| Salaries and wages | 26,420 |  |
| Bad debts | 877 |  |
| Provision for doubtful debts |  | 130 |
| Debtors | 12,120 |  |
| Creditors |  | 6,471 |
| Cash on hand | 177 |  |
| Cash at bank | 1,002 |  |
| Stock as at 1 June 20X5 | 11,927 |  |
| Equipment |  |  |
|   at cost | 58,000 |  |
|   accumulated depreciation |  | 19,000 |
| Capital |  | 53,091 |
|  | 216,770 | 216,770 |

The following additional information as at 31 May 20X6 is available.

(a) Rent is accrued by £210.
(b) Rates have been prepaid by £880.
(c) £2,211 of carriage represents carriage inwards on purchases.
(d) Equipment is to be depreciated at 15% per annum using the straight line method.
(e) The provision for bad debts to be increased by £40.
(f) Stock at the close of business has been valued at £13,551.

*Required*

Prepare a trading and profit and loss account for the year ended 31 May 20X6 and a balance sheet as at that date.

> *If you are stuck, look at the next page for detailed help as to how you should tackle this question.*

## Questions and answers

**APPROACHING THE ANSWER**

**Step 1** Presentation is always important, but especially so in accounts preparation questions. It is best to draw up a pro forma profit and loss account and balance sheet using the headings given to you in the trial balance, and allowing a whole side of paper for each. Do not enter any numbers at this stage.

**Step 2** Now work through all of the additional information that you are given and perform any calculations that are required. For example the information in (a) is the only additional information you are given about stock, so you can go ahead and enter the figures for opening stock in your pro forma profit and loss account and for closing stock in the P & L and balance sheet. Other calculations (for example the depreciation provision) can best be done in a separate working. In other cases you may be able to do your workings on the face of your pro forma P & L or balance sheet (for example 'Provision for bad debts (130 + 40)). When you check your own answers you will see a variety of such presentation techniques demonstrated in our suggested solutions to the questions in this section and you should try to emulate them.

**Step 3** The golden rule while you are doing your calculations is to keep the double entry going. The depreciation provision affects fixed assets in the balance sheet and the depreciation charge in the P & L. Accruals affect the relevant P & L account and the accruals provision in the balance sheet. Make both entries as soon as you have the relevant figures.

ie the depreciation charge is 15% × £58,000 = £8,700

So the entries are:

| | | £ | £ |
|---|---|---|---|
| DEBIT | Depreciation charge (P & L) | 8,700 | |
| CREDIT | Provision for depreciation | | 8,700 |

The provision for deprecation thus increases to £(19,000 + 8,700) = £27,700.

**Step 4** Finally, insert any remaining figures, taking them straight from the trial balance, and add up your profit and loss account and balance sheet. If it does not balance you have made a mistake. Work out the difference and see if it matches any of the figures you have been given or have calculated - this should enable you to correct your mistake. If not divide the difference by two and see if the resulting figure matches another one (this will mean that you have treated a debit as a credit or vice versa). If this fails it is probably not worth spending more time on the question, unless you have plenty of spare time left. Assuming time is short, just leave a note ('Difference: £X') to show the examiner that you are aware that there is still a problem and get on with the next question.

# 1 ANSWER TO QUESTION WITH HELP: ACCOUNTS PREPARATION

**MR YOUSEF**
**PROFIT AND LOSS ACCOUNT FOR THE YEAR ENDED 31 MAY 20X6**

|  | £ | £ |
|---|---:|---:|
| Sales |  | 138,078 |
| Opening stock | 11,927 |  |
| Purchases (W1) | 84,561 |  |
|  | 96,488 |  |
| Less closing stock | 13,551 |  |
| Cost of goods sold |  | 82,937 |
| Gross profit |  | 55,141 |
| Carriage out (W2) | 2,933 |  |
| Rent, rates and insurance (W3) | 5,952 |  |
| Postage and stationery | 3,001 |  |
| Advertising | 1,330 |  |
| Salaries and wages | 26,420 |  |
| Bad debts | 877 |  |
| Depreciation charge (W4) | 8,700 |  |
| Increase in provision for bad debts | 40 |  |
|  |  | 49,253 |
| Net profit |  | 5,888 |

**MR YOUSEF**
**BALANCE SHEET AS AT 31 MAY 20X6**

|  | Cost £ | Accumulated depreciation £ | NBV £ |
|---|---:|---:|---:|
| *Fixed assets* |  |  |  |
| Equipment | 58,000 | 27,700 | 30,300 |
| *Current assets* |  |  |  |
| Stock |  | 13,551 |  |
| Debtors | 12,120 |  |  |
| Less provision for bad debts | 170 |  |  |
|  |  | 11,950 |  |
| Prepayment |  | 880 |  |
| Cash |  | 177 |  |
| Bank |  | 1,002 |  |
|  |  | 27,560 |  |
| *Current liabilities* |  |  |  |
| Creditors |  | 6,471 |  |
| Accrual |  | 210 |  |
|  |  | 6,681 |  |
| Net current assets |  |  | 20,879 |
|  |  |  | 51,179 |
| *Capital* |  |  |  |
| At 1 June 20X5 |  |  | 53,091 |
| Profit for year |  |  | 5,888 |
|  |  |  | 58,979 |
| Drawings |  |  | (7,800) |
| At 31 May 20X6 |  |  | 51,179 |

## Questions and answers

*Workings*

1. Purchases

|  | £ |
|---|---|
| Per trial balance | 82,350 |
| Add carriage inwards | 2,211 |
| Per P & L a/c | 84,561 |

2. Carriage out = £5,144 – £2,211 = £2,933.

3. *Rent, rates and insurance*

|  | £ |
|---|---|
| Per trial balance | 6,622 |
| Add rent accrual | 210 |
| Less rates prepayment | (880) |
| Per P & L a/c | 5,952 |

4. Depreciation charge = 15% × £58,000 = £8,700

## 2 LIMITED COMPANY ISSUES (6/00)

A client of your firm has been trading successfully as a sole trader in the UK for a number of years. However, her business has grown so much that she now thinks it is time to consider converting the business into a limited company.

*Required*

Prepare some brief notes for the meeting that explain:

(a) The main advantages and disadvantages of operating as a limited company rather than as a sole trader (6 marks)

(b) The main types of share capital and their characteristics (5 marks)

(c) The main differences between share capital and debentures (4 marks)

**(15 marks)**

---

**Helping hand**

1 Both the advantages and disadvantages of trading as a limited company follow from the same fact.

2 Parts (b) and (c) are straightforward tests of knowledge.

## 2   ANSWER: LIMITED COMPANY ISSUES

> **Examiner's comment.** Those candidates who were familiar with this area of the syllabus were able to write good and concise answers. However, a number of candidates compensated for their lack of knowledge by producing lengthy and incorrect answers.

### NOTES FOR MEETING WITH CLIENT

(a) **Advantages and disadvantages of operating as a limited company**

   (i) **Limited liability.** Limited companies offer limited liability to their owners. This means that the maximum amount that an owner stands to lose in the event that the company becomes insolvent and cannot pay off its debts is his share of the capital in the business.

   (ii) **Ease of raising finance.** Providers of finance would be more prepared to lend to a company with limited liability than to a sole trader or partnership.

   (iii) **Perpetual succession.** With a partnership, a new partnership must be formed when one partner dies or retires. A share in a company is transferable.

   (iv) **Tax** advantages

**Disadvantages of operating as a limited company**

   (i) **Formation** and **annual registration costs**

   (ii) **Compliance with statute.** Under the Companies Act 1985 companies must prepare annual accounts and have them audited, keep statutory registers and publish accounts.

   (iii) **Compliance with SSAPs and FRSs.**

> **Helping hand**
> Pros and cons both follow from limited liability.

(b) **Types of share capital**

   (i) **Ordinary share capital**

   This is the most common type of share capital. Ordinary shareholders are in effect the **owners** of a company. They own the equity and the reserves.

   Ordinary shares carry **no right to a fixed dividend** but are entitled to all profits left after payment of any preference dividend.

   Should the company be wound up, any surplus not distributed is shared between the ordinary shareholders. Ordinary shares **normally carry voting rights.**

   (ii) **Preference share capital**

   Preference shares are shares which confer certain preferential rights on their holder. They carry the **right to a final dividend** which is expressed as a percentage of their nominal value. Preference dividends have priority over ordinary dividends; in other words if the directors of a company which to pay a dividend they must pay any preference dividend first.

   The rights attaching to preference shares vary according to the company's constitution. Generally preference shares **do not carry a right to vote.** They may give a priority right to **a return of capital** if the company goes into liquidation.

## Questions and answers

(c) **Differences between share capital and debentures**

  (i) **Shareholders** are **members** of a company while **debenture holders** are **creditors**.

  (ii) **Shareholders** receive **dividends** (appropriations of profit) whereas **debenture holders** are entitled to a fixed rate of **interest** (an expense charged against revenue.

  (iii) Debenture holders can take legal action against a company if their interest is not paid when due, whereas **shareholders cannot enforce the payment of dividends**.

  (iv) **Debentures** are often **secured on company assets,** whereas shares are not.

  (v) Debenture interest must be paid even if there are no profits. **Dividends are only paid when profits allow.**

## 3 CONCEPTS (6/98)

Your friend has just started studying accounting and has asked for some help in understanding certain accounting concepts.

*Required*

Produce brief notes for your friend which explain the following accounting concepts. Give an example of each.

(a) Business entity (3 marks)
(b) Going concern (3 marks)
(c) Materiality (3 marks)
(d) Prudence (3 marks)
(e) Substance over form (3 marks)

**(15 marks)**

## 3  ANSWER: CONCEPTS

> **Helping hand.** This question was designed to establish whether candidates understood some of the important accounting concepts that underpin the financial reporting framework
>
> **Examiner's comment.** This was the most poorly answered question on the examination paper. Too many candidates resorted to guesswork and produced some interesting but wrong answers.

*Notes on accounting concepts*

When preparing accounts, certain **fundamental concepts** or assumptions apply and are generally accepted.

(a) *Business entity*

Under this convention, the business is regarded as a **separate entity** from its owner(s) for the purposes of accounting. This applies whether or not the business is a separate legal entity, as is the case with a limited company.

For example, a sole trader takes some money from the till of his shop for his own purposes. Although the shop belongs to the trader, the transaction must be recorded in the accounts as '**drawings**'.

(b) *Going concern*

Under this convention it is assumed that the **business will continue to operate** for the foreseeable future and that operations will not be cut back or the business closed down. The going concern convention is implied unless it is stated otherwise.

The significance of this can be seen when applied to an example. Suppose a business has a number of machines which are used in the making of a bicycle. Together, as they are being used in the manufacture of the end product, the machines are worth far more than they would be if sold off individually, as they would have to be if the business closed.

(c) *Materiality*

This means that **significant items need to be disclosed**. Accounting standards, for instance apply to material items. A material item is one which is likely to influence the decisions of accounts users.

For example, it is normal to capitalise fixed assets and depreciate them. If, however, a company with a £20m turnover purchased a wastepaper bin, the item would be expensed as it is not material in the context of the financial statements.

(d) *Prudence*

Under this convention revenue and profits are treated differently from expenses and losses. **Losses and expenses** must be **provided for** as soon as they are known or can be estimated, but **revenue and profits** must **not be anticipated**.

For example if it were probable that a company would lose a court case, the loss would have to be provided for. If it were likely to win, this fact would merely be noted.

(e) *Substance over form*

Under this convention, transactions are accounted for and disclosed according to their **substance and not their legal form**.

An obvious example of this is to be found in the rules on consolidation of subsidiaries. A company may not legally **own** another, in that it may not possess more than 50% of the share capital. However, if it **controls** the other company, the latter is a subsidiary and must be consolidated.

## 4 INTERESTED PARTIES (6/99)

Your company regularly publishes financial statements for its shareholders. However, the director of resources is aware that there may be other groups who are also interested in the company's financial statements.

*Required*

You have been asked to prepare a memorandum for the director of resources which:

(a) Outlines the objectives of producing financial statements (3 marks)

(b) Identifies the main qualitative characteristics of financial information (4 marks)

(c) Identifies five other potential users of the company's financial statements and explains their specific information requirements (8 marks)

**(15 marks)**

---

**Helping hand**

1 A good approach would be to answer in terms of the ASB's *Statement of Principles*, but you do not have to, provided the points you make are valid.

2 Our answer is longer than you would need to do in an exam.

# 4 ANSWER: INTERESTED PARTIES

> **Examiner's comment.**
> This was most candidates' weakest answer. Candidates simply did not develop their answers properly.

**MEMORANDUM**

To: Director of Resources
     XYZ Ltd
From: C A Technician
Date: 14 January 20X0

*Objectives, qualitative characteristics and users of financial statements*

(a) *Objectives of financial statements*

The objective of producing financial statements is explained in the *Statement of Principles*, a document published by the Accounting Standards Board in December 1999. It is 'to provide information about the reporting entity's **financial performance and financial position** that is **useful** to a wide range of users for assessing the **stewardship** of the entity's management for making **economic decisions**'.

The *Statement* goes on to state that **investors**, ie shareholders are the **most important class of user**, and that the information they need must enable them to assess the entity's ability to generate cash and to assess its **financial adaptability**.

The main financial statements aim to achieve these objectives as follows.

(i) The **performance statements**, that is the profit and loss account and the statement of total recognised gains and losses show the **return on the resources** that the entity controls.

(ii) The **balance sheet** provides information on the **financial position** of the company by identifying the economic resources it controls and its liquidity and solvency.

(iii) The **cash flow statement** specifies the principle sources of the company's cash inflows and outflows, thereby showing the company's **ability to generate cash** in accordance with the objective.

> **Helping hand**
> This material is from the *Statement of Principles*.

(b) *Qualitative characteristics of financial statements*

Below are some features that accounting information should have if it is to be useful.

(i) **Relevance.** The information provided should satisfy the needs of information users. In the case of company accounts, clearly a wide range of information will be needed to satisfy a wide range of users.

(ii) **Comprehensibility.** Information may be difficult to understand because it is skimpy or incomplete; but too much detail is also a defect which can cause difficulties of understanding.

(iii) **Reliability.** Information will be more reliable if it is independently verified. The law requires that the accounts published by limited companies should be verified by auditors, who must be independent of the company and must hold an approved qualification.

## Questions and answers

(iv) **Completeness**. A company's accounts should present a rounded picture of its economic activities.

(v) **Objectivity**. Information should be as objective as possible. This is particularly the case where conflicting interests operate and an unbiased presentation of information is needed. In the context of preparing accounts, where many decisions must be based on judgement rather than objective facts, this problem often arises. Management are often inclined to paint a rosy picture of a company's profitability to make their own performance look impressive. By contrast, auditors responsible for verifying the accounts are inclined to take a more prudent view so that they cannot be held liable by, say, a supplier misled into granting credit to a shaky company.

(vi) **Timeliness**. The usefulness of information is reduced if it does not appear until long after the period to which it relates, or if it is produced at unreasonably long intervals. What constitutes a long interval depends on the circumstances: management of a company may need very frequent (perhaps daily) information on cash flows to run the business efficiently; but shareholders are normally content to see accounts produced annually.

(vii) **Comparability**. Information should be produced on a consistent basis so that valid comparisons can be made with information from previous periods and with information produced by other sources (for example the accounts of similar companies operating in the same line of business).

> **Helping hand**
> Any four of these points would be sufficient.

(c) The other people who might be interested in financial information about the company may be classified as follows.

(i) **Managers of the company**. These are people appointed by the company's owners to supervise the day-to-day activities of the company. They need information about the company's financial situation as it is currently and as it is expected to be in the future. This is to enable them to manage the business efficiently and to take effective control and planning decisions.

(ii) **Trade contacts**, including suppliers who provide goods to the company on credit and customers who purchase the goods or services provided by the company. Suppliers will want to know about the company's ability to pay its debts; customers need to know that the company is a secure source of supply and is in no danger of having to close down.

(iii) **Providers of finance to the company**. These might include a bank which permits the company to operate an overdraft, or provides longer-term finance by granting a loan. The bank will want to ensure that the company is able to keep up with interest payments, and eventually to repay the amounts advanced.

(iv) **The Inland Revenue**, who will want to know about business profits in order to assess the tax payable by the company, and also the Customs and Excise.

(v) **Employees of the company**. These should have a right to information about the company's financial situation, because their future careers and the size of their wages and salaries depend on it.

## 5 LECTURE NOTES (12/99)

Your director of finance is to present a lecture to a group of accounting trainees at a local college entitled 'Accounting Under Inflationary Conditions'. She has asked you to help with her preparation for the lecture.

*Required*

Prepare some brief notes which identify and explain:

(a) The main criticisms of historic cost accounting during periods of inflation (10 marks)

(b) The alternatives to historic cost accounting which have been developed (5 marks)

**(15 marks)**

> **Helping hand**
> 1  You should try to explain your points as well as listing them.
> 2  Give examples where appropriate.

# 5 ANSWER: LECTURE NOTES

> **Examiner's comment**
>
> Those candidates who had thoroughly revised were able to achieve a high mark on this question. However, too many candidates made token attempts or produced completely wrong answers.

## ACCOUNTING UNDER INFLATIONARY CONDITIONS
## NOTES FOR LECTURE

(a) It has become increasingly clear that accounts prepared on a traditional historical cost basis can present financial information in a misleading manner. The greatest criticisms of traditional accounting concepts have stemmed from their inability to reflect the effects of changing price levels.

(i) **Fixed asset values are unrealistic.** The most striking example is **property**. Although it is a statutory requirement that the market value of an interest in land should be disclosed in the directors' report if it is significantly different from the balance sheet figure, and although some companies have periodically updated the balance sheet values, revaluations have not been reported consistently.

(ii) If fixed assets are retained in the books at their historical cost, **unrealised holding gains are not recognised**. This means that the total holding gain, if any, will be brought into account during the year in which the asset is realised, rather than spread over the period during which it was owned.

(iii) **Depreciation is inadequate to finance the replacement of fixed assets.** Depreciation is not provided for in order to enforce retention of profits and thus ensure that funds are available for asset replacement. It is intended as a measure of the contribution of fixed assets to the company's activities in the period. However, an incidental effect of providing for depreciation is that not all liquid funds can be paid out to investors and so funds for asset replacement are on hand. What is important is not the replacement of one asset by an identical new one (something that rarely happens) but the replacement of the operating capability represented by the old asset.

(iv) **Holding gains on stocks are included in profit.** During a period of high inflation the monetary value of stocks held may increase significantly while they are being processed. The conventions of historical cost accounting lead to the unrealised part of this holding gain (known as stock appreciation) being included in profit for the year. It is estimated that in the late 1970s nearly half the declared profits of companies were due to stock appreciation.

> **Helping hand**
>
> Here we have explained what holding gains are.

(v) **Profits (or losses) on holdings of net monetary items are not shown.** In periods of inflation the purchasing power, and thus the value, of money falls. It follows that an investment in money will have a lower real value at the end of a period of time than it did at the beginning. A loss has been incurred. Similarly, the real value of a monetary liability will reduce over a period of time and a gain will be made.

(vi) **The true effect of inflation on capital maintenance is not shown.** To a large extent this follows from the points already mentioned. It is a widely held

## Questions and answers

principle that distributable profits should only be recognised after full allowance has been made for any erosion in the capital value of a business. In historical cost accounts, although capital is maintained in nominal money terms, it may not be in real terms. In other words, profits may be distributed to the detriment of the long-term viability of the business. This criticism may be made by those who advocate capital maintenance in physical terms and those who prefer money capital maintenance as measured by pounds of current purchasing power.

(vii) **Comparisons over time are unrealistic.** This will tend to an exaggeration of growth. For example, if a company's profit in 1967 was £100,000 and in 2001 £500,000, a shareholder's initial reaction might be that the company had done rather well. If, however, it was then revealed that with £100,000 in 1967 he could buy exactly the same goods as with £500,000 in 2001, the apparent growth would seem less impressive.

> **Helping hand**
>
> A hypothetical example helps make the point.

(b) The two principal alternatives to historic cost accounting are **current purchasing power** accounting and **current cost accounting.**

**Current purchasing power**

In accounting, the value of income and capital is measured in terms of money. In simple terms, profit is the difference between the closing and opening balance sheet values (after adjustment for new sources of funds and applications such as dividend distribution). If, because of inflation, the value of assets in the closing balance sheet is shown at a higher monetary amount than assets in the opening balance sheet, a profit has been made. In historic cost accounting, it is assumed that a monetary unit of £1 is a stable measurement; inflation removes this stability.

CPP accounting attempts to provide a more satisfactory methods of valuing profit and capital by establishing a stable unit of monetary measurement, **£1 of current purchasing power,** as at the end of the accounting period under review.

CPP arguably provides a more satisfactory system of accounting since **transactions are expressed in terms of 'today's money'** and similarly, the **balance sheet values are adjusted for inflation,** so as to give users of financial information a set of figures with which they can:

**Current cost accounting**

CPP and CCA accounting are different concepts, in that CCP accounting makes adjustments for general inflationary price changes, whereas CCA makes adjustments to allow for **specific price movements** (changes in the deprival value of assets). The two conventions use different concepts of capital maintenance (namely operating capability with CCA, and general purchasing power with CPP).

In addition CPP is based on the use of a general price index. In contrast, CCA only makes use of a specific price index where it is not possible to obtain the current value of an asset by other means (eg direct valuation).

Arguably, CCA is **more soundly based** than CPP, and the reported current operating profit is considered to be **more relevant** to many decisions such as wages, tax and dividends.

# DO YOU KNOW? - PREPARATION OF FINAL ACCOUNTS

- *Check that you can fill in the blanks in the statements below before you attempt any questions. If in doubt, you should go back to your BPP Interactive Text and revise first.*

- Trading accounts, profit and loss accounts and balance sheets have standard formats depending on the type of business. These must be committed to memory.

- Sole traders' accounts are not (strictly speaking) governed by legislation or accounting standards, but accountants should always follow best practice when preparing accounts of any kind.

- In tackling an incomplete records question you should take the following steps.

  o Prepare an opening statement of affairs if no balance sheet is given in the question.

  o Write up or complete any bank account transactions and write up the cash receipts and payments account. There will usually be a balancing figure on the cash account, usually ................., ................. or ................. .

  o Write up or complete the debtors and creditors control account. This will give you sales and purchases.

  o Make any adjustments for ................. and ................. . Write up the trading account, the profit and loss account and the balance sheet.

  TRY QUESTION 9

- The liability of a *partnership* to its owners is recorded in two accounts.

  o .................: records fixed capital of each partner

  o .................: records each partner's share of profits and losses less any drawings made

- When a new partner is admitted goodwill is brought in in the ................. profit-sharing ratio and eliminated in the ................. .

- Whenever two or more partnerships amalgamate the accounting problems are much the same as when a partner retires or a new partner is admitted in terms of:

  o revaluing assets
  o valuing goodwill
  o establishing new profit share

  TRY QUESTION 13

- On dissolution of a partnership, a ................. is prepared.

- Bodies such as *clubs and societies* do not set out primarily to make a profit, therefore it is inappropriate to prepare a profit and loss account. Instead an ................. is prepared.

- There is no capital account in the balance sheet, instead there is an accumulated fund (= net assets).

  TRY QUESTION 7

- *Limited companies* also have special features. Their accounts include certain items that are not found in the accounts of an unincorporated business such as ................. , ................. and ................. . There are specialised accounting transactions associated with these items.

- The accounting records and financial statements of a limited company are strictly regulated by statute.

  TRY QUESTION 19

- *Possible pitfalls*

  Write down the mistakes you know you should avoid.

## Questions and answers

### DID YOU KNOW? - PREPARATION OF FINAL ACCOUNTS

- *Could you fill in the blanks? The answers are in bold. Use this page for revision purposes as you approach the exam.*

- Trading accounts, profit and loss accounts and balance sheets have standard formats depending on the type of business. These must be committed to memory.

- Sole traders' accounts are not (strictly speaking) governed by legislation or accounting standards, but accountants should always follow best practice when preparing accounts of any kind.

- In tackling an incomplete records question you should take the following steps.
    - Prepare an opening statement of affairs if no balance sheet is given in the question.
    - Write up or complete any bank account transactions and write up the cash receipts and payments account. There will usually be a balancing figure on the cash account, usually **drawings, bankings** or **cash sales**.
    - Write up or complete the debtors and creditors control account. This will give you sales and purchases.
    - Make any adjustments for **accruals** and **prepayments**. Write up the trading account, the profit and loss account and the balance sheet.

    TRY QUESTION 9

- The liability of a *partnership* to its owners is recorded in two accounts.
    - **Capital account**: records fixed capital of each partner
    - **Current account**: records each partner's share of profits and losses less any drawings made

- When a new partner is admitted goodwill is brought in in the **old** profit-sharing ratio and eliminated in the **new**.

- Whenever two or more partnerships amalgamate the accounting problems are much the same as when a partner retires or a new partner is admitted in terms of:
    - revaluing assets
    - valuing goodwill
    - establishing new profit share

    TRY QUESTION 13

- On dissolution of a partnership, a **realisation account** is prepared.

- Bodies such as *clubs and societies* do not set out primarily to make a profit, therefore it is inappropriate to prepare a profit and loss account. Instead an **income and expenditure account** is prepared.

- There is no capital account in the balance sheet, instead there is an accumulated fund (= net assets).

    TRY QUESTION 7

- *Limited companies* also have special features. Their accounts include certain items that are not found in the accounts of an unincorporated business such as **dividends, share capital and debentures**. There are specialised accounting transactions associated with these items.

- The accounting records and financial statements of a limited company are strictly regulated by statute.

    TRY QUESTION 19

- *Possible pitfalls*
    - **Panic with incomplete records questions. These are actually very straightforward if you adopt a systematic approach.**
    - **Confusing capital and current accounts in partnership questions.**
    - **Confusing workings with notes to the financial statements.**

# 6 QUESTION WITH HELP: INCOME AND EXPENDITURE ACCOUNTS

The HB tennis club was formed on 1 April 20X0 and has the following receipts and payments account for the six months ended 30 September 20X0.

| Receipts | £ | Payments | £ |
|---|---|---|---|
| Subscriptions | 12,600 | Purchase of equipment | 4,080 |
| Tournament fees | 465 | Groundsman's wages | 4,520 |
| Bank interest | 43 | Rent and business rates | 636 |
| Sale of club ties | 373 | Heating and lighting | 674 |
| Life membership fees | 4,200 | Postage and stationery | 41 |
|  |  | Court maintenance | 1,000 |
|  |  | Tournament prizes | 132 |
|  |  | Purchase of club ties | 450 |
|  |  | Balance c/d | 6,148 |
|  | 17,681 |  | 17,681 |

*Notes*

(a) The annual subscription fee is £300. On 30 September there were still five members who had not paid their annual subscription, but this money was received on 4 October 20X0.

(b) The equipment is expected to be used by the club for five years, after which time it will need to be replaced. Its estimated scrap value at that time is £50.

(c) During the six months, the club purchased 100 ties printed with its own design. Forty of these ties remained unsold at 30 September 20X0.

(d) The club had paid business rates in advance on 30 September 20X0 of £68.

(e) The club treasurer estimates that the following amounts should be accrued for expenses.

| | £ |
|---|---|
| Groundsman's wages | 40 |
| Postage and stationery | 12 |
| Heating and lighting | 53 |

(f) The life membership fees received relate to payments made by four families. The scheme allows families to pay £1,050 which entitles them to membership for life without further payment. It has been agreed that such receipts would be credited to income and expenditure in equal instalments over ten years.

*Required*

(a) Prepare the club's income and expenditure account for the six months ended 30 September 20X0.

(b) Prepare the club's balance sheet at 30 September 20X0.

*If you are stuck, look at the next page for detailed help as to how you should tackle this question.*

## Questions and answers

**APPROACHING THE ANSWER**

**Step 1** The only real difference between an income and expenditure account and a profit and loss account is the format. Group together all the items of income and have a line for the total. Then do the same for expenditure. The net figure is called a 'surplus' and it is transferred to an accumulated fund which replaces the 'retained profit' on the balance sheet.

|  | £ | £ |
|---|---|---|
| *Income* |  |  |
| Subscriptions |  | X |
| Net income from tournaments |  | X |
| Bank interest received |  | X |
| Net income from sale of club ties |  | X |
| Life membership fees |  | <u>X</u> |
|  |  | X |
| *Expenditure* |  |  |
| Depreciation of equipment | X |  |
| Groundsman's wages | X |  |
| Rent and business rates | X |  |
| Heating and lighting | <u>X</u> |  |
|  |  | <u>X</u> |
| Surplus transferred to accumulated fund |  | <u>X</u> |

Don't forget that, in this question, you are preparing accounts for six months, whereas much of the information given relates to a full year.

**Step 2** Work out the subscriptions income. First take the figure for the full year, then divide it by 6/12. Then add the subscriptions owing: £5 × £300, again divided by 6/12 because £300 is the *annual* subscription.

Subscriptions will appear in the income and expenditure account, and there will also be headings under current assets for subscriptions due and under current liabilities for subscriptions paid in advance. Be especially careful here to think through the implications of the fact that you are preparing accounts for six months.

**Step 3** You need to do a 'trading' account to calculate the figure for income from the sale of club ties. These trading accounts are very common in club accounts questions - often there is a bar trading account. The formula is, of course:

|  | £ | £ |
|---|---|---|
| Sales |  | X |
| Opening stock (if any) | X |  |
| Purchases | X |  |
| Less closing stock (if any) | (X) |  |
| Cost of goods sold |  | <u>X</u> |
| Net income |  | <u>X</u> |

**Step 4** Now calculate the life membership fees. Again, remember that this is *six months'* income, so you will need to divide the total amount received by 10 and then by 6/12.

**Step 5** Calculate the depreciation. Assume straight line depreciation and do not forget the scrap value.

**Step 6** Slot the figures you have calculated into your income and expenditure account and balance sheet.

**Questions and answers**

## 6 ANSWER TO QUESTION WITH HELP: INCOME AND EXPENDITURE ACCOUNTS

(a) HB TENNIS CLUB
INCOME AND EXPENDITURE ACCOUNT
FOR THE SIX MONTHS ENDED 30 SEPTEMBER 20X0

|  | £ | £ |
|---|---:|---:|
| *Income* |  |  |
| Subscriptions (W1) |  | 7,050 |
| Net income from tournaments £(465 – 132) |  | 333 |
| Bank interest received |  | 43 |
| Net income from sale of club ties (W2) |  | 103 |
| Life membership fees (W3) |  | 210 |
|  |  | 7,739 |
| *Expenditure* |  |  |
| Depreciation of equipment (W4) | 403 |  |
| Groundsman's wages (4,520 + 40) | 4,560 |  |
| Rent and business rates (636 – 68) | 568 |  |
| Heating and lighting (674 + 53) | 727 |  |
| Postage and stationery (41 + 12) | 53 |  |
| Court maintenance | 1,000 |  |
|  |  | 7,311 |
| Surplus transferred to accumulated fund |  | 428 |

(b) HB TENNIS CLUB
BALANCE SHEET AS AT 30 SEPTEMBER 20X0

|  | £ | £ | £ |
|---|---:|---:|---:|
| *Fixed assets* |  |  |  |
| Equipment at cost |  |  | 4,080 |
| Depreciation to date |  |  | 403 |
|  |  |  | 3,677 |
| *Current assets* |  |  |  |
| Stock of ties (W2) |  | 180 |  |
| Subscriptions owing (W1) |  | 750 |  |
| Prepaid business rates |  | 68 |  |
| Bank |  | 6,148 |  |
|  |  | 7,146 |  |
| *Current liabilities* |  |  |  |
| Subscriptions in advance (W1) | 6,300 |  |  |
| Accrued expenses | 105 |  |  |
|  |  | 6,405 |  |
| Net current assets |  |  | 741 |
|  |  |  | 4,418 |
| *Financed by* |  |  |  |
| Accumulated fund |  |  | 428 |
| Life membership fund £(4,200 – 210) |  |  | 3,990 |
|  |  |  | 4,418 |

*Workings*

1  *Subscriptions income*

|  | £ |
|---|---:|
| Subscriptions received for full year | 12,600 |
| ∴ subscriptions for six months | 6,300 |
| Plus subscriptions outstanding (5 × £150) | 750 |
|  | 7,050 |

## Questions and answers

2  *Sale of club ties*

|  | £ | £ |
|---|---|---|
| Sales income |  | 373 |
| Purchases of ties | 450 |  |
| less closing stock (40/100 × £450) | 180 |  |
|  |  | 270 |
| Net income from sale of club ties |  | 103 |

3  *Life membership fees*

|  | £ |
|---|---|
| Fees received (4 × £1,050) | 4,200 |
| One years' instalment (÷ 10) | 420 |
| ∴ income for six months | 210 |

4  *Depreciation of equipment*

|  | £ |
|---|---|
| Purchase cost of equipment | 4,080 |
| Estimated scrap value | 50 |
|  | 4,030 |
| Annual depreciation (÷ 5 assuming straight line depreciation) | 806 |
| Charge for six months | 403 |

*Questions and answers*

## 7  HAPPY TICKERS

The accounting records of the Happy Tickers Sports and Social Club are in a mess. You manage to find the following information to help you prepare the accounts for the year to 31 December 20Y0.

SUMMARISED BALANCE SHEET 31 DECEMBER 20X9

|  | £ |  | £ |
|---|---|---|---|
| Half-share in motorised roller | 600 | Insurance (3 months) | 150 |
|  |  | Subscriptions 20Y0 | 120 |
| New sports equipment unsold | 1,000 | Life subscriptions | 1,400 |
|  |  |  | 1,670 |
| Used sports equipment at valuation | 700 | Accumulated fund | 2,900 |
| Rent (2 months) | 200 |  |  |
| Subscriptions 20X9 | 60 |  |  |
| Cafe stocks | 800 |  |  |
| Cash and bank | 1,210 |  |  |
|  | 4,570 |  | 4,570 |

*Receipts in year to 31 December 20Y0*

|  | £ |
|---|---|
| Subscriptions - 20X9 | 40 |
|       - 20Y0 | 1,100 |
|       - 20Y1 | 80 |
|       - life | 200 |
| From sales of new sports equipment | 900 |
| From sales of used sports equipment | 14 |
| Cafe takings | 4,660 |
|  | 6,994 |

*Payments in the year to 31 December 20Y0*

|  | £ |
|---|---|
| Rent (for 12 months) | 1,200 |
| Insurance (for 18 months) | 900 |
| To suppliers of sports equipment | 1,000 |
| To cafe suppliers | 1,900 |
| Wages of cafe manager | 2,000 |
| Total cost of repairing motorised roller | 450 |
|  | 7,450 |

*Notes*

(a) Ownership and all expenses of the motorised roller are agreed to be shared equally with the Carefree Conveyancers Sports and Social Club which occupies a nearby site. The roller cost a total of £2,000 on 1 January 20X6 and had an estimated life of 10 years.

(b) Life subscriptions are brought into income equally over 10 years, in a scheme begun in 20X5. Since the scheme began the cost of £200 per person has been constant. Prior to 31 December 20X9 10 life subscriptions had been received.

(c) Four more annual subscriptions of £20 each had been promised relating to 20Y0, but not yet received. Annual subscriptions promised but unpaid are carried forward for a maximum of 12 months.

(d) New sports equipment is sold to members at cost plus 50%. Used equipment is sold off to members at book valuation. Half the sports equipment bought in the year (all from a cash and carry supplier) has been used within the club, and half made available for sale,

## Questions and answers

new, to members. The 'used equipment at valuation' figure in the 31 December 20Y0 balance sheet is to remain at £700.

(e) Closing cafe stocks are £850, and £80 is owed to suppliers at 31 December 20Y0.

*Required*

(a) Calculate profit on cafe operations and profit on sale of sports equipment. (6 marks)

(b) Prepare statement of subscription income for 20Y0. (4 marks)

(c) Prepare income and expenditure statement for the year to 31 December 20Y0, and balance sheet as at 31 December 20Y0. (11 marks)

(d) Why do life subscriptions appear as a liability? (4 marks)

**(25 marks)**

---

**Helping hand**

1  In part (a) there is an incomplete records element.

2  When calculating the life subscriptions allocation to the current year, you need to think how many life members there are.

3  In the income and expenditure account, the used sports equipment at valuation figure must remain constant.

# 7 ANSWER: HAPPY TICKERS

(a) *Cafe operations*

|  | £ | £ |
|---|---:|---:|
| Sales |  | 4,660 |
| Stocks at 1.1.Y0 | 800 |  |
| Purchases | 1,980 |  |
|  | 2,780 |  |
| Stocks at 31.12.Y0 | (850) |  |
|  |  | 1,930 |
| Gross profit |  | 2,730 |
| Wages |  | 2,000 |
| Net profit |  | 730 |

> **Helping hand**
>
> Use the mark-up techniques from your studies of incomplete records to calculate the profit on the sale of sports equipment.

Sales of sports equipment

|  | £ | £ |
|---|---:|---:|
| Sales |  | 900 |
| Opening stock | 1,000 |  |
| Purchases | 500 |  |
|  | 1,500 |  |
| Closing stock (balancing figure) | (900) |  |
| Cost of sales (900 × 100/150) |  | 600 |
| Profit |  | 300 |

(b)

|  | £ |
|---|---:|
| Annual subscriptions (W1) | 1,300 |
| Life subscriptions (W2) | 220 |
|  | 1,520 |

> **Helping hand**
>
> £200 represents 1 new life member, so there are 10+1=11 altogether. This means that 11 × 20 = £220 is allocated to the current year.

*Workings*

1 *Annual subscriptions*

|  | £ |
|---|---:|
| b/f 31.12.X9 (in advance) | 120 |
| Received in year | 1,100 |
| Owed for 20Y0 at 31.12.20Y0 (4 × 20) | 80 |
|  | 1,300 |

2 *Life subscriptions*

|  | £ |
|---|---:|
| Life member subscriptions at 31.12.X9 | 1,400 |
| New subscriptions in year to 31.12.Y0 | 200 |
|  | 1,600 |
| Less 11 × £20 allocated to current year | 220 |
| Life subscriptions c/f at 31.12.Y0 | 1,380 |

## Questions and answers

(c) HAPPY TICKERS SPORTS AND SOCIAL CLUB
INCOME AND EXPENDITURE STATEMENT
FOR THE YEAR TO 31 DECEMBER 20Y0

|  | £ | £ |
|---|---:|---:|
| *Income* |  |  |
| Subscriptions |  | 1,520 |
| Cafe operations |  | 730 |
| Sale of sports equipment |  | 300 |
|  |  | 2,550 |
| *Expenses* |  |  |
| Rent | 1,200 |  |
| 20X9 subscription written off | 20 |  |
| Insurance 900 × 12/18 | 600 |  |
| Roller repairs (½ × 450) | 225 |  |
| Write down of used sports equipment* | 486 |  |
| Depreciation of roller | 100 |  |
|  |  | 2,631 |
| Excess of expenditure over income |  | 81 |
| Accumulated fund brought forward at 1 January 20Y0 |  | 2,900 |
| Accumulated fund carried forward at 31 December 20Y0 |  | 2,819 |

> **Helping hand**
>
> The used sports equipment at valuation figure must remain constant, so any additions must be written down. The write-down is calculated as follows.
>
> |  | £ |
> |---|---:|
> | Total purchases of sports equipment | 1,000 |
> | ∴ Used in club (½ × 1,000) | 500 |
> | Less: used equipment sold | (14) |
> | Additions to be written down | 486 |

HAPPY TICKERS SPORTS AND SOCIAL CLUB
BALANCE SHEET AS AT 31 DECEMBER 20Y0

|  | £ | £ | £ |
|---|---:|---:|---:|
| *Fixed assets* |  |  |  |
| Half share in motorised roller |  | 500 |  |
| New sports equipment unsold (part (a)) |  | 900 |  |
| Used sports equipment at valuation |  | 700 |  |
|  |  |  | 2,100 |
| *Current assets* |  |  |  |
| Rent pre-paid (2 months) | 200 |  |  |
| Insurance pre-paid (900 – 150 – 600) | 150 |  |  |
| Carefree Conveyancers (half repairs of roller) | 225 |  |  |
| Subscriptions in arrears (4 × £20) | 80 |  |  |
| Cafe stocks | 850 |  |  |
| Cash (1,210 + 6,994 – 7,450) | 754 |  |  |
|  |  | 2,259 |  |
| *Current liabilities* |  |  |  |
| Subscriptions in advance | 80 |  |  |
| Life subscriptions (part (b) W2) | 1,380 |  |  |
| Cafe supplies | 80 |  |  |
|  |  | 1,540 |  |
| *Net current assets* |  |  | 719 |
| *Net assets* |  |  | 2,819 |
| Accumulated fund brought forward |  | 2,900 |  |
| Less: loss for year |  | (81) |  |
| Accumulated fund carried forward |  |  | 2,819 |

(d) Life subscriptions are treated as a **liability** because they are monies which have been received from members for services in future periods. They are therefore 'owing' to future periods. Strictly speaking they are not liabilities but **deferred income**.

The principle is similar to that seen at work in the treatment of subscriptions received in advance. These too are shown as credit balances because they are 'owed' to the following year. The life subscriptions are similar but received for many years in advance, not just one.

## 8  RACKETS

You have been appointed the bookkeeper of a tennis club called Rackets Unlimited. The club began on 1 July 20W9, and no accounts have yet been prepared. The club has three ways of receiving subscriptions.

(a) £10 per year.

(b) If two years' subscriptions are paid at once £1 may be deducted from the second year. If three year's subscriptions are paid at once, £2 may also be deducted from the third year.

(c) If 10 years' subscriptions are paid at once no deductions are allowed, but members are regarded as members for life.

You have completed the following table of subscription receipts.

| Member | Relevant to membership year ended 30.6.X0 Date received | Amount £ | Relevant to membership year ended 30.6.X1 Date received | Amount £ | Relevant to membership year ended 30.6.X2 Date received | Amount £ |
|---|---|---|---|---|---|---|
| A | July 'W9 | 10 | | | | |
| B | July 'W9 | 10 | July 'X0 | 10 | | |
| C | July 'W9 | 10 | June 'X0 | 10 | July 'X1 | 10 |
| D | Sept 'W9 | 10 | Sept 'X0 | 27 | | |
| E | Oct 'W9 | 27 | | | | |
| F | Oct 'W9 | 10 | July 'X0 | 10 | June 'X1 | 27 |
| G | Oct 'W9 | 100 | | | | |
| H | Oct 'W9 | 10 | June 'X0 | 10 | June 'X1 | 100 |
| I | Oct 'W9 | 10 | June 'X0 | 19 | | |
| J | | | July 'X1 | 10 | | |
| K | | | July 'X0 | 27 | | |
| L | Dec 'W9 | 10 | | | June 'X1 | 10 |
| M | July 'X0 | 19 | | | | |
| N | | | July 'X1 | 100 | | |

The club does not intend to accrue for any income not received by the date of preparation of financial statements.

*Required*

(a) To assist in the preparation of some accounts, complete a table with the following headings.

| Member | Income year to 30.6.X0 | Income year to 30.6.X1 | Balance c/f at 30.6.X1 Dr | Cr |
|---|---|---|---|---|

(13 marks)

(b) State *two* comments about your table which you think might be helpful to the club committee. (2 marks)

**(15 marks)**

**Helping hand**

This question is helpful, since it actually gives you the format of the table you are to use.

# 8 ANSWER: RACKETS

(a)

> **Helping hand**
>
> Try to keep your table as neat and methodical as possible.

RACKETS UNLIMITED
TABLE OF SUBSCRIPTIONS INCOME

| Member | Income year to 30.6.X0 £ | Income year to 30.6.X1 £ | Balance c/f at 30.6.X1 Dr £ | Cr £ |
|---|---|---|---|---|
| A | 10 | – | – | – |
| B | 10 | 10 | – | – |
| C | 10 | 10 | – | – |
| D | 10 | 10 | – | 17 |
| E | 10 | 9 | – | 8 |
| F | 10 | 10 | – | 27 |
| G | 10 | 10 | – | 80 |
| H | 10 | 10 | – | 100 |
| I | 10 | 10 | – | 9 |
| J | – | 10 | 10 | – |
| K | – | 10 | – | 17 |
| l | 10 | – | – | 10 |
| M | 10 | 9 | – | – |
| N | – | 10 | 10 | – |

(b) Any two of the following.

   (i) It is **not clear** what **amount is due for a period paid in advance** or how this is to be accounted for.

   (ii) **Life subscriptions** appear to be spread **over ten years**. It is **not clear why** this figure has been chosen.

   (iii) **Reductions** are made for **payments in advance**. It might be more realistic to treat these reductions as **discounts** and show the gross amount of the subscription and the discount separately.

*Questions and answers*

## 9 K GUY (6/01)

K Guy runs a small business and has asked you to help him prepare his financial statements for the year ended 31 May 20X1. He does not use a double entry system of accounting to maintain his accounts, but is able to provide you with the following summaries of his cash account and bank account.

CASH ACCOUNT SUMMARY

|  | £ | £ |
|---|---|---|
| *Balance at 1 June 20X1* |  | 150 |
| *Receipts* |  |  |
| Cash sales | 16,400 |  |
| Debtors | 3,000 |  |
|  |  | 19,400 |
|  |  | 19,550 |
| *Payments* |  |  |
| Drawings | 11,655 |  |
| Repairs | 2,680 |  |
| Motor van expenses | 3,225 |  |
| Miscellaneous expenses | 300 |  |
| Cash banked | 1,460 |  |
|  |  | 19,320 |
| *Balance at 31 May 20X1* |  | 230 |

BANK ACCOUNT SUMMARY

|  | £ | £ |
|---|---|---|
| *Balance at 1 June 20X1* |  | 8,560 |
| *Receipts* |  |  |
| Debtors | 65,600 |  |
| Cash banked | 1,460 |  |
|  |  | 67,060 |
|  |  | 75,620 |
| *Payments* |  |  |
| Electricity | 1,450 |  |
| Insurance | 1,000 |  |
| Interest on loan | 1,545 |  |
| Rent | 1,350 |  |
| Telephone | 490 |  |
| Trade creditors | 50,560 |  |
| Wages | 15,750 |  |
|  |  | 72,145 |
| *Balance at 31 May 20X1* |  | 3,475 |

K Guy also provides you with the following information for the year ended 31 May 20X1.

(a) Goods costing £2,510 were withdrawn from the business for K Guy's own use.

(b) Bad debts of £350 were written off.

(c) Rent owing was £330 at 1 June 20X0.

(d) Insurance was prepaid by £250 at 31 May 20X1.

(e) Depreciation on fixed assets is provided for annually at 25% using the reducing balance method.

(f) The machinery and motor van had written down values of £12,560 and £4,580 respectively at 1 June 20X0.

(g) There was £255 owing to the bank for interest on the loan at 31 May 20X1.

(h) Discounts received for the year were £1,770 and discounts given to customers were £2,000. These discounts are for prompt payment.

## Questions and answers

*Other information relating to K Guy's business*

|  | 1 June 20X1 | 31 May 20X1 |
|---|---|---|
|  | £ | £ |
| Stocks | 4,500 | 8,760 |
| Debtors | 15,400 | 16,680 |
| Creditors | 8,050 | 9,425 |
| Bank loan | 12,000 | 12,000 |

*Required*

(a) Calculate the value of K Guy's capital at 1 June 20X0. (5 marks)

(b) Prepare:

  (i) K Guy's trading and profit and loss account for the year ended 31 May 20X1.

  (18 marks)

  (ii) K Guy's balance sheet as at 31 May 20X1. (13 marks)

(c) Briefly explain prepaid and accrued expenses and explain why it is necessary to account for them in the financial statements. (4 marks)

**(40 marks)**

---

**Helping hand**

1  The good thing about this question is that it is broken down into parts. These tell you the order in which to approach the question.

2  Start off with the control accounts for sales and purchases, but don't forget cash sales or good withdrawn.

# Questions and answers

## 9 ANSWER: K GUY

> **Examiner's comment** Most candidates made a good attempt at Part (a) of the question, although the format and presentation of answers could have been better. In Part (b)(i) the calculation of the sales figure and the purchases figure caused the most difficulty for candidates. However, even those candidates that incorrectly calculated these figures were still able to pick up some of the marks if they also included workings which the examiner was able to follow. Part (c) was reasonably well attempted, those candidates who also included reference to the matching concept in their answer were able to gain maximum marks.

(a) K GUY
CAPITAL AS AT 1 JUNE 20X0

|  | £ | £ |
|---|---:|---:|
| *Assets* | | |
| Cash in hand | | 150 |
| Bank | | 8,560 |
| Machinery | | 12,560 |
| Van | | 4,580 |
| Stock | | 4,500 |
| Debtors | | 15,400 |
| | | 45,750 |
| *Liabilities* | | |
| Creditors | 8,050 | |
| Accruals: rent | 330 | |
| Bank loan | 12,000 | |
| | | 20,380 |
| | | 25,370 |

> **Helping hand**
>
> You are asked to calculate the opening capital in order to feed into the balance sheet in Part (c).

43

## Questions and answers

(b) (i) K GUY
TRADING AND PROFIT AND LOSS ACCOUNT
FOR THE YEAR ENDED 31 MAY 20X1

|  | £ | £ |
|---|---:|---:|
| Sales (W1) |  | 88,630 |
| Opening stock | 4,500 |  |
| Purchases (W2) | 51,195 |  |
| Closing stock | (8,760) |  |
| Cost of sales |  | 46,935 |
| Gross profit |  | 41,695 |
| Discounts received |  | 1,770 |
|  |  | 43,465 |
| Less expenses |  |  |
| Electricity | 1,450 |  |
| Insurance (W3) | 750 |  |
| Interest on loan (W4) | 1,800 |  |
| Rent (W5) | 1,020 |  |
| Telephone | 490 |  |
| Wages | 15,750 |  |
| Discounts allowed | 2,000 |  |
| Repairs | 2,680 |  |
| Motor van expenses | 3,225 |  |
| Miscellaneous expenses | 300 |  |
| Bad debts | 350 |  |
| Depreciation (W6) | 4,285 |  |
|  |  | 34,100 |
| Net profit |  | 9,365 |

(ii) K GUY
BALANCE SHEET AS AT 31 MAY 20X1

|  | £ | £ |
|---|---:|---:|
| *Fixed assets* (W6) |  | 12,855 |
| *Current assets* |  |  |
| Stock | 8,760 |  |
| Debtors | 16,680 |  |
| Prepayments: insurance | 250 |  |
| Bank | 3,475 |  |
| Cash | 230 |  |
|  | 29,395 |  |
| *Current liabilities* |  |  |
| Creditors | 9,425 |  |
| Accrual: loan interest | 255 |  |
|  | 9,680 |  |
|  |  | 19,715 |
| *Net current assets* |  | 32,570 |
| *Long-term liabilities* |  |  |
| Loan |  | 12,000 |
|  |  | 20,570 |
| *Capital* |  |  |
| At 1 June 20X0 (part (a)) |  | 25,370 |
| Profit for year |  | 9,365 |
| Drawings (W7) |  | (14,165) |
|  |  | (20,570) |

*Workings*

1   *Sales*

DEBTORS CONTROL ACCOUNT

|  | £ |  | £ |
|---|---:|---|---:|
| Bal b/fwd | 15,400 | Receipts from debtors (65,600 + 3,000) | 68,600 |
|  |  | Discounts allowed | 2,000 |
|  |  | Bad debts | 350 |
| Credit sales (bal fig) | 72,230 | Balance c/fwd 31 May 20X1 | 16,680 |
|  | 87,630 |  | 87,630 |

Total sales = £72,230 + £16,400

            = £88,630

> **Helping hand**
> You must remember to add on cash sales.

2   *Purchases*

CREDITORS CONTROL ACCOUNT

|  | £ |  | £ |
|---|---:|---|---:|
| Bank | 50,560 | Bal b/fwd 1 June 20X0 | 8,050 |
| Discounts | 1,770 |  |  |
| Balance c/fwd 31 May 20X1 | 9,425 | ∴ Credit purchases (bal fig) | 53,705 |
|  | 61,755 |  | 61,755 |

| Purchases | 53,705 |
|---|---:|
| Less goods withdrawn | 2,510 |
|  | 51,195 |

> **Helping hand**
> Goods taken from stock are a deduction from purchases.

3   *Insurance*

|  | £ |
|---|---:|
| Bank | 1,000 |
| Less prepayment | 250 |
|  | 750 |

4   *Interest on loan*

|  | £ |
|---|---:|
| Bank | 1,545 |
| Accrual | 255 |
|  | 1,800 |

5   *Rent*

|  | £ |
|---|---:|
| Bank | 1,350 |
| Accrual | (330) |
|  | 1,020 |

6   *Depreciation and fixed assets*

|  | Machinery £ | Van £ | Total £ |
|---|---:|---:|---:|
| NBV at 1 June 20X0 | 12,560 | 4,580 | 17,140 |
| Depreciation charge 25% | 3,140 | 1,145 | 4,285 |
| NBV at 31 May 20X1 | 9,420 | 3,435 | 12,855 |

## Questions and answers

7   Drawings

|  | £ |
|---|---|
| Cash | 11,655 |
| Stock | 2,510 |
|  | 14,165 |

(c) **Prepaid expenses** are **payments in advance**, that is for goods or services which will not be used up until the following accounting period. **Accrued expenses** are the opposite, that is expenses on goods and services used in the current accounting period but only **paid for in a subsequent accounting period**.

The accruals or matching concept states that, in computing profit, revenue earned must be **matched** against the expenditure incurred in earning it. The preparer of accounts must include expenditure relating to a particular period regardless of when it is paid.

**Accrued expenses**, though paid in the next accounting period, **relate to the current one** and must be **charged in the current period's** profit and loss account In the **balance sheet** accrued expenses appear as **a liability**.

**Prepaid expenses**, though paid in this accounting period **relate to the next one**. They should therefore **be excluded from the current period's profit and loss account**. In the **balance sheet** prepayments appear as a **liability**.

## 10  R THOMAS (6/99)

R Thomas is a successful sole trader, but is not particularly good at maintaining financial records. He asks you to prepare his final accounts for the year to 31 May 20X9. You establish that at 1 June 20X8 he had the following balances.

|  |  | £'000 |
|---|---|---|
| Vehicles at cost |  | 100 |
| Equipment at cost |  | 200 |
| Provisions for depreciation: | Vehicles | 50 |
|  | Equipment | 80 |
| Trade creditors |  | 170 |
| Trade debtors |  | 225 |
| Prepayments: | Rent | 12 |
|  | Insurance | 15 |
| Accruals: | Telephone | 4 |
|  | Electricity | 6 |
| Bank |  | 28 |
| Stock |  | 150 |
| Capital |  | 420 |

In addition, R Thomas is also able to provide the following information for the financial year to 31 May 20X9.

(i) Receipts from customers were £1,200,000 and there are trade debtors at 31 May 20X9 of £230,000.

(ii) Bad debts of £35,000 were written off during the year and discounts to customers amounted to £30,000.

(iii) Personal drawings amounted to £100,000.

(iv) Payments to suppliers were £650,000 and £155,000 was owing to suppliers as at 31 May 20X9.

(v) Stock at 31 May 20X9 was £190,000.

(vi) Rent of £10,000 and telephone bills of £1,000 were paid in advance at 31 May 20X9.

(vii) A £15,000 electricity bill was still to be paid at 31 May 20X9.

(viii) Other payments made during the year were as follows.

|  | £'000 |
|---|---|
| Insurance | 25 |
| Rent | 40 |
| Rates | 5 |
| Electricity | 30 |
| Telephone | 14 |
| Motor vehicle expenses | 20 |
| Wages | 120 |
|  | 254 |

(ix) Depreciation on vehicles is provided annually at a rate of 25% on their original cost. Depreciation on equipment is based on 20% of its written down value.

*Required*

Prepare the following statements for R Thomas.

(a) The trading and profit and loss account for the year ended 31 May 20X9.  (26 marks)
(b) The balance sheet as at 31 May 20X9.  (14 marks)

Show any necessary supporting workings.  **(40 marks)**

## Questions and answers

**Helping hand**

1 It is always best in this kind of question, to start off with the bank account. This will enable you to arrive at a figure for sales and purchases using control accounts simply by following through the double entry. It is a good idea to tick off each item on the question paper as you deal with it.

2 Be careful, with T accounts for accruals and prepayments, to get the figures on the right side of the account.

# 10 ANSWER: R THOMAS

> **Examiner's comment**
>
> Most candidates performed well, showing detailed workings. Problem areas were accruals and prepayments and using the straight-line method of depreciation where the reducing balance was required.

(a) R THOMAS
TRADING, PROFIT AND LOSS ACCOUNT
FOR THE YEAR ENDED 31 MAY 20X9

|  | £'000 | £'000 |
|---|---|---|
| Sales (W2) |  | 1,270 |
| Cost of goods sold |  |  |
|     Opening stock | 150 |  |
|     Purchases (W3) | 635 |  |
|  | 785 |  |
| Closing stock | 190 |  |
|  |  | 595 |
|  |  | 675 |
| Expenses |  |  |
|     Rent (W4) | 42 |  |
|     Insurance (W5) | 40 |  |
|     Rates | 5 |  |
|     Electricity (W6) | 39 |  |
|     Telephone (W7) | 9 |  |
|     Motor vehicle expenses | 20 |  |
|     Wages | 120 |  |
|     Bad debts | 35 |  |
|     Discounts allowed | 30 |  |
|     Depreciation (W9) | 49 |  |
|  |  | 389 |
| Net profit |  | 286 |

## Questions and answers

(b) R THOMAS
BALANCE SHEET AS AT 31 MAY 20X9

|  | Cost £'000 | Accum. Depn. £'000 | Net book value £'000 |
|---|---|---|---|
| *Fixed assets* |  |  |  |
| Vehicles (W9) | 100 | 75 | 25 |
| Equipment | 200 | 104 | 96 |
|  | 300 | 179 | 121 |

*Current assets*
| Stock | 190 | | |
| Debtors | 230 | | |
| Prepayments (W8) | 11 | | |
| Bank (W1) | 224 | | |
|  |  | 655 | |

*Current liabilities*
| Creditors | 155 | | |
| Accruals (electricity) | 15 | | |
|  |  | 170 | |

| Net current assets | | | 485 |
|  | | | 606 |

*Proprietor's capital*
| As at 1 June 20X8 | | | 420 |
| Profit for the year | | | 286 |
|  | | | 706 |
| Less drawings | | | 100 |
|  | | | 606 |

*Workings*

1   *Bank account*

BANK

| | £'000 | | £'000 |
|---|---|---|---|
| Balance | 28 | Creditors control a/c | 650 |
| Debtors control | 1,200 | Insurance | 25 |
|  |  | Rent | 40 |
|  |  | Rates | 5 |
|  |  | Electricity | 30 |
|  |  | Telephone | 14 |
|  |  | Motor vehicle exp. | 20 |
|  |  | Wages | 120 |
|  |  | Drawings | 100 |
|  |  | Balance c/f | 224 |
|  | 1,228 |  | 1,228 |

> **Helping hand.**
> Don't forget drawings, or the bank account won't balance – neither will your balance sheet!

2   *Sales*

### DEBTORS CONTROL ACCOUNT

|  | £'000 |  | £'000 |
|---|---|---|---|
| Balance b/f | 225 | Bad debts | 35 |
| Sales (bal. fig.) | 1,270 | Discounts allowed | 30 |
|  |  | Bank | 1,200 |
|  |  | Bal. c/f | 230 |
|  | 1,495 |  | 1,495 |

3   *Purchases*

### CREDITORS CONTROL ACCOUNTS

|  | £'000 |  | £'000 |
|---|---|---|---|
| Bank | 650 | Bal b/f | 170 |
| Bal c/f | 155 | Purchases (bal. fig.) | 635 |
|  | 805 |  | 805 |

4   *Rent*

### RENT

|  | £'000 |  | £'000 |
|---|---|---|---|
| Prepayment b/f | 12 | Prepayment c/f | 10 |
| Bank | 40 | P & L a/c (bal. fig.) | 42 |
|  | 52 |  | 52 |

5   *Insurance*

### INSURANCE

|  | £'000 |  | £'000 |
|---|---|---|---|
| Balance b/d | 15 | P & L a/c (bal. fig.) | 40 |
| Bank | 25 |  |  |
|  | 40 |  | 40 |

6   *Electricity*

### ELECTRICITY

|  | £'000 |  | £'000 |
|---|---|---|---|
| Bank | 30 | Bal b/f | 6 |
| Bal c/f | 15 | P & L a/c (bal. fig.) | 39 |
|  | 45 |  | 45 |

7   *Telephone*

### TELEPHONE

|  | £'000 |  | £'000 |
|---|---|---|---|
| Bank | 14 | Bal b/f | 4 |
|  |  | P & L a/c (bal. fig.) | 9 |
|  |  | Bal c/f | 1 |
|  | 14 |  | 14 |

**Helping hand.**

Make sure you get the figures on the right side of the account. You have an opening accrual and a closing prepayment.

## Questions and answers

8 *Prepayments*

|  | £'000 |
|---|---|
| Rent | 10 |
| Telephone | 1 |
|  | 11 |

9 *Depreciation*

|  | Vehicles £'000 | Equipment £'000 |
|---|---|---|
| Accumulated depn. at 1 June 20X8 | 50 | 80 |
| Charge for year |  |  |
|    Vehicles 25% × 100 | 25 |  |
|    Equipment 20% × (200 – 80) |  | 24 |
| Accumulated depn. at 31 May 20X9 | 75 | 104 |

Total charge for year = 25 + 24 = 49

## 11 MR BENDS

On 1 January Mr Bends starts a business buying and selling motor cars. He gives you a summary of the business receipts and payments account as follows, for the year to 31 December (all figures are in £'000).

| *Receipts* | £'000 |
|---|---:|
| Capital introduced (1 January) | 100 |
| From customers (after deducting worthless cheque, see note (c) below) | 400 |
| 10% loan from his mother (1 January) | 50 |
| | 550 |
| *Payments* | |
| To suppliers of new cars | 320 |
| To suppliers of second-hand cars | 93 |
| Wages | 36 |
| Rent | 15 |
| Purchase of furniture | 5 |
| Purchase of showroom display equipment | 5 |
| Insurance, electricity and stationery | 7 |
| Bank charges | 1 |
| Transfers to private bank account | 26 |
| | 508 |

You are informed that:

(a) Rent payable is £3,000 for each 3-month period.

(b) Mr Bends has bought a total of 37 new cars at a cost of £10,000 each. One of these was destroyed by fire the day before Mr Bends signed his insurance policy, two were taken into use by Mr Bends and his senior salesman, and 27 have been sold at a markup of 20% on cost (one of which has not yet been paid for).

(c) Mr Bends had a problem with the very first second-hand car which he sold. He accepted a cheque for £5,000 which proved worthless, and he has been unable to trace the customer. Since then all sales of second-hand cars have been for cash. All purchases of second-hand cars have also been for cash.

(d) Four second-hand cars remain in stock at 31 December. The cost of these to Mr Bends was £6,000, £6,000, £7,000 and £8,000 respectively.

(e) All fixed assets are to be depreciated at the rate of 20% for the year.

*Required*

Prepare in good order:

A trading account for new cars
A trading account for second-hand cars
A profit and loss account for the business for the year
A balance sheet as at 31 December

Indicate clearly the calculation of all figures in your solution.

**(25 marks)**

---

**Helping hand**

1. You need to think carefully about which cars to include in the trading accounts.
2. You will need to calculate the cash received for second hand cars.
3. A separate working will be required for depreciation.

# 11 ANSWER: MR BENDS

> **Helping hand**
>
> Remember to take out the car destroyed, and the car used by the salesman.

## TRADING ACCOUNT FOR NEW CARS

|  | £'000 | £'000 | £'000 |
|---|---|---|---|
| Sales (27 × 10,000 × 120%) |  |  | 324 |
| Purchases (37 × 10,000) |  | 370 |  |
| Less: car destroyed by fire | 10 |  |  |
| cars taken to fixed assets | 20 |  |  |
|  |  | (30) |  |
|  |  | 340 |  |
| Less: closing stock (ie 37 – 27 sales – 3) = 7 cars |  | (70) |  |
|  |  |  | (270) |
| Gross profit |  |  | 54 |

> **Helping hand**
>
> Cash received from second hand cars will be a balancing figure.

## TRADING ACCOUNT FOR SECOND HAND CARS

| | | |
|---|---|---|
| Sales (W) |  | 93 |
| Purchases (per question) | 93 |  |
| Closing stock | 27 |  |
| Cost of sales |  | 66 |
| Gross profit |  | 27 |

*Working*

| | |
|---|---|
| Total receipts of cash | 400 |
| Less: cash from new cars (324 – 12 debtor) | 312 |
| ∴ cash received from second hand cars | 88 |
| Plus car sold but not paid for | 5 |
|  | 93 |

> **Helping hand**
>
> To calculate depreciation, find total fixed assets and take 20%.

## PROFIT AND LOSS ACCOUNT FOR THE YEAR

| | | |
|---|---|---|
| Gross profit |  |  |
| New cars | 54 |  |
| Second hand cars | 27 |  |
|  |  | 81 |
| Less: Wages | 36 |  |
| Rent (4 × 3) | 12 |  |
| Depreciation (W) | 6 |  |
| Insurance, electricity, stationery | 7 |  |
| Loss by fire | 10 |  |
| Bad debt | 5 |  |
| Bank charges | 1 |  |
| Interest on loan from mother (10% × 50) | 5 |  |
|  |  | 82 |
| Net loss |  | 1 |

## Questions and answers

*Working*

| Total fixed assets: | furniture | 5 |
|---|---|---|
| | display equipment | 5 |
| | cars | 20 |
| | | 30 |

∴ depreciation @ 20% = 6

BALANCE SHEET AT 31 DECEMBER

| | Cost £'000 | Acc'd dep'n £'000 | NBV £'000 |
|---|---|---|---|
| *Fixed assets* | | | |
| Cars | 20 | 4 | 16 |
| Furniture | 5 | 1 | 4 |
| Equipment | 5 | 1 | 4 |
| | 30 | 6 | 24 |
| *Current assets* | | | |
| Stock (70 + 27) | | 97 | |
| Debtors | | 12 | |
| Prepayments: rent (15 – 12) | | 3 | |
| Cash at bank (550 – 508) | | 42 | |
| | | 154 | |
| *Current liabilities* | | | |
| Creditors for new cars (370 – 320) | 50 | | |
| Interest accrued on loan | 5 | | |
| | | (55) | |
| *Net current assets* | | | 99 |
| | | | 123 |
| Long term loan | | | 50 |
| *Net assets* | | | 73 |
| | | | |
| *Represented by:* | | | |
| Capital | | | 100 |
| Less: loss | | 1 | |
| drawings | | 26 | |
| *Proprietor's funds* | | | 27 |
| | | | 73 |

## 12 OPENING BALANCE SHEET

You are given the following information about a sole trader.

TRIAL BALANCE 31 DECEMBER 20X8

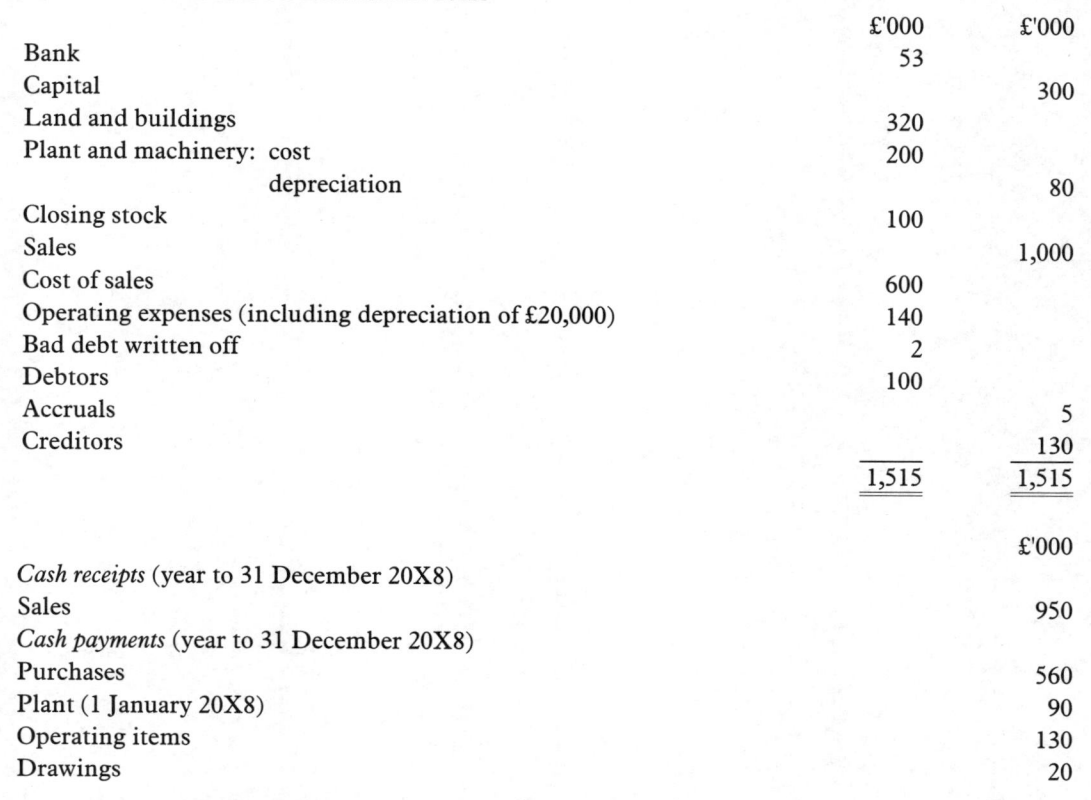

|  | £'000 | £'000 |
|---|---|---|
| Bank | 53 |  |
| Capital |  | 300 |
| Land and buildings | 320 |  |
| Plant and machinery: cost | 200 |  |
|     depreciation |  | 80 |
| Closing stock | 100 |  |
| Sales |  | 1,000 |
| Cost of sales | 600 |  |
| Operating expenses (including depreciation of £20,000) | 140 |  |
| Bad debt written off | 2 |  |
| Debtors | 100 |  |
| Accruals |  | 5 |
| Creditors |  | 130 |
|  | 1,515 | 1,515 |

|  | £'000 |
|---|---|
| *Cash receipts* (year to 31 December 20X8) |  |
| Sales | 950 |
| *Cash payments* (year to 31 December 20X8) |  |
| Purchases | 560 |
| Plant (1 January 20X8) | 90 |
| Operating items | 130 |
| Drawings | 20 |

The creditors figure has doubled since 1 January 20X8.

*Required*

Open appropriate T accounts to enable you to calculate the items in the opening balance sheet at 1 January 20X8. Submit the summarised 1 January 20X8 balance sheet and all workings.

**(20 marks)**

---

**Helping hand**

1. First set out the pro forma balance sheet.
2. Then think what T accounts you need.
3. Then put in what you know from the question.

## 12 ANSWER: OPENING BALANCE SHEET

> **Helping hand**
>
> The items in the question should tell you what headings to have in your balance sheet.

BALANCE SHEET AS AT 1 JANUARY 20X8

|  | £'000 | £'000 |
|---|---|---|
| *Fixed assets* | | |
| Land and buildings (given) | | 320 |
| Plant and machinery: cost (W1) | 110 | |
| depreciation (W2) | 60 | |
| | | 50 |
| | | 370 |
| *Current assets* | | |
| Stock (W4) | 75 | |
| Debtors (W5) | 52 | |
| | 127 | |
| *Current liabilities* | | |
| Bank overdraft (W6) | 97 | |
| Creditors (W3) | 65 | |
| Accruals (W7) | 15 | |
| | 177 | |
| Net current liabilities | | (50) |
| | | 320 |
| *Capital* (W8) | | 320 |

*Workings*

> **Helping hand**
>
> You will need T accounts for plant and machinery, depreciation on plant and machinery, creditors, cost of sales, debtors, bank and operating expenses.

1     PLANT AND MACHINERY - COST

|  | £'000 |  | £'000 |
|---|---|---|---|
| ∴ Balance b/d | 110 | Balance c/d | 200 |
| Bank | 90 | | |
| | 200 | | 200 |

2     PLANT AND MACHINERY - DEPRECIATION

|  | £'000 |  | £'000 |
|---|---|---|---|
| Balance c/d | 80 | ∴ Balance b/d | 60 |
| | | Charge for the year | 20 |
| | 80 | | 80 |

3     CREDITORS

|  | £'000 |  | £'000 |
|---|---|---|---|
| Bank | 560 | Balance b/d (£130,000 ÷ 2) | 65 |
| Balance c/d | 130 | ∴ Purchases | 625 |
| | 690 | | 690 |

## Questions and answers

**4**

### COST OF SALES

| | £'000 | | £'000 |
|---|---|---|---|
| ∴ Opening stock | 75 | Closing stock | 100 |
| Purchases (W3) | 625 | P & L account | 600 |
| | 700 | | 700 |

**5**

### DEBTORS

| | £'000 | | £'000 |
|---|---|---|---|
| ∴ Balance b/d | 52 | Bank | 950 |
| Sales | 1,000 | Bad debts written off | 2 |
| | | Balance c/d | 100 |
| | 1,052 | | 1,052 |

**6**

### BANK

| | £'000 | | £'000 |
|---|---|---|---|
| Debtors | 950 | Opening balance | 97 |
| | | Creditors | 560 |
| | | Plant and machinery - cost | 90 |
| | | Operating expenses | 130 |
| | | Drawings | 20 |
| | | Balance c/d | 53 |
| | 950 | | 950 |

**7**

### OPERATING EXPENSES

| | £'000 | | £'000 |
|---|---|---|---|
| Bank | 130 | ∴ Accruals b/d | 15 |
| Accruals c/d | 5 | P & L account | 120 |
| | 135 | | 135 |

**8** *Capital*

As no drawings account is shown on the trial balance, you must assume that drawings during the year have been debited to the capital account.

∴ Opening balance = £300,000 + £20,000 = £320,000.

## 13 SMITH, JONES AND MATTHEWS (12/98)

Smith, Jones and Matthews are in partnership and their trial balance for the year ended 30 September 20X8 was as follows.

|  | Dr £ | Cr £ |
|---|---:|---:|
| Motor vans at cost | 43,750 |  |
| Office equipment at cost | 29,400 |  |
| Provisions for depreciation at 1 October 20X7: Motor vans |  | 14,700 |
| Office equipment |  | 9,450 |
| Sales |  | 736,750 |
| Carriage inwards | 5,250 |  |
| Stock at 1 October 20X7 | 149,975 |  |
| Discounts allowed | 385 |  |
| Returns inwards | 23,800 |  |
| Bad debts | 4,319 |  |
| Provision for doubtful debts |  | 2,800 |
| General expenses | 3,308 |  |
| Rent and rates | 8,978 |  |
| Postages | 8,575 |  |
| Motor expenses | 13,790 |  |
| Salaries and wages | 64,036 |  |
| Purchases | 480,165 |  |
| Drawings: Smith | 44,135 |  |
| Jones | 29,460 |  |
| Matthews | 21,756 |  |
| Current accounts at 1 October 20X7: Smith |  | 7,260 |
| Jones |  | 4,865 |
| Matthews | 536 |  |
| Capital accounts: Smith |  | 105,000 |
| Jones |  | 56,000 |
| Matthews |  | 42,000 |
| Creditors |  | 85,246 |
| Debtors | 130,123 |  |
| Cash at bank | 2,330 |  |
|  | 1,064,071 | 1,064,071 |

The following additional information is also available.

(a) Stock at 30 September 20X8 was £178,710.

(b) Rates of £420 were paid in advance at 30 September 20X8.

(c) The provision for doubtful debts is to be increased to £3,045 and any adjustment charged to bad debts.

(d) The provision for depreciation for year ended 30 September 20X8 is to be: motor vans £8,750 and office equipment £5,880.

(e) Included in drawings are salaries as follows: Smith £4,200, Jones £2,450 and Matthews £3,500.

(f) Interest on drawings is: Smith £595, Jones £385 and Matthews £420.

(g) Interest on each partner's capital is to be allowed for at 10% per annum.

(h) Smith, Jones and Matthews have agreed that profits and losses should be shared in the ratio 6:4:2 respectively.

## Questions and answers

*Required*

You are required to prepare the following statements for the partnership for the year ended 30 September 20X8.

(a) The trading and profit and loss account (including an appropriation account)

(20 marks)

(b) The partners' current accounts (6 marks)

(c) The balance sheet as at 30 September 20X8. (14 marks)

**(40 marks)**

Supporting workings are required.

> **Helping hand**
> 1 There are no hidden traps in this question. Much of it is straightforward accounts preparation, and the partnership aspects are fairly easy.
> 2 Make sure you know which items are in the expenses and which are appropriations.
> 3 Take care to get interest on capital / drawings on the right side of the current accounts.

## 13 ANSWER: SMITH, JONES AND MATTHEWS

> **Examiner's comment.** Most candidates performed well on this question and were able to adjust the balances correctly. Answers were well presented.

(a) SMITH, JONES AND MATTHEWS
TRADING, PROFIT AND LOSS AND APPROPRIATION ACCOUNT
FOR THE YEAR ENDED 30 SEPTEMBER 20X8

|  | £ | £ |
|---|---:|---:|
| Sales (W1) |  | 712,950 |
| Cost of goods sold (W2) |  | 456,680 |
| Gross profit |  | 256,270 |
| Less expenses |  |  |
|   Discounts allowed | 385 |  |
|   General expenses | 3,308 |  |
|   Rent and rates (W3) | 8,558 |  |
|   Postages | 8,575 |  |
|   Motor expenses | 13,790 |  |
|   Salaries and wages | 64,036 |  |
|   Bad debts (W4) | 4,564 |  |
|   Depreciation (W5) | 14,630 |  |
|  |  | 117,846 |
| Net profit before appropriation |  | 138,424 |
| Add: interest on drawings: Smith | 595 |  |
|     Jones | 385 |  |
|     Matthews | 420 |  |
|  |  | 1,400 |
|  |  | 139,824 |
| Less: interest on capital: Smith | 10,500 |  |
|     Jones | 5,600 |  |
|     Matthews | 4,200 |  |
|  |  | 20,300 |
| Salaries: Smith | 4,200 |  |
|     Jones | 2,450 |  |
|     Matthews | 3,500 |  |
|  |  | 10,150 |
|  |  | 109,374 |
| Balance of profit share: Smith 6/12 |  | 54,687 |
|     Jones 4/12 |  | 36,458 |
|     Matthews 2/12 |  | 18,229 |
|  |  | 109,374 |

> **Helping hand**
>
> Salaries, interest on capital and interest on drawings are appropriations; the others are expenses.

(b) PARTNERS' CURRENT ACCOUNTS

|  | Smith £ | Jones £ | Matthews £ |  | Smith £ | Jones £ | Matthews £ |
|---|---:|---:|---:|---|---:|---:|---:|
| Bal b/f |  |  | 536 | Bal b/f | 7,260 | 4,865 | - |
| Drawings | 44,135 | 29,460 | 21,756 | Salaries | 4,200 | 2,450 | 3,500 |
| Interest on drawings | 595 | 385 | 420 | Interest on capital | 10,500 | 5,600 | 4,200 |
| Bal c/f | 31,917 | 19,528 | 3,217 | Share of profit | 54,687 | 36,458 | 18,229 |
|  | 76,647 | 49,373 | 25,929 |  | 77,647 | 49,373 | 25,929 |

> **Helping hand**
>
> Just think about the double entry. Interest on capital is a debit to the appropriation account, so it must be a credit to the current account. Interest on drawings goes the other way round.

## Questions and answers

(c) SMITH, JONES AND MATTHEWS
BALANCE SHEET AS AT 30 SEPTEMBER 20X8

|  | Cost £ | Acc Depn £ | NBV £ |
|---|---|---|---|
| *Fixed assets* |  |  |  |
| Motor vans | 43,750 | 23,450 | 20,300 |
| Office equipment | 29,400 | 15,330 | 14,070 |
|  | 73,150 | 38,780 | 34,370 |
| *Current assets* |  |  |  |
| Stock |  | 178,710 |  |
| Debtors (130,123 – 3,045) |  | 127,078 |  |
| Prepayments |  | 420 |  |
| Cash at bank |  | 2,330 |  |
|  |  | 308,538 |  |
| *Current liabilities* |  |  |  |
| Creditors |  | 85,246 |  |
| Net current assets |  |  | 223,292 |
|  |  |  | 257,662 |
| *Capital accounts* |  |  |  |
| Smith |  | 105,000 |  |
| Jones |  | 56,000 |  |
| Matthews |  | 42,000 |  |
|  |  |  | 203,000 |
| *Current accounts* |  |  |  |
| Smith |  | 31,917 |  |
| Jones |  | 19,528 |  |
| Matthews |  | 3,217 |  |
|  |  |  | 54,662 |
|  |  |  | 257,662 |

*Workings*

1  Sales

|  | £ |
|---|---|
| Sales | 736,750 |
| Less returns inwards | 23,800 |
|  | 712,950 |

2  Cost of goods sold

|  | £ |
|---|---|
| Opening stock | 14,997 |
| Purchases | 480,165 |
| Carriage inwards | 5,250 |
|  | 635,390 |
| Less closing stock | 178,710 |
|  | 456,680 |

3  Rent and rates

|  | £ |
|---|---|
| Per trial balance | 8,978 |
| Less prepayment | (420) |
| Profit and loss account | 8,558 |

4  Bad debts

|  | £ |
|---|---|
| Provision per trial balance | 2,800 |
| Provision needed | 3,045 |
| Increase | 245 |
| Bad debts per trial balance | 4,319 |
| Profit and loss account | 4,564 |

5   *Depreciation*

|  | Motor vans £ | Office equipment £ |
|---|---|---|
| Per trial balance | 14,700 | 9,450 |
| Charge for year | 8,750 | 5,880 |
| Provision at 30.9.X8 | 23,450 | 15,330 |

Total depreciation charge for year: £8,750 + £5,880 = £14,630

## 14 SMITH AND JONES (Pilot Paper)

You are responsible for preparing the books and accounts of a sole trader Smith who owns three convenience stores. Smith has been approached by another sole trader Jones who owns four convenience stores in the same region, with a view to forming a partnership. Smith is undecided and before making a final decision has asked you to explain the accounting of the proposed amalgamation and the rule in *Garner v Murray*.

The following assumptions are made to assist in the explanation of the rule in *Garner v Murray*.

(a) Partners are Smith, Jones and A N Other who share profits in the ratio 3:4:1.

(b) Balances on partners' accounts are as follows.

|  | Smith £ | Jones £ | A N Other £ |
|---|---|---|---|
| Capital (Cr) | 25,000 | 50,000 | 4,000 |
| Current (Cr) | 4,000 | 7,000 | 1,000 |

(c) The partnership is to be dissolved and the loss on realisation amounts to £64,000.

(d) A N Other is insolvent.

*Required*

(a) Explain the accounting implications of the amalgamation of Smith and Jones to the proposed partnership. (7 marks)

(b) Prepare and close off the partners' accounts applying the rule in *Garner v Murray* to the assumptions given. (8 marks)

**(15 marks)**

---

**Helping hand**

1. Unusually, you are asked to explain accounting implications rather than to do the calculations. Make sure your explanation is clear and comprehensible to non-accountants.

2. Remember, in part (b) you need to think what to do with any deficit arising on AN Other's account, given that he is insolvent.

## 14 ANSWER: SMITH AND JONES

(a)

> **Helping hand**
>
> Aspects to consider are introduction of capital, appropriation of net profit, partnership agreement and treatment of the old firm's assets and liabilities.

The basic principles of accounts preparation are similar for partnerships and sole traders. However, where partnerships differ is in the treatment of **capital** and **profits**. Capital will be introduced into the new business by both Smith and Jones and net profits will be **appropriated** between the partners in a profit sharing ratio.

It is likely that a formal **partnership agreement** will be drawn up in respect of the proposed business. The agreement will probably detail the following.

(i) The profit sharing ratio
(ii) Rate of interest, if any, on capital
(iii) Limit (if any) on partners' drawings
(iv) Details of partners' salaries, if any
(v) Whether the rule in *Garner v Murray* is to be applied on dissolution (as here)

The old firms' assets and liabilities are **realised** by 'sale' to the new partnership, not for cash but for a share in the capital of the new business, the amount of capital being determined by the value of net assets contributed.

A **revaluation account** is used in each of the old firms' existing set of books to account for and apportion to the sole traders their share of the profit or loss on revaluation of assets and liabilities. If necessary, a goodwill account is used to introduce (or increase) the goodwill and to credit the sole traders with their share.

Once both firms have adjusted their asset, liability and capital accounts to take into account the agreed values, the separate books may be merged. The traders' agreed capital accounts are transferred to the new partnership capital accounts, and, if agreed, goodwill written off in the profit sharing ratio.

(b)

> **Helping hand**
>
> Because A N Other is unable to make good the deficit, the rule in Garner v Murray applies. By this rule, the loss of £3,000 is shared between the partners in the ratio of their last agreed capital balances.

## Questions and answers

### PARTNERS' ACCOUNTS

|  | Smith £ | Jones £ | A N Other £ | Smith £ | Jones £ | A N Other £ |
|---|---|---|---|---|---|---|
| Bal b/f: capital account |  |  |  | 25,000 | 50,000 | 4,000 |
| current account |  |  |  | 4,000 | 7,000 | 1,000 |
| Loss on realisation |  |  |  |  |  |  |
| £64,000 apportioned 3:4:1 | 24,000 | 32,000 | 8,000 |  |  |  |
| Balance c/d | 5,000 | 25,000 |  |  |  | 3,000 |
|  | 29,000 | 57,000 | 8,000 | 29,000 | 57,000 | 8,000 |
| Balance b/f |  |  | 3,000 | 5,000 | 25,000 |  |
| A N Other's deficit |  |  |  |  |  |  |
| Smith 25/75 × 3,000 | 1,000 |  |  |  |  |  |
| Jones 50/75 × 3,000 |  | 2,000 |  |  |  |  |
| Smith and Jones |  |  |  |  |  | 3,000 |
| Bank | 4,000 | 23,000 |  |  |  |  |
|  | 5,000 | 25,000 | 3,000 | 5,000 | 25,000 | 3,000 |

## 15 CAIN AND ABEL (12/00)

Cain and Abel have been in partnership for several years and share profits and losses in the ratio 3:2. The following is the trial balance from the partnership books as at 31 October 20X0.

|  | Dr £ | Cr £ |
|---|---|---|
| Provision for doubtful debts |  | 6,000 |
| Sales |  | 1,483,400 |
| Accumulated depreciation: vans |  | 66,600 |
|     fittings |  | 12,800 |
| Office expenses | 72,000 |  |
| Purchases | 1,143,400 |  |
| Bank |  | 7,650 |
| Vans at cost | 90,000 |  |
| Fittings at cost | 28,000 |  |
| Debtors | 137,200 |  |
| Creditors |  | 47,200 |
| Stock at 1 November 20W9 | 195,300 |  |
| Insurance | 8,650 |  |
| Motor vehicle expenses | 44,500 |  |
| Motor car, at cost (purchased 1 November 20W9) | 18,000 |  |
| Discounts allowed | 28,800 |  |
| Wages and salaries | 82,800 |  |
| Capital accounts at 1 November 20W9: Cain |  | 154,000 |
|     Abel |  | 138,000 |
| Drawings: Cain | 40,000 |  |
|     Abel | 27,000 |  |
|  | 1,915,650 | 1,915,650 |

The following additional information as at 31 October 20X0 is available.

(a) Bank charges of £655 have not been entered into the accounts.

(b) Depreciation is to be provided for using the reducing balance method at 10% on fittings and 20% on vans and the motor car. Abel is to accept personally £5,000 of the motor vehicle expenses and half of the depreciation charge on the motor car.

(c) Stock was valued at £296,700.

(d) The partners are entitled to 10% a year interest on capital.

(e) Insurance of £850 has been paid in advance.

(f) There are outstanding wages of £3,475.

(g) The annual payment for rent of £9,000 is still outstanding.

(h) £2,200 of bad debts are to be written off.

(i) The provision for doubtful debts is to be adjusted to 5% of the remaining debtors and the adjustment charged to bad debts.

(j) Interest on drawings for the year is: Cain £2,400; Abel £1,420

(k) There were no current account balances at 1 November 20W9

*Required*

(a) Prepare the following statements for the partnership.

    (i) The trading and profit and loss account (including an appropriation account) for the year ended 31 October 20X0     *(18 marks)*

## Questions and answers

      (ii)    The partners' current accounts for the year ended 31 October 20X0    (6 marks)

      (iii)   The balance sheet as at 31 October 20X0    (12 marks)

(b)  Briefly outline the advantages and disadvantages of operating as a partnership rather than as a sole trader.    (4 marks)

**(40 marks)**

> **Helping hand**
>
> 1    Although this is a partnership accounts question, many of the principles and procedures are the same as for sole traders.
>
> 2    It is important that you know which side of the current accounts the entries go.

## 15 ANSWER: CAIN AND ABEL

> **Examiner's comment.** In part (a) candidates were required to prepare a trading, profit and loss account (including appropriation account) and balance sheet. Nearly all candidates made a good attempt at this part of the question and were able to perform most of the adjustments required. The appropriation account caused the most difficulty for candidates. Part (b) was reasonably well attempted, but some candidates used this part of the question to state all their knowledge on partnerships rather than focusing on the requirements of the questions.

(a) (i) CAIN AND ABEL
TRADING, PROFIT AND LOSS AND APPROPRIATION ACCOUNT
FOR THE YEAR ENDED 31 OCTOBER 20X0

|  | £'000 | £'000 |
|---|---|---|
| Sales |  | 1,483,400 |
| Opening stock | 195,300 |  |
| Purchases | 1,143,400 |  |
|  | 1,338,700 |  |
| Less closing stock | 296,700 |  |
| Cost of goods sold |  | 1,042,000 |
| Gross profit |  | 441,400 |
|  |  |  |
| Expenses |  |  |
|     Office expenses | 72,000 |  |
|     Insurance (8,650 – 850) | 7,800 |  |
|     Motor vehicle expenses (W1) | 39,500 |  |
|     Discounts allowed | 28,800 |  |
|     Wages and salaries (82,800 + 3,475) | 86,275 |  |
|     Depreciation (W2) | 8,000 |  |
|     Bank charges | 655 |  |
|     Rent | 9,000 |  |
|     Bad debts (W3) | 2,950 |  |
|  |  | 254,980 |
| Net profit before appropriation |  | 186,420 |
|  |  |  |
| Interest on drawings: Cain | 2,400 |  |
|                           Abel | 1,420 |  |
|  |  | 3,820 |
|  |  | 190,240 |
| Interest on capital: Cain (154,000 × 10%) | 15,400 |  |
|                    Abel (138,000 × 10%) | 13,800 |  |
|  |  | 29,200 |
|  |  | 161,040 |
| Share on profit: Cain $^3/_5$ |  | 96,624 |
|                 Abel $^2/_5$ |  | 64,416 |
|  |  | 161,040 |

> **Helping hand.** Up to 'net profit before appropriation' is just like a sole trader.

(ii)

CAIN: CURRENT ACCOUNT

|  | £'000 |  | £'000 |
|---|---|---|---|
| Drawings | 40,000 | Interest on capital | 15,400 |
| Interest on drawings | 2,400 | Share of profit | 96,624 |
| Bal c/f | 69,624 |  |  |
|  | 112,024 |  | 112,024 |

73

## Questions and answers

### ABEL: CURRENT ACCOUNT

|  | £'000 |  | £'000 |
|---|---|---|---|
| Drawings | 27,000 | Interest on capital | 13,800 |
| Motor vehicle expenses | 5,000 | Share of profit | 64,416 |
| Depn on motor vehicle | 1,800 |  |  |
| Interest on drawings | 1,420 |  |  |
| Bal c/f | 42,996 |  |  |
|  | 78,216 |  | 78,216 |

> **Helping hand.** Drawings and interest on drawings both go on the debit side. Likewise capital and interest on capital are both credits.

(iii) CAIN AND ABEL
BALANCE SHEET AS AT 31 OCTOBER 20X0

|  | Cost £ | Acc depn £ | NBV £ |
|---|---|---|---|
| *Fixed assets* |  |  |  |
| Van | 90,000 | 71,280 | 18,720 |
| Fittings | 28,000 | 14,320 | 13,680 |
| Motor car | 18,000 | 3,600 | 14,400 |
|  | 136,000 | 89,200 | 46,800 |
| *Current assets* |  |  |  |
| Stock |  | 296,700 |  |
| Debtors (W3) | 135,000 |  |  |
| Less provision (W3) | 6,750 |  |  |
|  |  | 128,250 |  |
| Prepayment: insurance |  | 850 |  |
|  |  | 425,800 |  |
| *Current liabilities* |  |  |  |
| Creditors |  | 47,200 |  |
| Bank overdraft (W4) |  | 8,305 |  |
| Accruals |  |  |  |
| Wages | 3,475 |  |  |
| Rent | 9,000 |  |  |
|  |  | 12,475 |  |
|  |  | 67,980 |  |
| Net current assets |  |  | 357,820 |
|  |  |  | 404,620 |
| *Capital accounts* |  |  |  |
| Cain |  | 154,000 |  |
| Abel |  | 138,000 |  |
|  |  |  | 292,000 |
| *Current accounts* |  |  |  |
| Cain |  | 69,624 |  |
| Abel |  | 42,996 |  |
|  |  |  | 112,620 |
|  |  |  | 404,620 |

*Workings*

1  *Motor vehicle expenses*

|  | £ |
|---|---|
| Per trial balance | 44,500 |
| Less accepted by Abel | 5,000 |
|  | 39,500 |

*Questions and answers*

2 **Depreciation**

|  | £ |
|---|---:|
| *Vans* | |
| Cost | 90,000 |
| Acc depn at 1 November 20W9 | 66,600 |
| NBV at 1 November 20W9 | 23,400 |
| Charge for year (23,400 × 20%) | 4,680 |
| NBV at 31 October 20X0 | 18,720 |
| *Fittings* | |
| Cost | 28,000 |
| Acc depn at 1 November 20W9 | 12,800 |
| NBV at 1 November 20W9 | 15,200 |
| Charge for year (15,200 × 10%) | 1,520 |
| NBV at 31 October 20X0 | 13,680 |
| *Motor car* | |
| Cost | 18,000 |
| Depn charge (18,000 × 20%) | 3,600 |
| NBV at 31 October 20X0 | 14,400 |
| *Total depreciation charge* | |
| Vans | 4,680 |
| Fittings | 1,520 |
| Motor car (3,600 × ½)* | 1,800 |
| | 8,000 |

*Note.* Half of the depreciation charge on the motor car has been accepted by Abel and will be shown in his current account.

3 **Bad debts**

|  | £ |
|---|---:|
| Debtors per trial balance | 137,200 |
| Less bad debt written off | (2,200) |
| Balance for provision calculation | 135,000 |
| Provision required | 6,750 |
| Provision per trial balance | 6,000 |
| Increase charged to P & L | 750 |

Total charged to P & L: 2,200 + 750 = £2,950.

4 **Bank overdraft**

|  | £ |
|---|---:|
| Per trial balance | 7,650 |
| Add bank charges | 655 |
| | 8,305 |

(b) **Advantages of a partnership**

The main problem with trading as a sole trader is the limitation on resources. As the business grows, there will be a need for the following items.

(i) **Additional capital.** Although some capital may be provided by a bank, it would not be desirable to have the business entirely dependent on borrowing.

(ii) **Additional expertise.** A sole trader technically competent in his own field may not have, for example, the financial skills that would be needed in a larger business.

(iii) **Additional management time.** Once a business grows to a certain point, it becomes impossible for one person to look after all aspects of it without help.

## Questions and answers

(iv) **Additional business contacts.** Partners may have access to a wider network.

**Disadvantages of a partnership**

(i) **Disputes over management of the business.** Partners may disagree on the best way to run and develop the business.

(ii) **Joint and several liability.** A partner may end up sharing the blame for another partner's mistake.

(iii) **Less profit.** Profits are spread over more than one person.

(iv) **Disputes over financial matters.** Examples might be level of drawings or interest on capital

## 16 GREEN, BROWN AND GRAY

Green, Brown and Gray are in partnership sharing profits and losses in the ratio 2:1:1. The balance sheet of the firm as at 31 May 20X9 was as follows.

BALANCE SHEET OF GREEN, BROWN AND GRAY

|  | £ | £ |  | £ Cost | £ Depn | £ Net |
|---|---|---|---|---|---|---|
| *Capital accounts* |  |  | *Fixed assets* |  |  |  |
| Green | 40,000 |  | Premises | 60,000 | - | 60,000 |
| Brown | 20,000 |  | Plant and equipment | 10,000 | 3,440 | 6,560 |
| Gray | 20,000 |  |  | 70,000 | 3,440 | 66,560 |
|  |  | 80,000 |  |  |  |  |
| *Current liabilities* |  |  | *Current assets* |  |  |  |
| Bank overdraft | 1,300 |  | Stock | 16,000 |  |  |
| Trade creditors | 5,500 |  | Debtors | 4,240 |  |  |
|  |  | 6,800 |  |  |  | 20,240 |
|  |  | 86,800 |  |  |  | 86,800 |

On 31 May 20X9 it was agreed to dissolve the partnership and as Brown is continuing in business on his own account he agrees to take over the stock, plant and debtors at valuations of £18,000, £5,500 and £4,100 respectively. He also agrees to acquire the premises at a cost of £105,000 and obtains a mortgage loan of £80,000 which is paid to the partnership. The balance owing by Brown is charged against Green's capital account as the two parties have agreed that Brown will repay the loan to Green over a period of three years. Realisation expenses amounting to £1,000 are paid in cash and the creditors of the firm are paid in full.

You are required to record the above transactions in the ledger accounts of the partnership.

**(20 marks)**

---

**Helping hand**

1   You need to open up a realisation account and a bank account.
2   The other accounts you need are the partner's capital accounts.
3   Think carefully how you should deal with the loan from Green to Brown.

# 16 ANSWER: GREEN, BROWN AND GRAY

> **Helping hand**
>
> Open up a realisation account. Put in all the assets in the old valuation and take them out in the new. The gain on realisation goes to the partners' capital accounts.

## REALISATION ACCOUNT

| 20X9 | | £ | 20X9 | | £ |
|---|---|---:|---|---|---:|
| 31 May | Premises | 60,000 | 31 May | Assets taken over by Brown: | |
| | Plant and equipment | 6,560 | | Stock | 18,000 |
| | Stock | 16,000 | | Plant and equipment | 5,500 |
| | Debtors | 4,240 | | Debtors | 4,100 |
| | Realisation expenses | 1,000 | | Premises | 105,000 |
| | Gain on realisation: | | | | |
| | Green | 22,400 | | | |
| | Brown | 11,200 | | | |
| | Gray | 11,200 | | | |
| | | 44,800 | | | |
| | | 132,600 | | | 132,600 |

> **Helping hand**
>
> You are paying off the creditors, Green and Gray, and the realisation expenses.

## BANK ACCOUNT

| 20X9 | | £ | 20X9 | | £ |
|---|---|---:|---|---|---:|
| 31 May | Brown - on account | 80,000 | 31 May | Balance | 1,300 |
| | | | | Creditors | 5,500 |
| | | | | Realisation expenses | 1,000 |
| | | | | Green capital | 41,000 |
| | | | | Gray capital | 31,200 |
| | | 80,000 | | | 80,000 |

## GREEN CAPITAL ACCOUNT

| 20X9 | | £ | 20X9 | | £ |
|---|---|---:|---|---|---:|
| 31 May | Loan to Brown | 21,400 | 31 May | Balance | 40,000 |
| | Cash (balance) | 41,000 | | Gain on realisation | 22,400 |
| | | 62,400 | | | 62,400 |

> **Helping hand**
>
> Don't forget that Brown owes to Green the balance on his capital account.

## BROWN CAPITAL ACCOUNT

| 20X9 | | £ | 20X9 | | £ |
|---|---|---:|---|---|---:|
| 31 May | Assets taken over | 132,600 | 31 May | Balance | 20,000 |
| | | | | Gain on realisation | 11,200 |
| | | | | Cash | 80,000 |
| | | | | Loan from Green (bal) | 21,400 |
| | | 132,600 | | | 132,600 |

## Questions and answers

### GRAY CAPITAL ACCOUNT

|  | £ |  | £ |
|---|---|---|---|
| *20X9* |  | *20X9* |  |
| 31 May Cash | 31,200 | 31 May Balance | 20,000 |
|  |  | Gain on realisation | 11,200 |
|  | 31,200 |  | 31,200 |

## 17　G PADGETT (12/01)

You are provided with the following accounting ratios for G Padgett for the year ended 31 October 20X1.

| | |
|---|---|
| Current ratio | 1.5 times |
| Acid test ratio | 1.25 times |
| Net assets to turnover | 2.5 times |
| Stock turnover | 6 times |
| Debtors turnover | 5 times |

In addition, the following information is also available.

(a) G Padgett started in business on 1 November 20X0.

(b) Working capital at 31 October 20X1 was £15,000.

(c) Drawings during the year were £6,000.

(d) Depreciation of fixed assets during the year was £4,000 and is based on 20% of their cost.

(e) General expenses, excluding depreciation, were 26% of sales.

*Required*

Prepare G Padgett's trading and profit and loss account for the year ended 31 October 20X1 and his balance sheet as at 31 October 20X1 in so far as the above information permits.

**(15 marks)**

---

**Helping hand**

1. This question is unusual in that you are having to prepare the accounts from the ratios rather than the other way round.

2. Start off with what you know – working capital. You can then get current assets and liabilities.

3. The other figures can be calculated in a similar way.

# Questions and answers

## 17 ANSWER: G PADGETT

> **Examiner's comment.** Clearly, some candidates found this question challenging. Those candidates who worked methodically and calmly through the question were able to calculate most of the figures required and present them appropriately. There were some easy marks to be gained, eg correctly showing the depreciation figure (which was given in the question) and the profit and loss account and balance sheet. Where appropriate, candidates were given credit for their own figures, provided they demonstrated some level of understanding.

G PADGETT
TRADING AND PROFIT AND LOSS ACCOUNT
FOR THE YEAR ENDED 31 OCTOBER 20X1

|  | £'000 |
|---|---:|
| Turnover (W3) | 77,500 |
| Cost of sales (W6) | 45,000 |
| Gross profit | 32,500 |
| General expenses (W4) | 20,150 |
| Depreciation | 4,000 |
| Net profit | 8,350 |

G PADGETT
BALANCE SHEET AS AT 31 OCTOBER 20X1

|  | £'000 | £'000 |
|---|---:|---:|
| Fixed assets at NBV (W2) |  | 16,000 |
| Current assets |  |  |
|   Stock (W5) | 7,500 |  |
|   Debtors (W7) | 15,500 |  |
|   Cash (W8) | 22,000 |  |
|  | 45,000 |  |
| Current liabilities (W1) | 30,000 |  |
| Net current assets |  | 15,000 |
|  |  | 31,000 |
| Proprietor's capital |  |  |
|   At 1 November 20X0 (bal fig) |  | 28,650 |
|   Profit for the year |  | 8,350 |
|   Less drawings |  | (6,000) |
|  |  | 31,000 |

*Workings*

1    *Current assets and liabilities*

     Working capital = current assets less current liabilities
                        = £15,000

     Current ratio = $\dfrac{\text{current assets}}{\text{current liabilities}}$ = 1.5

     $\therefore$ £15,000 = 0.5 × current liabilities

     $\therefore$ Current liabilities = £30,000; current assets = £45,000

> **Helping hand.** You could also do this by algebra:
>      'let x = current assets, etc'

2    *Fixed assets*

     Depreciation     = £4,000

     $\therefore$ Cost            = £4,000 × $\dfrac{100}{20}$ = £20,000

     Net book value = £20,000 − 4,000 = £16,000

83

## Questions and answers

> **Helping hand.** This is a good working to do next, because you know the depreciation figure.

3 *Turnover*

|  | £'000 |
|---|---|
| Net assets | |
| Fixed assets (W2) | 16,000 |
| Net current assets (W1) | 15,000 |
| | 31,000 |

$$\text{Asset turnover ratio} = \frac{\text{Turnover}}{\text{Net assets}} = 2.5 \text{ times}$$

∴ Turnover = £31,000 × 2.5 = £77,500

4 *General expenses*

26% of sales = £77,500 × 26%
= £20,150

5 *Stock*

$$\text{Acid test ratio} = \frac{\text{Current assets} - \text{stock}}{\text{Current liabilities}}$$

$$\frac{£45,000 - \text{stock}}{30,000} = 1.25$$

£45,000 − stock = 1.25 × 30,000
= £37,500

∴ Stock = £7,500

6 *Cost of sales*

$$\text{Stock turnover} = \frac{\text{Cost of sales}}{\text{Stock}} = 6 \text{ times}$$

∴ Cost of sales = £7,500 × 6 = £45,000

7 *Debtors*

$$\text{Debtors turnover} = \frac{\text{Sales}}{\text{Debtors}} = 5 \text{ times}$$

$$\frac{77,500}{\text{Debtors}} = 5$$

$$\text{Debtors} = \frac{77,500}{5} = £15,500$$

8 *Cash*

Current liabilities = stock + debtors + cash

∴ Cash = £45,000 − (£7,500 + 15,500)
= £22,000

> **Helping hand**
> You don't have to do the workings in this order, as long as you get there in the end.

*Questions and answers*

## 18 CHEAPSTAKE (Pilot paper, amended)

You are the newly appointed accounting assistant in Cheapstake plc and your chief accountant has presented you with the following trial balance which has been prepared by your predecessor.

TRIAL BALANCE AS AT 31 DECEMBER 20X6

|  | £'000 | £'000 |
|---|---|---|
| Administration and general expenses | 850 |  |
| Debenture interest (to 30.6.X6) | 25 |  |
| Distribution expenses | 346 |  |
| Directors' emoluments | 150 |  |
| Purchases | 4,329 |  |
| Sales |  | 9,000 |
| Rates and insurance | 350 |  |
| Interim dividend on ordinary shares | 16 |  |
| Authorised and issued £1 ordinary shares |  | 400 |
| Authorised and issued 10% preference shares |  | 600 |
| Revaluation reserve |  | 650 |
| Profit and loss account reserve |  | 550 |
| Debentures 5% |  | 1,000 |
| Goodwill | 300 |  |
| Land and buildings | 4,600 |  |
| accumulated depreciation to 31.12.X5 |  | 1,750 |
| Plant and machinery | 1,500 |  |
| accumulated depreciation to 31.12.X5 |  | 600 |
| Stock | 2,150 |  |
| Trade debtors and creditors | 1,704 | 1,750 |
| Bank balance | 200 |  |
| Provision for bad and doubtful debts |  | 100 |
| Deferred taxation |  | 120 |
|  | 16,520 | 16,520 |

You have been advised of the following additional information.

(a) The credit controller has stated that a bad debt of £25,000 needs to be written off and that the bad debts provision should be increased by 50%. He has also advised that a debt previously written off of £15,000 will be recovered and should be accrued.

(b) Goodwill currently valued at £300,000 has been reviewed and should be amortised over the next 10 years with effect from the year ended 31 December 20X6.

(c) The directors propose to pay a final dividend on the ordinary shares of 6p per share and to pay the preference dividend in full.

(d) The stock check at year end has been completed and the balance sheet as at 31 December 20X6 is £1,950,000.

(e) The corporation tax on profits for 20X6 is estimated to be £105,000.

(f) The land and buildings are to be depreciated at 10% per annum on cost and the plant and machinery at 20% per annum on cost. The land and buildings are the subject of an external revaluation every three years and you have been told that the latest review carried out in December 20X6 reduces the carrying value of land and buildings by £300,000. The revaluation reserve included in the trial balance wholly relates to previous reviews of the land and buildings.

(g) The allocation of expenditure between distribution and administration expenses is as follows.

## Questions and answers

|  | Distribution % | Administration % |
|---|---|---|
| Rates and insurance | 50 | 50 |
| Land and buildings depreciation | 40 | 60 |
| Plant and machinery depreciation | 75 | 25 |
| Goodwill amortisation | - | 100 |

(h) There is an outstanding legal dispute with a customer who is claiming damages for faulty goods. This is not covered by insurance, the outcome is uncertain and the amount of any damages is not quantifiable. You have been asked what, if any, action should be taken.

*Required*

(a) Draft a profit and loss account and balance sheet for Cheapstake plc for the year ended 31 December 20X6 in compliance with the Companies Act 1985. Notes to the account are not required. (35 marks)

(b) State what action you recommend in respect of the legal dispute and your reasons.
(5 marks)

**(40 marks)**

---

**Helping hand**

1 You should be able to set out your pro formas quite quickly as the financial statements are in Companies Act Format.

2 Many of the figures can be taken from the trial balance; others will require separate workings. Take care with the earnings per share working.

3 The best approach to part (b) is to think which accounting standard applies.

## 18 ANSWER: CHEAPSTAKE

(a) CHEAPSTAKE PLC
PROFIT AND LOSS ACCOUNT
FOR THE YEAR ENDED 31 DECEMBER 20X6

|  | £'000 |
|---|---|
| Turnover | 9,000 |
| Cost of sales (W1) | 4,529 |
| Gross profit | 4,471 |
| Distribution expenses (W2) | 918 |
| Administration expenses (W2) | 1,598 |
| Operating profit | 1,955 |
| Interest payable and similar charges (1,000 × 5%) | 50 |
| Profit on ordinary activities before tax | 1,905 |
| Tax on profit on ordinary activities | 105 |
| Profit on ordinary activities after tax | 1,800 |
| Dividends (W4) | 100 |
| Retained profit for the year | 1,700 |
| Profit and loss account at 1.X.96 | 550 |
| Profit and loss account at 31.12.X6 | 2,250 |
| Earnings per share (W5) | £4.35 |

CHEAPSTAKE PLC
BALANCE SHEET AS AT 31 DECEMBER 20X6

|  | £'000 | £'000 |
|---|---|---|
| *Fixed assets* |  |  |
| Intangible asset: goodwill (300 – 30) |  | 270 |
| Tangible assets (W6) |  | 2,720 |
|  |  | 2,990 |
| *Current assets* |  |  |
| Stock | 1,950 |  |
| Debtors (W7) | 1,544 |  |
| Bank | 200 |  |
|  | 3,694 |  |
| *Creditors: amounts falling due within one year* (W8) | (1,964) |  |
|  |  | 1,730 |
| *Total assets less current liabilities* |  | 4,720 |
| *Creditors: amounts falling due after one year* |  | 1,000 |
| *Provisions for liabilities and charges:* deferred tax |  | 120 |
|  |  | 3,600 |
| *Capital and reserves* |  |  |
| £1 Ordinary shares |  | 400 |
| 10% preference shares |  | 600 |
| Revaluation reserve (650 – 300) |  | 350 |
| Profit and loss account |  | 2,250 |
|  |  | 3,600 |

*Workings*

1 Cost of sales

|  | £'000 |
|---|---|
| Opening stock | 2,150 |
| Purchases | 4,329 |
|  | 6,479 |
| Closing stock | 1,950 |
|  | 4,529 |

## Questions and answers

### 2 Distribution and administration expenses

> **Helping hand**
> 
> This is the largest working but there is nothing difficult about it.

|  | Total £'000 | Distribution £'000 | Admin £'000 |
|---|---|---|---|
| Directors' emoluments | 150 |  | 150 |
| Rates and insurance (50:50) | 350 | 175 | 175 |
| Depreciation: land and buildings $((4,600 - 300) \times 10\%)$ | 430 | 172 | 258 |
| plant and machinery $(1,500 \times 20\%)$ | 300 | 225 | 75 |
| Goodwill amortisation $(300 \times 10\%)$ | 30 |  | 30 |
| Bad debts (W3) | 60 |  | 60 |
| Distribution expenses per trial balance | 346 | 346 |  |
| Administration expenses per trial balance | 850 |  | 850 |
| Total | 2,516 | 918 | 1,598 |

### 3 Bad debt expense

|  | £'000 |
|---|---|
| Increase in provision $(100 \times 50\%)$ | 50 |
| Bad debt written off | 25 |
|  | 75 |
| Less bad debt recovered | 15 |
|  | 60 |

### 4 Dividends

|  | £'000 |
|---|---|
| Final ordinary dividend $(6p \times 400,000)$ | 24 |
| Interim dividend | 16 |
| Total ordinary dividends | 40 |
| Preference dividend $10\% \times 600$ | 60 |
|  | 100 |

### 5 Earnings per share

> **Helping hand**
> 
> Do not forget to deduct the preference dividend.

|  | £'000 |
|---|---|
| Profit after tax | 1,800 |
| Less preference dividend | 60 |
| Earnings | 1,740 |

$$\text{EPS} = \frac{1,740}{400} = £4.35$$

### 6 Tangible fixed assets

|  | Cost/ valuation £'000 | Accumulated depreciation £'000 | NBV £'000 |
|---|---|---|---|
| Land and buildings | 4,300 | 2,180 | 2,120 |
| Plant and machinery | 1,500 | 900 | 600 |
| Total | 5,800 | 3,080 | 2,720 |

*Questions and answers*

7    *Debtors*

|  | £'000 |
|---|---|
| Trade debtors | 1,704 |
| Less provision for doubtful debts (100 × 150%) | (150) |
| Less bad debt written off | (25) |
|  | 1,529 |
| Add bad debt recovered | 15 |
|  | 1,544 |

8    *Creditors: amounts falling due within one year*

|  | £'000 |
|---|---|
| Trade creditors | 1,750 |
| Debenture interest accrued | 25 |
| Corporation tax provision | 105 |
| Proposed dividends (24 + 60) | 84 |
|  | 1,964 |

**Issued share capital** is the number of shares which the company has in issue at the present time, ie a proportion of the authorised share capital up to a maximum amount of the authorised share capital. Issued share capital could include ordinary and preference shares and appears in the balance sheet.

(b) The potential damages payable following an unfavourable outcome to the legal dispute may be classified as a 'contingent liability'. The treatment of contingent liabilities is governed by FRS 12 *Provisions, contingent assets and contingent liabilities*. The FRS defines a contingent liability as:

> 'A present obligation that arises from past events but is not recognised because it is not probable that a transfer of economic benefits will be required to settle the obligation or because the amount of the obligation cannot be measured with sufficient reliability.'

**Helping hand**

Now you have established which FRS applies, you must deal with the accounting treatment.

FRS 12 states that a contingent liability must not be recognised. However, disclosure is required of:

(i)    An estimate of its financial effect

(ii)   An indication of the uncertainties relating to the amount or timing of any outflow

(iii)  The possibility of any reimbursement

## 19 MUGGERIDGE (6/00)

The trial balance of Muggeridge Ltd at 31 December 20X9 was as follows.

|  | Dr £'000 | Cr £'000 |
|---|---|---|
| 7% Preference shares of 50p |  | 500 |
| Ordinary shares of £1 |  | 250 |
| Share premium account |  | 180 |
| Profit and loss account at 1 January 20X9 |  | 40 |
| Stock, 1 January 20X9 | 450 |  |
| Land at cost | 300 |  |
| Buildings at cost | 900 |  |
| Buildings, accumulated depreciation, 1 January 20X9 |  | 135 |
| Plant at cost | 1,020 |  |
| Plant, accumulated depreciation, 1 January 20X9 |  | 370 |
| Trade creditors |  | 900 |
| Debtors | 600 |  |
| Provision for doubtful debts at 1 January 20X9 |  | 25 |
| Purchases | 1,900 |  |
| Discounts received |  | 70 |
| Discounts allowed | 60 |  |
| Carriage in | 90 |  |
| Wages | 215 |  |
| Sales |  | 3,000 |
| Directors' remuneration | 50 |  |
| Heating and lighting | 230 |  |
| Other expenses | 50 |  |
| Fixed asset replacement reserve |  | 30 |
| Bank balance | 135 |  |
| 10% Debentures |  | 500 |
|  | 6,000 | 6,000 |

*Additional information as at 31 December 20X9*

(a) Depreciation on buildings is provided at 5% per annum on cost.

(b) Plant is depreciated at 20% per annum using the reducing balance method.

(c) Closing stock is valued at £500,000

(d) The provision for doubtful debts is to be made equal to 5% of debtors.

(e) There is a wages accrual of £30,000.

(f) Debenture interest has not been paid during the year

(g) On 1 January 20X9 the company purchased and absorbed another business as a going concern. Muggeridge Ltd acquired the business's sole asset of stock for £40,000 and, in addition, paid £100,000 for goodwill. The consideration of £140,000 was paid for by the issue of 100,000 ordinary shares. This transaction has not yet been recorded in the books of Muggeridge Ltd. The purchased goodwill has an estimated economic life of 10 years from 1 January 20X9.

(h) During December a bonus (or scrip) issue of two for five was made to ordinary shareholders. This has not been entered into the books. The share premium account is to be used for this purpose.

(i) The Directors wish to provide for:

(i) The preference dividend for the year

## Questions and answers

      (ii)    An ordinary dividend of 10p per share. (The bonus shares do not rank for dividend until the following year.)

      (iii)   A transfer of £20,000 to the fixed asset replacement reserve

(j)   Provision for corporation tax of £55,000 for the year is to be made.

*Required*

(a)   Prepare the following statements for Muggeridge Ltd for internal use.

      (i)     The trading and profit and loss account for the year ended 31 December 20X9

                                                                                                                                                                               (18 marks)

      (ii)    The balance sheet as at 31 December 20X9                        (16 marks)

(b)   Briefly explain the nature and purpose of:

      (i)     A provision for doubtful debts                                            (3 marks)

      (ii)    A bonus (or scrip) issue                                                          (3 marks)

                                                                                                                                                                                  **(40 marks)**

> **Helping hand.**
> 1   The issue of shares to acquire another business is tricky.
> 2   So are the fixed assets and the provision for doubtful debts.

# 19 ANSWER: MUGGERIDGE

> **Examiner's comment.** Most candidates performed well on this question, although some had difficulty with the above adjustments. Answers to Part (b) were generally weak.

(a) (i) MUGGERIDGE LIMITED
PROFIT AND LOSS ACCOUNT
FOR THE YEAR ENDED 31 DECEMBER 20X9

|  | £'000 | £'000 |
|---|---|---|
| Sales |  | 3,000 |
| Cost of sales (W1) |  | 1,980 |
| Gross profit |  | 1,020 |
| Discounts received |  | 70 |
|  |  | 1,090 |
| Less expenses |  |  |
| Discounts allowed | 60 |  |
| Wages (215 + 30) | 245 |  |
| Directors' remuneration | 50 |  |
| Heating and lighting | 230 |  |
| Other expenses | 50 |  |
| Goodwill amortisation 100/10 | 10 |  |
| Increase in provision for doubtful debts (W2) | 5 |  |
| Depreciation (W3) | 175 |  |
|  |  | 825 |
| Net profit before interest and tax |  | 265 |
| Debenture interest 500 × 10% |  | 50 |
| Net profit before tax |  | 215 |
| Corporation tax |  | 55 |
| Net profit after tax |  | 160 |
| Proposed dividends |  |  |
| Preference (500 × 7%) | 35 |  |
| Ordinary (10p × (250 + 100)) | 35 |  |
|  |  | 70 |
| Transfer to fixed asset |  | 90 |
| Replacement reserve |  | (20) |
|  |  | 70 |
| Profit and loss account at 1 January 20X9 |  | 40 |
| Profit and loss account at 31 December 20X9 |  | 110 |

## Questions and answers

(ii) **MUGGERIDGE LIMITED**
**BALANCE SHEET AS AT 31 DECEMBER 20X9**

|  | Cost £'000 | Accum. depn £'000 | Net book value £'000 |
|---|---|---|---|
| *Fixed assets* |  |  |  |
| Intangible |  |  |  |
| Goodwill | 100 | 10 | 90 |
| Tangible |  |  |  |
| Land | 300 | – | 300 |
| Buildings | 900 | 180 | 720 |
| Plant (W3) | 1,020 | 500 | 520 |
|  | 2,220 | 680 | 1,540 |
|  |  |  | 1,630 |

| | £'000 | £'000 |
|---|---|---|
| *Current assets* | | |
| Stock | | 500 |
| Debtors | 600 | |
| Less provision | (30) | |
| | | 570 |
| Bank | | 135 |
| | | 1,205 |
| *Creditors: amounts falling due within one year* | | |
| Trade creditors | | 900 |
| Corporation tax | | 55 |
| Accruals | | |
| Wages | 30 | |
| Interest | 50 | |
| | | 80 |
| Dividends proposed | | 70 |
| | | 1,105 |

|  | £'000 |
|---|---|
| Net current assets | 100 |
|  | 1,730 |
| *Creditors: amounts falling due after one year* |  |
| 10% debentures | 500 |
|  | 1,230 |
| *Capital and reserves* |  |
| Ordinary shares of £1 (W4) | 490 |
| 7% preference shares of 50p | 500 |
| Share premium account (W5) | 80 |
| Fixed asset replacement reserve (30 + 20) | 50 |
| Profit and loss account | 110 |
|  | 1,230 |

*Workings*

1  Cost of sales

|  | £'000 |
|---|---|
| Opening stock | 450 |
| Purchases (1,900 + 40) | 1,940 |
| Carriage inwards | 90 |
| Closing stock | (500) |
|  | 1,980 |

## Questions and answers

**2** *Increase in provision for doubtful debts*

|  | £'000 | £'000 |
|---|---|---|
| Debtors per trial balance | 600 | |
| 5% of debtors (required provision) | | 30 |
| Existing provision for doubtful debts | | 25 |
| Increase in provision | | 5 |

> **Helping hand.** Remember it is the **increase** in provision that goes to the profit and loss accounts.

**3** *Fixed assets and depreciation*

|  | £'000 | £'000 |
|---|---|---|
| *Buildings* | | |
| Cost | | 900 |
| Accumulated depn 1.1.X9 | 135 | |
| Depn, charge per year (900 × 5%) | 45 | |
| Acc. dep. 31.12.X9 | | 180 |
| NBV 31.12.X9 | | 720 |
| *Plant* | | |
| Cost | | 1,020 |
| Acc. depn. 1.1.X9 | | 370 |
| NBV at 1.1.X9 | | 650 |
| ∴ Depn charge for year: 650 × 20% | | 130 |
| NBV at 31.12.X9 | | 520 |
| Depreciation charge for year: 45 + 130 = 175 | | |

> **Helping hand.** Don't forget the reducing balance method.

**4** *Ordinary shares*

|  | £'000 |
|---|---|
| Per trial balance | 250 |
| Shares issued to acquire business | 100 |
| | 350 |
| Bonus issue: 350 × 2/5 | 140 |
| | 490 |

> **Helping hand.** 100,000 £1 shares were issued for £140,000, so £40,000 must be share premium.

**5** *Share premium*

|  | £'000 |
|---|---|
| Per trial balance | 180 |
| Premium on share issued to acquire business (140 – 100) | 40 |
| Bonus issue | (140) |
| | 80 |

(b) (i) A **provision for doubtful debts** is a general estimate of the percentage of debts which are not expected to be repaid. A business may know from past experience that, say, 5% of debtors' balances are unlikely to be collected. It may be that no particular customers are regarded as suspect and so it is not possible to write off any individual customer balances as bad debts. The provision aims to match doubtful debts to the right year so that the profits and the assets of the business are not overstated.

## Questions and answers

(ii) **Bonus share issues** or scrip issues arise when a company wishes to increase its share capital without raising new finance. In effect, **reserves are re-classified as share capital**. This is purely a paper exercise which raises no funds. Any reserve may be re-classified in this way – in this case it is the share premium account. Such a re-classification increases the capital base of the company and gives creditors greater protection.

## 20 ARNFIELD (12/99)

The following trial balance has been prepared for Arnfield Ltd for the year ended 31 October 20X9.

|  | Dr £'000 | Cr £'000 |
|---|---|---|
| Buildings at cost | 2,000 |  |
| Motor vehicles at cost | 70 |  |
| Land at cost | 600 |  |
| Furniture and equipment at cost | 1,000 |  |
| Fixed assets replacement reserve |  | 100 |
| Share premium account |  | 40 |
| Cash in hand | 140 |  |
| Stock at 1 November 20X8 | 700 |  |
| Rates | 100 |  |
| Advertising | 30 |  |
| Insurance | 70 |  |
| Wages and salaries | 750 |  |
| Heating and lighting | 80 |  |
| Discounts received |  | 130 |
| Profit and loss account at 1 November 20X8 |  | 100 |
| Provision for doubtful debts |  | 40 |
| Returns inward | 30 |  |
| General expenses | 20 |  |
| Telephone | 40 |  |
| Sales |  | 7,900 |
| Creditors |  | 320 |
| Bank |  | 300 |
| Debtors | 1,960 |  |
| Purchases | 3,500 |  |
| Debenture interest | 50 |  |
| Bad debts | 600 |  |
| Provisions for depreciation at 1 November 20X8 |  |  |
|     Furniture and equipment |  | 350 |
|     Buildings |  | 400 |
|     Motor vehicles |  | 20 |
| 10% Debentures |  | 500 |
| 6% £1 Preference shares |  | 300 |
| £1 Ordinary shares |  | 1,240 |
|  | 11,740 | 11,740 |

You have also been provided with the following notes.

(a) Stock at 31 October 20X9 was valued at £900,000.

(b) The advertising expenditure included £10,000 which relates to a newspaper advertising campaign to be run during November and December 20X9.

(c) There are wages and salaries outstanding of £70,000 for the year ended 31 October 20X9.

(d) The provision for doubtful debts is to be increased to £50,000 and any adjustments charged to bad debts.

(e) Depreciation is to be provided for as follows.

    Motor vehicles at 20% of written down value.
    Furniture and equipment at 20% of written down value.

## Questions and answers

(f) Buildings are depreciated at 10% of cost. At 31 October 20X9 the buildings were professionally valued at £2,300,000 and the directors wish this valuation to be incorporated into the accounts.

(g) The directors have declared an ordinary dividend of 20p per share. No dividends were paid during the year.

(h) An additional £150,000 is to be transferred to the fixed assets replacement reserve.

(i) Corporation tax of £700,000 is to be provided for the year.

*Required*

Prepare the following statements, for internal use.

(a) The trading, profit and loss account for the year ended 31 October 20X9     (25 marks)
(b) The balance sheet as at 31 October 20X9     (15 marks)

**(40 marks)**

You are advised to show workings where appropriate.

---

**Helping hand**

The trickiest thing about this question is remembering to put everything in, specifically to follow through profit and loss account and balance sheet items. Remember, for example:

1 The preference dividend
2 The fixed asset replacement reserve
3 The revaluation reserve

# 20 ANSWER: ARNFIELD

> **Examiner's comment**
>
> Most candidates coped well with this question, although the depreciation on the building caused problems. Those candidates that produced a well presented balance sheet with appropriate headings, sub-totals and main totals did well.

(a) ARNFIELD LIMITED
TRADING, PROFIT AND LOSS ACCOUNT
FOR THE YEAR ENDED 31 OCTOBER 20X9

|  | £ | £ |
|---|---:|---:|
| Sales (W1) |  | 7,870 |
| Cost of sales (W2) |  | 3,300 |
| Gross profit |  | 4,570 |
| Discounts received |  | 130 |
|  |  | 4,700 |
| Less expenses |  |  |
|     Rents | 100 |  |
|     Advertising (30–10) | 20 |  |
|     Insurance | 70 |  |
|     Wages and salaries (750+70) | 820 |  |
|     Heating and lighting | 80 |  |
|     General expenses | 20 |  |
|     Telephone | 40 |  |
|     Debenture interest | 50 |  |
|     Bad debts (W3) | 610 |  |
|     Depreciation (W4) | 340 |  |
|  |  | 2,150 |
| Profit on ordinary activities before tax |  | 2,550 |
| Corporation tax |  | 700 |
| Profit after tax |  | 1,850 |
| Appropriations |  |  |
| Dividends: ordinary (1,240 × 20p) | 248 |  |
|           preference 6% × 300 | 18 |  |
|  | 266 |  |
| Transfer to fixed assets replacement reserve | 150 |  |
|  |  | 416 |
| Retained profit for the year |  | 1,434 |
| Profit and loss account as at 1.11.X8 |  | 100 |
| Profit and loss account as at 31.10.X9 |  | 1,534 |

> **Helping hand**
>
> The preference dividend isn't directly mentioned in the question, but you should know from the trial balance that it is 6%.

## Questions and answers

(b) ARNFIELD LIMITED
BALANCE SHEET AS AT 31 OCTOBER 20X9

|  | Cost £ | Acc. Depn. £ | NBV £ |
|---|---|---|---|
| Land | 600 | - | 600 |
| Buildings (at valuation) | 2,300 | - | 2300 |
| Motor vehicles | 70 | 30 | 40 |
| Furniture and equipment | 1,000 | 480 | 520 |
|  | 3,970 | 510 | 3,460 |

Current assets
| | | | |
|---|---|---|---|
| Stock | | 900 | |
| Debtors | | 1,920 | |
| Cash in hand | | 140 | |
| | | 2,960 | |

Current liabilities
| | | | |
|---|---|---|---|
| Creditors | | 320 | |
| Bank overdraft | | 300 | |
| Accrued wages | | 70 | |
| Corporation tax payable | | 700 | |
| Proposed dividends | | 266 | |
| | | 1,656 | |
| | | | 1,304 |
| Total assets less current liabilities | | | 4,764 |

Long-term liabilities
| | | |
|---|---|---|
| 10% debentures | | 500 |
| | | 4,264 |

Capital and reserves
| | | |
|---|---|---|
| Ordinary share capital | | 1,240 |
| Preference shares | | 300 |
| Share premium | | 40 |
| Fixed assets replacement reserve (100+150) | | 250 |
| Revaluation reserve (W4) | | 900 |
| Profit and loss account | | 1,534 |
| | | 4,264 |

---

**Helping hand**

Remember to put in the transfer to the fixed asset replacement reserve, already dealt with in the profit and loss account.

---

*Workings*

1  *Sales*

| | £ |
|---|---|
| Per trial balance | 7,900 |
| Less returns inwards | (30) |
| | 7,870 |

2  *Cost of sales*

| | £ |
|---|---|
| Opening stock | 700 |
| Purchases | 3,500 |
| | 4,200 |
| Less closing stock | 900 |
| | 3,300 |

## Questions and answers

3   *Increase in provision for doubtful debts*

|  | £ |
|---|---|
| Provision | 40 |
| Provision required | 50 |
| Increase | 10 |

Total bad debts charge: 600+10=610

4   *Fixed assets and depreciation*

Buildings:

Cost/valuation on = £2,300,000

∴ Transfer to revaluation reserve is calculated as follows

|  | £ |
|---|---|
| Cost | 2,000 |
| Accumulated depreciation = 400 (10% × 2,000) | (600) |
| Net book value | 1,400 |
| Revalued amount | 2,300 |
| ∴ Transfer to revaluation reserve | 900 |

> **Helping hand**
> Don't forget this when you do the bottom part of the balance sheet.

Land:
Cost = NBV = £600,000

Furniture and equipment:

|  | £ |
|---|---|
| Cost | 1,000 |
| Acc. depn. at 1.11.X8 | 350 |
| NBV at 1.11.X8 | 650 |
| Charge for year: 20% × 650 | 130 |
| NBV at 31.10.X9 | 520 |

Motor vehicles:

|  | £ |
|---|---|
| Cost | 70 |
| Acc. depn. at 1.11.X8 | 20 |
| NBV at 1.11.X8 | 50 |
| Charge for year : 20% × 50 | 10 |
| NBV at 31.10.X9 | 40 |

Total depreciation charges = 130+10+200=340

5   *Debtors*

|  | £ |
|---|---|
| Per trial balance | 1,960 |
| Less provision | 50 |
|  | 1,910 |
| Add prepayment (advertising) | 10 |
|  | 1,920 |

## 21 POLLARD (12/01)

The following is the trial balance of Pollard Ltd as at 31 October 20X1.

|  | Dr £'000 | Cr £'000 |
|---|---|---|
| Stock, at 31 October 20X0 | 600 |  |
| Land at cost | 400 |  |
| Trade creditors |  | 450 |
| Debtors | 900 |  |
| Buildings at cost | 800 |  |
| Buildings: accumulated depreciation at 31 October 20X0 |  | 120 |
| Plant at cost | 1,400 |  |
| Plant: accumulated depreciation at 31 October 20X0 |  | 200 |
| 7% preference shares of £1 |  | 300 |
| Ordinary shares of £1 |  | 700 |
| Share premium account |  | 200 |
| Profit and loss account at 31 October 20X0 |  | 80 |
| Provision for doubtful debts at 31 October 20X0 |  | 50 |
| Wages | 325 |  |
| Sales |  | 4,370 |
| Directors' fees | 100 |  |
| Heating and lighting | 85 |  |
| Insurance | 45 |  |
| Other expenses | 30 |  |
| 8% debentures |  | 800 |
| Purchases | 2,600 |  |
| Discounts received |  | 60 |
| Discounts allowed | 50 |  |
| Carriage in | 170 |  |
| Fixed asset replacement reserve |  | 100 |
| Bank balance |  | 75 |
|  | 7,505 | 7,505 |

*Additional information for the year ended 31 October 20X1*

(a) Closing stock is valued at £450,000.

(b) There are wages outstanding of £50,000.

(c) The provision for doubtful debts is to be made equal to 15% of outstanding debts.

(d) Debenture interest is to be accrued for the year.

(e) Insurance of £10,000 has been prepaid.

(f) Depreciation on buildings is provided at 5% per annum using the straight line method.

(g) Plant is depreciated at 20% per annum using the reducing balance method.

(h) Provision for corporation tax of £40,000 for the year is to be made.

(i) During October a bonus (or scrip) issue of one for five was made to ordinary shareholders. This has not been entered into the books. The share premium account is to be used for this purpose.

(j) The directors wish to provide for:

(i) The preference dividend for the year

(ii) A 5% dividend on the ordinary shares. (The bonus shares do not rank for dividend until the following year.)

(k) A provision is to be made for the audit fee of £55,000.

## Questions and answers

*Required*

(a) Prepare the following statements for Pollard Ltd for internal use.

   (i) The trading and profit and loss account for the year ended 31 October 20X1

   (17 marks)

   (ii) The balance sheet as at 31 October 20X1. (16 marks)

(b) Referring to items (b), (c) and (f) in the additional information above, state the main accounting concept which is being applied in each of these adjustments. (3 marks)

(c) Explain what is meant by 'relevance' and 'reliability' in the context of providing useful financial information. (4 marks)

**(40 marks)**

---

**Helping hand**

1 Don't forget that you are calculating the **increase** in doubtful debt provision for the P&L and the actual provision required for the balance sheet.

2 The bonus issue is to be written off the share premium account. So after the bonus issue, the total of share capital and share premium should be the same as before.

# 21 ANSWER: POLLARD

> **Examiner's comment.** Most candidates made a good attempt at this part of the question and were able to perform most of the adjustments required. The main difficulty experienced by candidates was dealing with the bonus issue of shares to ordinary shareholders. A significant number of candidates did not adjust the ordinary shares figure and the share premium account in the balance sheet. The other adjustment that caused difficulty was the outstanding audit fee of £55,000. Candidates needed to charge the £55,000 to the profit and loss account and to show an accrual in the balance sheet.
>
> Some candidates are still unsure (or confused) where, in the trading and profit and loss account, the discounts received and discounts allowed appear. Similarly, carriage inwards is another item which some candidates have difficulty in presenting correctly. The format and presentation of the trading and profit and loss account and balance sheet answers was generally better than in previous examinations.
>
> In part (b) most candidates identified the matching concept for the wages adjustment but not for depreciation.
>
> Part (c) was well answered.

(a) (i) POLLARD LIMITED
TRADING AND PROFIT AND LOSS ACCOUNT
FOR THE YEAR ENDED 31 OCTOBER 20X1

|  | £'000 | £'000 |
|---|---|---|
| Sales |  | 4,370 |
| Cost of sales (W1) |  | 2,920 |
| Gross profit |  | 1,450 |
| Discounts received |  | 60 |
|  |  | 1,510 |
| Less expenses |  |  |
| Discounts allowed | 50 |  |
| Wages (325 + 50) | 375 |  |
| Increase in provision for doubtful debts (W2) | 85 |  |
| Directors' fees | 100 |  |
| Heating and lighting | 85 |  |
| Insurance (45 – 10) | 35 |  |
| Other expenses | 30 |  |
| Depreciation (W3) | 280 |  |
| Audit fee | 55 |  |
|  |  | 1,095 |
| Net profit before interest and tax |  | 415 |
| Debenture interest (800 × 8%) |  | 64 |
| Net profit before tax |  | 351 |
| Corporation tax |  | 40 |
| Net profit after tax |  | 311 |
| Proposed dividends |  |  |
| Preference (300 × 7%) | 21 |  |
| Ordinary (700 × 5%) | 35 |  |
|  |  | 56 |
| Retained profit for the year |  | 255 |
| Profit and loss account at 1.11.X0 |  | 80 |
| Profit and loss account at 31.10.X1 |  | 335 |

## Questions and answers

(ii) POLLARD LIMITED
BALANCE SHEET AS AT 31 OCTOBER 20X1

|  | Cost £'000 | Accum depn £'000 | Net book value £'000 |
|---|---|---|---|
| *Fixed assets* | | | |
| Land | 400 | – | 400 |
| Buildings (W3) | 800 | 160 | 640 |
| Plant (W3) | 1,400 | 440 | 960 |
| | 2,600 | 600 | 2,000 |

|  | £'000 | £'000 |
|---|---|---|
| *Current assets* | | |
| Stock | | 450 |
| Debtors | 900 | |
| Less provision (W2) | 135 | |
| | | 765 |
| Prepayments: insurance | | 10 |
| | | 1,225 |
| *Creditors: amounts falling due within one year* | | |
| Trade creditors | | 450 |
| Corporation tax | | 40 |
| Accruals | | |
|   Wages | 50 | |
|   Interest | 64 | |
| | | 114 |
| Bank overdraft | | 75 |
| Audit fee | | 55 |
| Proposed dividends | | 56 |
| | | 790 |
| Net current assets | | 435 |
| | | 2,435 |
| *Creditors: amounts falling due after one year* | | |
| 8% debentures | | 800 |
| | | 1,635 |
| *Share capital and reserves* | | |
| Ordinary shares of £1 (W4) | | 840 |
| Share premium account (W5) | | 60 |
| 7% preference shares of £1 | | 300 |
| Fixed asset replacement reserve | | 100 |
| Profit and loss account | | 335 |
| | | 1,635 |

*Workings*

1    *Cost of sales*

|  | £'000 |
|---|---|
| Opening stock | 600 |
| Purchases | 2,600 |
| Carriage inwards | 170 |
| | 3,370 |
| Closing stock | (450) |
| | 2,920 |

2    *Increase in provision for doubtful debts*

|  | £'000 | £'000 |
|---|---|---|
| Debtors per trial balance | 900 | |
| 15% of debtors (required provision) | | 135 |
| Existing provision | | 50 |
| Increase in provision | | 85 |

> **Helping hand.** This working will feed into both the P&L and balance sheet.

3   *Fixed assets and depreciation*

|  | £'000 | £'000 |
|---|---|---|
| *Buildings* | | |
| Cost | | 800 |
| Accumulated depn 1.11.20X0 | 120 | |
| Depn charge for year 800 × 5% | 40 | |
| Accumulated depn 31.10.X1 | | 160 |
| NBV 31.10.X1 | | 640 |
| *Plant* | | |
| Cost | | 1,400 |
| Accumulated depn 1.11.20X0 | | 200 |
| NBV 1.1.20X0 | | 1,200 |
| Depn charge for year: 20% × 1,200 | | 240 |
| NBV 31.10.X1 | | 960 |

Depreciation charge for year: £240,000 + £40,000 = £280,000

> **Helping hand.** This working will also feed into the profit and loss account and the balance sheet.

4   *Ordinary shares*

|  | £'000 |
|---|---|
| Per trial balance | 700 |
| Bonus issue: 700 × 1/5 | 140 |
|  | 840 |

5   *Share premium*

|  | £'000 |
|---|---|
| Per trial balance | 200 |
| Bonus issue | (140) |
|  | 60 |

> **Helping hand.** Check:
>
> Before bonus issue, share capital + share premium = £(700,000 + 200,000) = £900,000
>
> After bonus issue, share capital + share premium = £(840,000 + 60,000) = £900,000

(b) (i) This is the **accruals concept**, which matches revenue to expenses incurred in the accounting period in earning that revenue. Although the wages will be paid in the next accounting period, they relate to the current one.

(ii) In operation here is the **prudence concept**. This means that revenue must not be anticipated. The element of doubt over the collectability of the debts means that a provision is necessary.

(iii) Depreciation is an example of the **matching (or accruals) concept**. The cost of a fixed asset is allocated to accounting periods which are likely to benefit from it.

(c) **Relevance** means that the information provided should **satisfy the needs of information users**. In the case of company accounts, clearly a wide range of information will be needed to satisfy a wide range of users.

**Reliability** means that the information presented in a set of financial statements **can be relied upon** to give an **accurate** description of the transactions of the enterprise in

The accounting records. This means that users should have **confidence** that the information is **correct** and that there are **no material errors** in the accounts.

# Questions and answers

## DO YOU KNOW? - REGULATORY AND CONCEPTUAL FRAMEWORK

- *Check that you can fill in the blanks in the statements below before you attempt any questions. If in doubt, you should go back to your BPP Interactive Text and revise first.*

- Accounting standards were formerly published by the ………………….. and called ………………….. (…………………….). In future, they will be published by the ………………….. and called ………………….. (…………………….). Make sure you know the differences between the old system and the new.

- You should also be able to discuss the role of the Urgent Issues Task Force and the Review Panel.

- All companies must prepare full statutory accounts for approval by their shareholders. For large companies, a copy of these accounts must also be made available to the public by filing with the ………………….. . Small and medium-sized companies may, if they wish, prepare an additional set of accounts disclosing less information.

- Listed companies must comply with Stock Exchange regulations contained in the ………………….. or ………………….. . The requirements are more stringent than for non-listed companies.

- You should ensure that you can discuss the arguments for and against a conceptual framework and that you understand what is meant by GAAP.

    TRY QUESTION 23

- FRS 3 introduced three new statements.
    - …………………..
    - …………………..
    - …………………..

- You should be aware of the FRS 3 definitions of:
    - Extraordinary items
    - Exceptional items
    - Prior year adjustments
    - Discontinued operations
    - Total recognised gains and losses

- The ASB's *Statement of Principles*, now in exposure draft form, should provide the backbone of the conceptual framework in the UK.

- Key elements in the *Statement* are as follows.
    - Financial statements should give financial information useful for assessing ………………….. of management and for making economic decisions.
    - Financial information should be ………………….., ………………….., ………………….. and ………………….. .
    - Assets and liabilities have conceptual priority over the profit and loss account.
    - Accounts should move towards ………………….. valuations.
    - ………………….. is for assets held for the business to continue trading.

- *Possible pitfalls*

    *Write down the mistakes you know you should avoid.*

## Questions and answers

### DID YOU KNOW? – REGULATORY AND CONCEPTUAL FRAMEWORK

- *Could you fill in the blanks? The answers are in bold. Use this page for revision purposes as you approach the exam.*

- Accounting standards were formerly published by the **Accounting Standards Committee** and called **SSAPs** (**statements of standard accounting practice**). In future, they will be published by the **Accounting Standards Board** and called **FRSs** (**financial reporting standards**). Make sure you know the differences between the old system and the new.

- You should also be able to discuss the role of the Urgent Issues Task Force and the Review Panel.

- All companies must prepare full statutory accounts for approval by their shareholders. For large companies, a copy of these accounts must also be made available to the public by filing with the **registrar of companies**. Small and medium-sized companies may, if they wish, prepare an additional set of accounts disclosing less information.

- Listed companies must comply with Stock Exchange regulations contained in the **Listing Rules** or **'Yellow Book'**. The requirements are more stringent than for non-listed companies.

- You should ensure that you can discuss the arguments for and against a conceptual framework and that you understand what is meant by GAAP.

    TRY QUESTION 23

- FRS 3 introduced three new statements.
    - **Statement of total recognised gains and losses**
    - **Reconciliation of movements in shareholders' funds**
    - **Note on historical cost profits and losses**

- You should be aware of the FRS 3 definitions of:
    - Extraordinary items
    - Exceptional items
    - Prior year adjustments
    - Discontinued operations
    - Total recognised gains and losses

- The ASB's *Statement of Principles*, now in exposure draft form, should provide the backbone of the conceptual framework in the UK.

- Key elements in the *Statement* are as follows.
    - Financial statements should give financial information useful for assessing **stewardship** of management and for making economic decisions.
    - Financial information should be **relevant**, **reliable**, **comparable** and **understandable**.
    - Assets and liabilities have conceptual priority over the profit and loss account.
    - Accounts should move towards **current cost** valuations.
    - **Statement of total recognised gains and losses** is for assets held for the business to continue trading.

- *Possible pitfalls*
    - **Questions on the regulatory framework tend to be written rather than computational. Do not underestimate the amount of time needed for such questions.**
    - **You need to know FRS 3 fairly well, but do not expect complicated calculations.**
    - **The *Statement of Principles* may seem theoretical but it will be tested in a practical context.**

## 22  QUESTION WITH HELP: REGULATORY FRAMEWORK

In the UK there are regulations governing the following aspects of accounting:

(a) Valuation of items in the financial statements
(b) Disclosure in the financial statements
(c) Format of the accounts
(d) Publication of the accounts

*Required*

Discuss each of these in turn, giving examples to show how they are affected by regulations.

> *If you are stuck, look at the next page for detailed help as to how you should tackle this question.*

## Questions and answers

**APPROACHING THE ANSWER**

This is a 'wordy' question. You will get at least one of these on the paper. Students tend to underestimate such questions because they get bogged down in calculations, or think they can waffle.

**Step 1** First look at the number of marks, ie 20. You therefore have 36 minutes for this question. Think of it as 8 minutes planning time and around 7 minutes for each of parts (a) to (d).

**Step 2** Plan your answer. Jot down the sources of regulation governing accounting, ie

SSAPs and FRSs
Company law
Stock Exchange

**Step 3** Still at the planning stage, divide a sheet of paper into four columns headed:

Valuation
Disclosure
Format
Publication

(*Note.* Use **lots of paper** in your exam - now is not the time to be thinking about saving trees!)

**Step 4** Still planning ...

Look at the column headed 'valuation'. Which of the three sources identified in Step 3 deals specifically with valuation? The answer is SSAPs and FRSs. Jot this down, then make a note of SSAPs or FRSs you can think of that deal with this. The obvious one is SSAP 9.

**Step 5** Still planning ...

Repeat this exercise for each of the other three columns. You should find that more than one source is used, eg for disclosure you have both the Companies Act 1985 and SSAPs and FRSs.

**Step 6** When you have completed your columns, write out your answer in full. Because you have the information at your fingertips your final answer will be that much better.

Because the question is divided into four parts, it is easier to structure. Pure 'essay' questions will require even more planning.

## 22 ANSWER TO QUESTION WITH HELP: REGULATORY FRAMEWORK

(a) The question of **valuation of items** is not generally addressed by company law, being left to the standard setters. Many SSAPs deal with questions of valuation, in particular FRS 15 *Tangible fixed assets*, SSAP 9 *Stocks and long-term contracts* and SSAP 19 *Accounting for investment properties*.

**Valuation** is a subjective and often complex process about which it is not easy to legislate. Some accounting standards dealing with valuation have been more 'successful' than others. **SSAP 9**, for example, has found general acceptance while **SSAP 16** on current cost accounting provoked so much opposition that it had to be withdrawn.

(b) **Disclosure in the financial statement**

Disclosure in the financial statements is governed by legislation and by accounting standards. Examples include the following.

(i) Disclosure of accounting policies is required by the **Companies Act 1985**, to enable a comparison to be made between companies with difference policies and to prevent possible abuse of the range of accounting bases available.

(ii) Certain **disclosures** are required by the Act for political reasons (the amount of political donations) or social reasons (policy on employment of disabled persons).

(iii) **SSAPs** and **FRSs** require certain disclosures not specifically dealt with in legislation but which are necessary in order to give the user of the accounts a full understanding of the issues. An example of this is FRS 12 *Provisions, contingent liabilities and contingent assets*.

(c) **Format of the accounts**

Statutory accounts are part of the price to be paid for **limited liability**, and statute lays down numerous rules on the information to be included in the published accounts and the format of its presentation. The Companies Act 1985 sets out two formats for the balance sheet and two for the profit and loss account.

It should be emphasised that the requirement that the accounts show a **true and fair view** is paramount, and any rule on the format of the accounts may be overridden if compliance with it would prevent the accounts from showing a true and fair view.

The format of the accounts is the province of legislation rather than accounting standards, with the exception of FRS 1 which prescribes the format of a cash flow statement.

(d) **Publication of the accounts**

Limited companies must produce statutory accounts annually and must appoint an independent person to audit and report on them. Once prepared, a copy of the accounts must be sent to the **Registrar of Companies** who maintains a separate file for every company. The Registrar's file may be inspected for a nominal fee by any member of the public. This is why the statutory accounts are often referred to as published accounts.

A listed company must conform with **Stock Exchange regulations** contained in the *Listing Rules* issued by the Council of The Stock Exchange. The company commits itself to certain procedures and standards, including matters concerning the disclosure of accounting information which are more extensive than the disclosure requirements of the Companies Act.

## 23 CONCEPTUAL FRAMEWORK (12/00)

*Required*

(a) Define the nature and purpose of an accounting conceptual framework. (4 marks)

(b) Outline the potential benefits and drawbacks of an accounting conceptual framework. (5 marks)

(c) Explain the following accounting concepts and give an example of how each is applied during the preparation of financial statements.

    (i) Accruals concept
    (ii) Consistency concept
    (iii) Prudence concept (6 marks)

**(15 marks)**

## 23 ANSWER: CONCEPTUAL FRAMEWORK

> **Helping hand.** The conceptual framework is an important and topical area and you should have a good overview of it. Since this question was set, SSAP 2, which referred to 'fundamental accounting concepts' has been replaced by FRS 18 *Accounting policies*, which has a slightly different emphasis and terminology. However, the concepts remain the same and will be applied in the same way.
>
> **Examiner's comment.** Part (a) was quite poorly answered with many candidates confusing the regulatory framework with the conceptual accounting framework. In part (b), those candidates who were unable to correctly define the conceptual framework in part (a) also struggled to gain marks on this part of the question. . Most candidates did well on Part (c) of the question. However, a number of candidates compensated for their lack of knowledge by producing lengthy and incorrect answers.

(a) A conceptual framework is a **statement of generally accepted theoretical principles** which form the frame of reference for financial reporting. These theoretical principles form the **basis for the development of new reporting standards** and the evaluation of those already in existence.

Such a framework will form the theoretical basis for determining which events should be accounted for, how they should be measured and how they should be communicated to the user. Thus the accounting profession should be able to develop standards and rules which **do not conflict.**

In the UK, the conceptual framework used by the Accounting Standards Board is the *Statement of Principles.* This is not an accounting standard, but is used in developing accounting standards.

(b) **Advantages**

  (i) The 'fire-fighting', **piecemeal approach** to standard setting is **avoided**.

  (ii) The standard setting process is **less likely to be influenced by interest groups.**

  (iii) The fundamental principles behind particular standards are available in a **single document** and do not have to be justified each time a new standard is published.

  (iv) It is a frame of reference for when **disputes** arise over the accounting treatment of items.

  **Disadvantages**

  (i) Financial statements are intended for a variety of users and it is **not certain** that a single conceptual framework **will suit all users.**

  (ii) **One financial statement may be favoured** at the expense of the other(s). It has been said that the *Statement of Principles* emphasises the balance sheet at the expense of the profit and loss account.

  (iii) **Users have different requirements.** There may be a need for a variety of accounting standards, each produced for a different purpose and with different concepts underlying them.

  (iv) The framework may be **too general** or theoretical to help much in producing accounting standards.

(c) (i) **Accruals concept**

  The accruals concept states that, in computing profit, revenue earned must be **matched** against the expenditure incurred in earning it.

  An example of this is the calculation of cost of sales. The cost of items unsold at the end of the year is matched against revenue for the following year.

(ii) **Consistency**

This concept states that similar items should be accorded **similar treatment**, both within one set of accounts or from one accounting period to the next.

An example of this would be the valuation of stock – if the basis changed from year to year, it would be very difficult to make comparisons and the profit figure would be distorted.

(iii) **Prudence**

The prudence concept states that where alternative procedures or valuations are possible, the one selected should be the one which gives the **most cautious** presentation of the business's financial position or results.

Stock valuation is a good example. If an item of stock cost £50, and could be sold for £70, it would be valued at £50 because profits must not be anticipated. However, if the sale value dropped to £30, the stock would be written down and the loss recorded.

This has led to profits and losses being treated unevenly. FRS 18 *Accounting policies* places less emphasis on prudence than SSAP 2, its predecessor did.

## 24 REGULATORS

State three different regulatory influences on the preparation of the published accounts of quoted companies and briefly explain the role of each one. Comment briefly on the effectiveness of this regulatory system.

(20 marks)

## 24 ANSWER: REGULATORS

A **listed company** is a public limited company whose shares are bought and sold on The Stock Exchange. This involves the signing of a listing agreement which requires compliance with the 'Listing Rules' (formerly known as the **Yellow Book**). This contains amongst other things The Stock Exchange's detailed rules on the information to be disclosed in listed companies' accounts. This, then, is one regulatory influence on a listed company's accounts. The Stock Exchange enforces compliance by monitoring accounts and reserving the right to withdraw a company's shares from **The Stock Exchange List**: ie the company's shares would no longer be traded through The Stock Exchange. There is, however, no statutory requirement to obey these rules.

All companies in the UK have to comply with the **Companies Acts**, which lay down detailed requirements on the preparation of accounts. Company law is becoming more and more detailed, partly because of **EU Directives**. Another reason to increase statutory regulation is that listed companies are under great pressure to show profit growth and an obvious way to achieve this is to manipulate accounting policies. If this involves breaking the law, as opposed to ignoring professional guidance, company directors may think twice before bending the rules - or, at least, this is the government's hope.

Professional guidance is given by the **Accounting Standards Board (ASB)**, overseen by the **Financial Reporting Council**. Prescriptive guidance is given in **Statements of Standard Accounting Practice (SSAPs)** and **Financial Reporting Standards (FRSs)** which must be applied in all accounts required to show a 'true and fair view' (ie all companies). SSAPs and FRSs are issued after extensive consultation and are revised as required to reflect economic or legal changes. Until fairly recently, companies have been able to disguise non-compliance if their auditors did not qualify the audit report. However, the **Companies Act 1989** requires details of non-compliance to be disclosed in the accounts. 'Defective' accounts will in future be revised under court order if necessary and directors signing such accounts can be prosecuted and fined (or even imprisoned). This sanction applies to breach of both accounting standards and company law.

# DO YOU KNOW? - ACCOUNTING STANDARDS

- *Check that you can fill in the blanks in the statements below before you attempt any questions. If in doubt, you should go back to your BPP Interactive Text and revise first.*

- SSAP 17 *Accounting for balance sheet events* amplifies the CA 1985 requirement to take account of post balance sheet liabilities and losses by distinguishing between ............................ and ............................ and giving examples.

- The SSAP also requires disclosure of ............................ transactions.

- Where an otherwise non-adjusting event indicates that the going concern concept is no longer appropriate then the accounts may have to be restated on a break-up basis.

- You should be able to define and discuss all these terms and apply them to practical examples.

  TRY QUESTION 26

- FRS 12 ............................................................................ defines these items and specifies the accounting treatment.

- You should learn the definition and required treatments and be able to discuss why losses and gains are treated differently. You should also be able to give examples of each.

- Be sure that you can explain the difference between the CA 1985's requirements and those of FRS 12.

  TRY QUESTION 25

- If a business has ............................, it means that the value of the business as a going concern is greater than the value of its separate tangible assets.
  - The valuation of goodwill is extremely subjective and fluctuates constantly.
  - For this reason, goodwill is not normally shown as an asset in the balance sheet.

- The exception to the rule is ............................, when someone purchases a business as a going concern. In this case the purchaser and vendor will fix an agreed price which includes an element in respect of goodwill. The way in which goodwill is then valued is not an accounting problem, but a matter of agreement between the two parties.

- Purchased goodwill may then either be amortised over its useful economic life in the profit and loss account, or be retained in the balance sheet as an intangible asset. If it is retained in the balance sheet, it must be reviewed for impairment every year.

  TRY QUESTION 27

- Companies pay ............................ on their profits. Taxable profits are net profit before dividends adjusted for items where the tax treatment differs from the accounts treatment.

- When a company pays certain expenses such as debenture interest it must deduct ............................ at a specified rate and pay this to the Revenue.

- Gross debentures is treated as ............................ and gross debenture interest paid is a tax ............................ .

- General VAT is ............ in the accounts of a trader in income and expenditure.

- *Possible pitfalls*

  *Write down the mistakes you know you should avoid.*

## Questions and answers

### DID YOU KNOW? - ACCOUNTING STANDARDS

- *Could you fill in the blanks? The answers are in bold. Use this page for revision purposes as you approach the exam.*

- SSAP 17 *Accounting for balance sheet events* amplifies the CA 1985 requirement to take account of post balance sheet liabilities and losses by distinguishing between **adjusting events** and **non-adjusting events** and giving examples.

- The SSAP also requires disclosure of **window dressing** transactions.

- Where an otherwise non-adjusting event indicates that the going concern concept is no longer appropriate then the accounts may have to be restated on a break-up basis.

- You should be able to define and discuss all these terms and apply them to practical examples.

  TRY QUESTION 26

- FRS 12 **Provisions, contingent liabilities and contingent assets** defines these items and specifies the accounting treatment.

- You should learn the definition and required treatments and be able to discuss why losses and gains are treated differently. You should also be able to give examples of each.

- Be sure that you can explain the difference between the CA 1985's requirements and those of FRS 12.

  TRY QUESTION 25

- If a business has **goodwill**, it means that the value of the business as a going concern is greater than the value of its separate tangible assets.
  - The valuation of goodwill is extremely subjective and fluctuates constantly.
  - For this reason, goodwill is not normally shown as an asset in the balance sheet.

- The exception to the rule is **purchased goodwill**, when someone purchases a business as a going concern. In this case the purchaser and vendor will fix an agreed price which includes an element in respect of goodwill. The way in which goodwill is then valued is not an accounting problem, but a matter of agreement between the two parties.

- Purchased goodwill may then either be amortised over its useful economic life in the profit and loss account, or be retained in the balance sheet as an intangible asset. If it is retained in the balance sheet, it must be reviewed for impairment every year.

  TRY QUESTION 27

- Companies pay **corporation tax** on their profits. Taxable profits are net profit before dividends adjusted for items where the tax treatment differs from the accounts treatment.

- When a company pays certain expenses such as debenture interest, it must deduct **income tax** at a specified rate and pay this to the Revenue.

- Gross debenture interest received is treated as **taxable profit** and gross debenture interest paid is a tax **allowable expense**.

- General VAT is **not included** in the accounts of a trader in income and expenditure.

- *Possible pitfalls*
  - **Confusing contingencies and post balance sheet events.**
  - **Confusing adjusting and non-adjusting events.**

## 25 QUESTION WITH HELP: MISCELLANEOUS ACCOUNTING STANDARDS

The directors of a company are reviewing the company's most recent draft financial statements and the following points have been raised for discussion:

(a) **Research and development**

This year the company has begun a substantial programme of research and development. To spread the cost fairly over the years, the draft financial statements have been prepared on the basis that all such costs are to be capitalised and written off on the straight-line basis over three years, beginning in the year in which the expenditure is incurred.

(b) **Post balance sheet events**

Shortly after the balance sheet date a major debtor of the company went into liquidation because of heavy trading losses and it is expected that little or nothing will be recoverable for the debt.

In the financial statements the debt has been written off, but one of the directors has pointed out that, as a post balance sheet event, the debt should not in fact be written off but disclosure should be made by note to this year's financial statements, and the debt written off next year.

(c) **Contingency**

An ex-director of the company has commenced an action against the company claiming substantial damages for wrongful dismissal. The company's solicitors have advised that the ex-director is unlikely to succeed with his claim. The solicitors' estimates of the company's potential liabilities are:

|  | £ |
|---|---|
| Legal costs (to be incurred whether the claim is successful or not) | 50,000 |
| Settlement of claim if successful | 500,000 |
|  | 550,000 |

At present there is no provision or note for this contingency.

*Required*

State with reasons whether you consider the accounting treatments in the draft financial statements, as described above, are acceptable. Include in your answer, where appropriate, an explanation of the relevant provisions of Statements of Standard Accounting Practice (SSAPs) or Financial Reporting Standards (FRSs).

> *If you are stuck, look at the next page for detailed help as to how you should tackle this question.*

## Questions and answers

**APPROACHING THE ANSWER**

**Step 1** If you are completely stuck, have a look at your BPP Interactive Text for material on SSAP 13 *Accounting for research and development,* SSAP 17 *Accounting for post balance sheet events* and FRS 12 *Provisions, contingent liabilities and contingent assets.*

**Step 2** Read the question carefully.

**Step 3** Think about the structure of your answer. The question is divided into 3 parts, so your structure is more or less given.

**Step 4** The most important point to make in part (a) is that SSAP 13 applies and that the accounting treatment adopted goes against SSAP 13. You should also state the SSAP 13 criteria for capitalisation to make the point clearer.

**Step 5** Part (b) is very straightforward if you know SSAP 17 as this is an example specifically mentioned as an adjusting post balance sheet event.

**Step 6** You may not have known that this situation is now governed by FRS 12. However, the treatment is logical.

## 25 ANSWER TO QUESTION WITH HELP: MISCELLANEOUS ACCOUNTING STANDARDS

(a) **Research and development**

(i) *Research costs*

The accounting treatment adopted in the draft financial statements violates the requirements of SSAP 13. This says that research costs should be written off in full to the profit and loss account in the accounting period in which they are incurred. There is no scope for capitalising such costs and amortising them over a number of years unless the expenditure relates to capital expenditure on research facilities.

(ii) *Development costs*

SSAP 13 states that development costs may only be deferred to future periods when all of the following criteria are met.

- Separately defined project
- Expenditure separately identifiable
- Commercially viable
- Technically feasible
- Overall profit expected
- Resources exist to complete project

(b) **Post balance sheet events**

These are defined in SSAP 17 as 'those events, both favourable and unfavourable, which occur between the balance sheet date and the date on which the financial statements are approved by the board of directors.' Post balance sheet events may be either adjusting or non-adjusting in nature.

An appendix to SSAP 17 cites a number of post balance sheet events which normally should be classified as adjusting events. The insolvency of a debtor is specifically included, since it is an event which provides additional evidence of a condition existing at the balance sheet date.

Under the requirements of SSAP 17 a provision for this bad debt should be made in the financial statements.

(c) **Contingency**

FRS 12 states that an entity should never recognise a contingent liability. The FRS requires a contingent liability to be disclosed unless the possibility of any outflow of economic benefits to settle it is remote.

The FRS also states that a provision should be recognised only when an entity has an obligation that requires the transfer of economic benefits in settlement which can be measured sufficiently reliably.

As the claim is unlikely to succeed, the potential settlement of £500,000 should be disclosed as a contingent liability. However, given that the legal costs of £50,000 must be paid whether the claim is successful or not, this amount should be provided for in the company's financial statements.

## 26 NEW COLLEAGUE (12/98)

A new colleague has just joined your accounting firm and has come across the terms 'post balance sheet events', 'contingent assets' and 'contingent liabilities' which she does not understand.

*Required*

Prepare some brief notes as follows.

(a) Define post balance sheet events. (2 marks)

(b) Define adjusting and non-adjusting events and give a clear example of each. (5 marks)

(c) Define contingent assets and contingent liabilities. (4 marks)

(d) Explain how material contingent assets and liabilities should be dealt with in the financial statements. (4 marks)

**(15 marks)**

---

**Helping hand**

1 Don't just learn the SSAP 17 definitions automatically; think about the logic of the classifications.

2 In part (d), prudence comes in.

## 26  ANSWER: NEW COLLEAGUE

> **Examiner's comment.** This question was the most poorly answered on the December 1998 paper, with too many candidates making 'token attempts'.

(a) **Post balance sheet events** are those events, both favourable and unfavourable, which occur between the balance sheet date and the date on which the financial statements are approved by the board of directors.

(b) **Adjusting events** are post balance sheet events which provide additional evidence of conditions existing at the balance sheet date. Examples include:

   (i)   The receipt of proceeds of sale or other evidence after the balance sheet date concerning the net realisable value of stock

   (ii)  The renegotiation of amounts owing by debtors or the insolvency of a debtor

**Non-adjusting events** are events which arise after the balance sheet date and concern conditions which did not exist at that time. Consequently, they do not result in changes in amounts in financial statements. They may, however, be of such materiality that their disclosure is required by way of notes to ensure that financial statements are not misleading. Examples include:

   (i)   Losses of fixed assets or stocks as a result of a catastrophe such as fire or flood.

   (ii)  Closing a significant part of the trading activities if this was not anticipated at the year end.

> **Helping hand**
> However disastrous such events may seem, they do not affect conditions at the balance sheet date.

(c) FRS 12 *Provisions, contingent assets and contingent liabilities* defines a **contingent assets** as:

> 'A possible asset that arises from past events and whose existence will be confirmed only by the occurrence of one or more uncertain future events not wholly within the entity's control.'

A **contingent liability** is defined as:

> '(i)   A possible obligation that arises from past events and whose existence will be confirmed only by the occurrence of one or more uncertain future events not wholly within the entity's control, or
>
> (ii)  A present obligation that arises from past events but is not recognised because:
>
>    (1) It is not probable that a transfer of economic benefits will be required to settle the obligation, or
>
>    (2) The amount of the obligation cannot be measured with sufficient reliability.'

(d) An entity **must not recognise a contingent asset,** because it could result in the recognition of profit that may never be realised. However, when the realisation of profit is virtually certain, then the related asset is not a contingent asset and its recognition is appropriate.

Contingent assets must be **disclosed** in the notes to the financial statements where an inflow of economic benefits is probable.

## Questions and answers

> **Helping hand**
>
> Prudence requires that a greater degree of caution is required in recognising assets than liabilities. Thus a contingent asset is only disclosed when an inflow is probable, not merely possible.

A contingent liability must not be recognised. It must be disclosed in the financial statements unless the possibility of a transfer of economic benefits is remote.

## 27 GOODWILL

(a) List three methods of accounting for purchased goodwill and briefly state the arguments in favour of each of the three. (12 marks)

(b) What are the main characteristics of goodwill which distinguish it from other intangible assets? To what extent do you consider that these characteristics should affect the accounting treatment of goodwill?

State your reasons. (8 marks)

**(20 marks)**

## 27 ANSWER: GOODWILL

(a) **Purchased goodwill** may be treated in one of the following ways.

(i) It may be eliminated from the accounts immediately against reserves.

(ii) It may be eliminated gradually by amortisation through the profit and loss account.

(iii) It is possible to leave it at cost in the balance sheet unless its value is permanently impaired.

Method (i), writing goodwill off to reserves, brings the treatment of purchased goodwill into line with that of non-purchased goodwill. It is felt that goodwill is a **unique asset, volatile, difficult to identify** and **without a structured relationship** with the costs incurred in building it up. Accordingly, it should not be capitalised but written off immediately. This was the treatment preferred by SSAP 22, however, the SSAP has now been superseded by FRS 10.

Method (ii), capitalisation and amortisation brings goodwill into line with other fixed assets. Goodwill may be volatile in value and not readily identifiable, but these are not sufficient reasons to disqualify it from recognition in the balance sheet. To show goodwill at a cost-based amount will provide information on the resources that have been deployed in acquisition on the shareholders' behalf and can therefore help provide a basis for assessing management's performance. Furthermore the cost of the asset is being matched with the benefits which it generates over its economic life, as is the case with other fixed assets. This treatment is generally required by **FRS 10**.

Method (iii), leaving goodwill at cost in the balance sheet, recognises that, unlike a piece of machinery, goodwill has **no predictable finite life**. Rather than diminishing in value, it may in fact be increasing, and may well last as long as the business itself. FRS 10 accordingly provides that in some circumstances goodwill may remain in the balance sheet, **subject to annual checks** to see if its value has been improved.

(b) Goodwill may be distinguished from other intangible fixed assets by reference to the following characteristics.

(i) It is incapable of realisation separately from the business as a whole.

(ii) Its value has no reliable or predictable relationship to any costs which may have been incurred.

(iii) Its value arises from various intangible factors such as skilled employees, effective advertising or a strategic location. These indirect factors cannot be valued.

(iv) The value of goodwill may fluctuate widely according to internal and external circumstances over relatively short periods of time.

(v) The assessment of the value of goodwill is highly subjective.

It could be argued that, because goodwill is so different from other intangible fixed assets it does not make sense to account for it in the same way. Thus the capitalisation and amortisation treatment would not be acceptable. Furthermore, because goodwill is so difficult to value, any valuation may be misleading, and it is best eliminated from the balance sheets altogether. However, there are strong arguments, as discussed in Part (a), for treating it like any other intangible fixed asset. This the approach favoured by the ASB.

# Questions and answers

## DO YOU KNOW? – INTERPRETATION OF ACCOUNTS

- *Check that you can fill in the blanks in the statements below before you attempt any questions. If in doubt, you should go back to your BPP Interactive Text and revise first.*

- Cash flow statements concentrate on the sources and uses of cash, are a useful indicator of a company's ..................... and ..................... . FRS 1 Cash flow statements was revised and the revised standard issued in October 1996.

- You need to be aware of the format of the statements. For cash flow statements in particular, setting out the format according to FRS 1 (revised) is an essential first stage in preparing the statement, so this format must be learnt.

- It is important that you are in a position to answer a written question discussing the advantages and disadvantages of cash flow statements.

  TRY QUESTION 32

- The profit and loss account and balance sheet provide useful information about the condition of a business. Ratios can be calculated and trends identified so that different businesses can be compared or the performance of a business over time can be judged.

- Ratios are often classified as follows.

  - ..................... (current ratio, acid test ratio, turnover periods)
  - ..................... (debt: equity, interest cover, dividend cover)
  - ..................... (ROCE, ROOE, asset turnover, profit margins)
  - ..................... (dividend yield, P/E ratio, earnings per share)

- Additional information may be gleaned from cash flow statements. These are intended to reveal how a business obtains its cash and how it uses it.

- The interpretation of financial statements requires a large measure of common sense. For example:
  - you should not expect a firm of solicitors (say) to have substantial plant and machinery;
  - you should not expect a chain of supermarkets to make many sales on credit; you should expect it to turn over its (perishable) stock quickly;
  - you should expect a business that 'piles 'em high and sells 'em cheap' to have a low gross profit margin;
  - you should expect a more upmarket organisation to have higher selling and administrative costs, reflecting the level of service given to customers.

  TRY QUESTION 36

- The limitations of ratio analysis are as follows.
  - .....................
  - .....................
  - .....................
  - .....................
  - .....................
  - .....................

- *Possible pitfalls*

  *Write down the mistakes you know you should avoid.*

## Questions and answers

### DID YOU KNOW? - INTERPRETATION OF ACCOUNTS

- *Could you fill in the blanks? The answers are in bold. Use this page for revision purposes as you approach the exam.*

- Cash flow statements concentrate on the sources and uses of cash, and are a useful indicator of a company's **liquidity** and **solvency**. FRS 1 *Cash flow statements* was revised and the revised standard issued in October 1996.

- You need to be aware of the format of the statements. For cash flow statements in particular, setting out the format according to FRS 1 (revised) is an essential first stage in preparing the statement, so this format must be learnt.

- It is important that you are in a position to answer a written question discussing the advantages and disadvantages of cash flow statements.

  TRY QUESTION 32

- The profit and loss account and balance sheet provide useful information about the condition of a business. Ratios can be calculated and trends identified so that different businesses can be compared or the performance of a business over time can be judged.

- Ratios are often classified as follows.
  - **Liquidity ratios** (current ratio, acid test ratio, turnover periods)
  - **Gearing ratios** ( debt: equity, interest cover, dividend cover)
  - **Profitability ratios** (ROCE, ROOE, asset turnover, profit margins)
  - **Investors' ratios** (dividend yield, P/E ratio, earnings per share)

- Additional information may be gleaned from cash flow statements. These are intended to reveal how a business obtains its cash and how it uses it.

- The interpretation of financial statements requires a large measure of common sense. For example:
  - you should not expect a firm of solicitors (say) to have substantial plant and machinery;
  - you should not expect a chain of supermarkets to make many sales on credit; you should expect it to turn over its (perishable) stock quickly;
  - you should expect a business that 'piles 'em high and sells 'em cheap' to have a low gross profit margin;
  - you should expect a more upmarket organisation to have higher selling and administrative costs, reflecting the level of service given to customers.

  TRY QUESTION 36

- The limitations of ratio analysis are as follows.
  - **Comparative information is not always available.**
  - **They sometimes use out of date information.**
  - **Interpretation requires thought and analysis. Ratios should not be considered in isolation.**
  - **The exercise is subjective and results can therefore be manipulated.**
  - **Ratios are not defined in standard form.**
  - **Companies may not always use the same accounting policies so the figures behind the ratios may not be comparable.**

- *Possible pitfalls*
  - **Confusing notes and workings for the cash flow statement.**
  - **Getting bogged down in calculating ratios at the expense of interpretation.**
  - **Not considering the purpose for which a ratio analysis report is prepared.**

## 28 QUESTION WITH HELP: EMMA

Set out below are the financial statements of Emma Ltd. You have been asked to prepare the cash flow statement of the company, implementing FRS 1 (revised) *Cash flow statements*.

**EMMA LIMITED**
**PROFIT AND LOSS ACCOUNT FOR THE YEAR ENDED 31 DECEMBER 20X2**

|  | £'000 |
|---|---:|
| Turnover | 2,553 |
| Cost of sales | 1,814 |
| Gross profit | 739 |
| Distribution costs | 125 |
| Administrative expenses | 264 |
| Operating profit | 350 |
| Interest received | 25 |
| Interest paid | 75 |
| Profit on ordinary activities before taxation | 300 |
| Taxation | 140 |
| Profit after tax | 160 |
| Dividends | 100 |
| Retained profit for the year | 60 |

**EMMA LIMITED**
**BALANCE SHEETS AS AT 31 DECEMBER**

|  | 20X2 £'000 | 20X1 £'000 |
|---|---:|---:|
| *Fixed assets* |  |  |
| Tangible assets | 380 | 305 |
| Intangible assets | 250 | 200 |
| Investments | - | 25 |
|  | 630 | 530 |
| *Current assets* |  |  |
| Stocks | 150 | 102 |
| Debtors | 390 | 315 |
| Short-term investments | 50 | - |
| Cash in hand | 2 | 1 |
|  | 592 | 418 |
| *Creditors: amounts falling due in less than one year* |  |  |
| Trade creditors | 127 | 119 |
| Bank overdraft | 85 | 98 |
| Taxation | 120 | 110 |
| Dividends proposed | 100 | 80 |
|  | 432 | 407 |
| *Net current assets* | 160 | 11 |
| *Total assets less current liabilities c/f* | 790 | 541 |

## Questions and answers

|  | 20X2 £'000 | 20X1 £'000 |
|---|---|---|
| Total assets less current liabilities b/f | 790 | 541 |
| *Creditors amounts falling due after more than one year* | | |
| Long-term loan | 100 | - |
| *Provisions for liabilities and charges* | | |
| Deferred taxation | 70 | 50 |
| | 620 | 491 |
| *Capital and reserves* | | |
| Share capital (£1 ordinary shares) | 200 | 150 |
| Share premium account | 160 | 150 |
| Revaluation reserve | 100 | 91 |
| Profit and loss account | 160 | 100 |
| | 620 | 491 |

The following information is available.

(a) The proceeds of the sale of fixed asset investments amounted to £30,000.

(b) Fixtures and fittings, with an original cost of £85,000 and a net book value of £45,000, were sold for £32,000 during the year.

(c) The current asset investments fall within the definition of liquid resources under FRS 1 (revised).

(d) The following information relates to tangible fixed assets.

|  | 31.12.20X2 £'000 | 31.12.20X1 £'000 |
|---|---|---|
| Cost | 720 | 595 |
| Accumulated depreciation | 340 | 290 |
| Net book value | 380 | 305 |

(e) 50,000 £1 ordinary shares were issued during the year at a premium of 20p per share.

*Required*

Prepare a cash flow statement for the year to 31 December 20X2 using the format laid out in FRS 1 (revised), together with the relevant notes to the statement.

> *If you are stuck, look at the next page for detailed help as to how you should tackle this question.*

## Questions and answers

**APPROACHING THE ANSWER**

**Step 1** Set out the proforma cash flow statement with all the headings required by FRS 1 (revised). You should leave plenty of space. Ideally, use three or more sheets of paper, one for the main statement, one for the notes (particularly if you have a separate note for the gross cash flows) and one for your workings. It is obviously essential to know the formats very well.

EMMA LIMITED
CASH FLOW STATEMENT
FOR THE YEAR ENDED 31 DECEMBER 20X2

*Reconciliation of operating profit to net cash inflow from operating activities*

|  | £ |
|---|---|
| Operating profit | X |
| Depreciation charge | X |
| Loss on sale of tangible fixed assets | X |
| Profit on sale of fixed asset investments | (X) |
| Increase/decrease in stocks | (X) |
| Increase/decrease in debtors | (X) |
| Increase/decrease in creditors | X |
| Net cash inflow from operating activities | X |

CASH FLOW STATEMENT

|  | £ |
|---|---|
| Net cash inflow from operating activities | X |
| Returns on investments and servicing of finance (note 1) | (X) |
| Taxation | (X) |
| Capital expenditure | (X) |
|  | (X) |
| Equity dividends paid | (X) |
|  | (X) |
| Management of liquid resources (note 1) | (X) |
| Financing (note 1) | X |
| Increase in cash | X |

*Reconciliation of net cash flow to movement in net debt (note 2)*

|  | £ | £ |
|---|---|---|
| Increase in cash in the period | X |  |
| Cash received from long-term loan | (X) |  |
| Cash used to increase liquid resources | X |  |
| Change in net debt |  | (X) |
| Net debt at 1.1.X2 |  | (X) |
| Net debt at 31.12.X2 |  | (X) |

**Step 2** Complete the reconciliation of operating profit to net cash inflow from operating activities. Most of the figures are very easy. You may have to do a separate working for the profit or loss on the sale of tangible fixed assets. Think carefully about which figures need adding and which need subtracting. For example an increase in debtors means less cash (cash has not come in), but an increase in creditors means more cash (we have not used it to pay them).

**Step 3** Calculate the figures for tax paid, dividends paid and purchase of tangible fixed assets.

**Step 4** Complete note 1, the gross cash flows. Alternatively, this information may go straight into the statement.

**Step 5** Complete the cash flow statement by slotting in the figures given or calculated.

**Step 6** Complete note 2, the analysis of change is net debt.

**Step 7** Complete the reconciliation of net cash flow to movement in net debt.

## 28 ANSWER TO QUESTION WITH HELP: EMMA

EMMA LIMITED
CASH FLOW STATEMENT
FOR THE YEAR ENDED 31 DECEMBER 20X2

*Reconciliation of operating profit to net cash inflow from operating activities*

|  | £'000 |
|---|---|
| Operating profit | 350 |
| Depreciation charge (W1) | 90 |
| Loss on sale of tangible fixed assets (45 – 32) | 13 |
| Profit on sale of fixed asset investments | (5) |
| Increase/decrease in stocks | (48) |
| Increase/decrease in debtors | (75) |
| Increase/decrease in creditors | 8 |
| *Net cash inflow from operating activities* | 333 |

### CASH FLOW STATEMENT

|  | £'000 |
|---|---|
| Net cash inflow from operating activities | 333 |
| Returns on investments and servicing of finance (note 1) | (50) |
| Taxation (W2) | (110) |
| Capital expenditure | (189) |
|  | (16) |
| Equity dividends paid | (80) |
|  | (96) |
| Management of liquid resources (note 1) | (50) |
| Financing (note 1) | 160 |
| Increase in cash | 14 |

*Reconciliation of net cash flow to movement in net debt (note 2)*

|  | £'000 | £'000 |
|---|---|---|
| Increase in cash in the period | 14 |  |
| Cash received from long-term loan | (100) |  |
| Cash used to increase liquid resources | 50 |  |
| Change in net debt |  | (36) |
| Net debt at 1.1.X2 |  | (97) |
| Net debt at 31.12.X2 |  | (133) |

### NOTES TO THE CASH FLOW STATEMENT

1   *Gross cash flows*

|  | £'000 | £'000 |
|---|---|---|
| *Returns on investments and servicing of finance* |  |  |
| Interest received | 25 |  |
| Interest paid | (75) |  |
|  |  | 50 |
| *Capital expenditure* |  |  |
| Payments to acquire intangible fixed assets | (50) |  |
| Payments to acquire tangible fixed assets (W3) | (201) |  |
| Receipts from sale of tangible fixed assets | 32 |  |
| Receipts from sale of fixed asset investments | 30 |  |
|  |  | (189) |
| *Management of liquid resources* |  |  |
| Purchase of short-term investments |  | (50) |
| *Financing* |  |  |
| Issue of ordinary share capital | 60 |  |
| Issue of long-term loan | 100 |  |
|  |  | 160 |

## Questions and answers

2 *Analysis of changes in net debt*

|  | At 1 Jan 20X2 £'000 | Cash flows £'000 | At 31 Dec 20X2 £'000 |
|---|---|---|---|
| Cash in hand, at bank | 1 | 1 | 2 |
| Overdraft | (98) | 13 | (85) |
|  |  | 14 |  |
| Debt due within 1 year | - | - | - |
| Debt due after 1 year | - | (100) | (100) |
| Current asset investments | - | 50 | 50 |
| Total | (97) | (36) | (133) |

*Workings*

1 *Depreciation charge*

|  | £'000 | £'000 |
|---|---|---|
| Depreciation at 31 December 20X2 |  | 340 |
| Depreciation 31 December 20X1 | 290 |  |
| Depreciation on assets sold (85 – 45) | 40 |  |
|  |  | 250 |
| Charge for the year |  | 90 |

2 *Tax paid*

### CORPORATION TAX

|  | £'000 |  | £'000 |
|---|---|---|---|
| Tax paid | 110 | 1.1.X2 balance b/d | 110 |
|  |  | Profit and loss |  |
|  |  | 140 – (70 – 50)* | 120 |
| 31.12.X2 balance c/d | 120 |  |  |
|  | 230 |  | 230 |

*Note. The taxation charge in the profit and loss account includes the increase in deferred taxation provision. This must be excluded when calculating the amount of corporation tax paid.

3 *Purchase of tangible fixed assets*

### TANGIBLE FIXED ASSETS

|  | £'000 |  | £'000 |
|---|---|---|---|
| 1.1.X2 Balance b/d | 595 | Disposals | 85 |
| Revaluation (100 – 91) | 9 |  |  |
| Purchases (bal fig) | 201 | 31.12.X2 Balance c/d | 720 |
|  | 805 |  | 805 |

## 29  RENE

The summarised accounts of Rene plc for the year ended 31 December 20X8 are as follows.

RENE PLC
BALANCE SHEET AS AT 31 DECEMBER 20X8

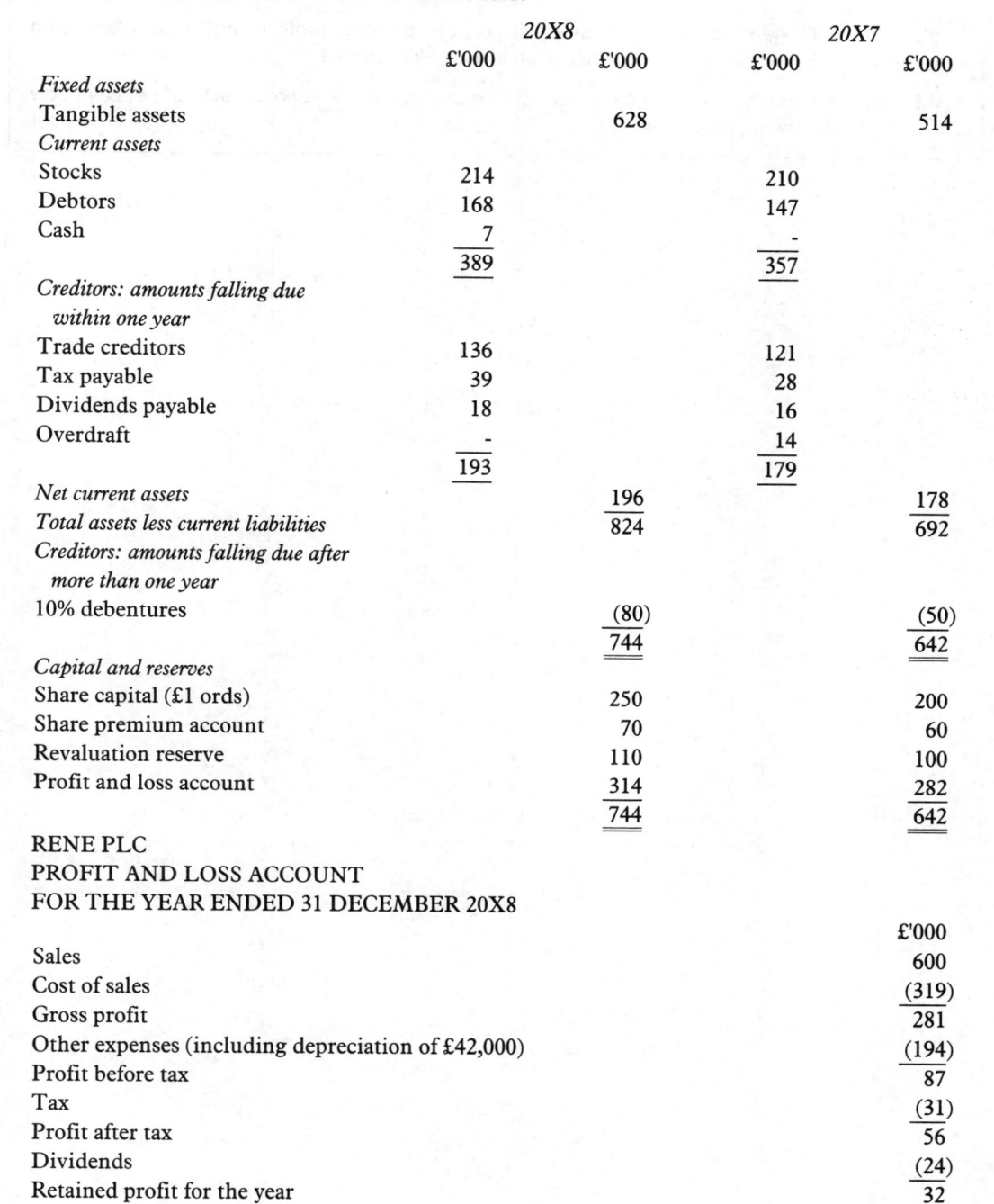

|  | 20X8 £'000 | 20X8 £'000 | 20X7 £'000 | 20X7 £'000 |
|---|---|---|---|---|
| *Fixed assets* | | | | |
| Tangible assets | | 628 | | 514 |
| *Current assets* | | | | |
| Stocks | 214 | | 210 | |
| Debtors | 168 | | 147 | |
| Cash | 7 | | - | |
| | 389 | | 357 | |
| *Creditors: amounts falling due within one year* | | | | |
| Trade creditors | 136 | | 121 | |
| Tax payable | 39 | | 28 | |
| Dividends payable | 18 | | 16 | |
| Overdraft | - | | 14 | |
| | 193 | | 179 | |
| Net current assets | | 196 | | 178 |
| Total assets less current liabilities | | 824 | | 692 |
| *Creditors: amounts falling due after more than one year* | | | | |
| 10% debentures | | (80) | | (50) |
| | | 744 | | 642 |
| *Capital and reserves* | | | | |
| Share capital (£1 ords) | | 250 | | 200 |
| Share premium account | | 70 | | 60 |
| Revaluation reserve | | 110 | | 100 |
| Profit and loss account | | 314 | | 282 |
| | | 744 | | 642 |

RENE PLC
PROFIT AND LOSS ACCOUNT
FOR THE YEAR ENDED 31 DECEMBER 20X8

|  | £'000 |
|---|---|
| Sales | 600 |
| Cost of sales | (319) |
| Gross profit | 281 |
| Other expenses (including depreciation of £42,000) | (194) |
| Profit before tax | 87 |
| Tax | (31) |
| Profit after tax | 56 |
| Dividends | (24) |
| Retained profit for the year | 32 |

You are additionally informed that there have been no disposals of fixed assets during the year. New debentures were issued on 1 January 20X8. Wages for the year amounted to £86,000.

*Required*

Produce a cash flow statement using the direct method suitable for inclusion in the financial statements, as per FRS 1 (revised 1996).

**(15 marks)**

## Questions and answers

> **Helping hand**
>
> 1 Unlike other cash flow statement questions, this requires the direct method. This is straightforward in theory, although in practice the figures would be more difficult to obtain.
>
> 2 You still need to provide a reconciliation of operating profit to net cash inflow from operating activities as this is laid down in the FRS 1 format.
>
> 3 Do the analysis of changes in net debt before you do the reconciliation of net-cash flow to movement in net debt.

## 29 ANSWER: RENE

**RENE PLC**
**CASH FLOW STATEMENT**
**FOR THE YEAR ENDED 31 DECEMBER 20X8**

|  | £'000 | £'000 |
|---|---:|---:|
| *Operating activities* | | |
| Cash received from customers (W1) | 579 | |
| Cash payments to suppliers (W2) | (366) | |
| Cash payments to and on behalf of employees | (86) | |
| | | 127 |
| *Returns on investments and servicing of finance* | | |
| Interest paid | (8) | |
| Net cash outflow from returns on investments and servicing of finance | | (8) |
| *Taxation* | | |
| UK corporation tax paid (W5) | (20) | |
| | | (20) |
| *Capital expenditure* | | |
| Purchase of tangible fixed assets (W6) | (146) | |
| Net cash outflow from investing activities | | (146) |
| | | (47) |
| Equity dividends paid (W4) | (22) | |
| | | (22) |
| *Financing* | | |
| Issue of share capital | 60 | |
| Issue of debentures | 30 | |
| Net cash inflow from financing | | 90 |
| Increase in cash | | 21 |

### NOTES TO THE CASHFLOW STATEMENT

1 *Reconciliation of operating profit to net cash inflow from operating activities*

|  | £'000 |
|---|---:|
| Operating profit (87 + 8) | 95 |
| Depreciation | 42 |
| Increase in stock | (4) |
| Increase in debtors | (21) |
| Increase in creditors | 15 |
| | 127 |

> **Helping hand**
>
> You'll be able to tell whether you have the right figure for net cash inflow from operating activities. It should be the same as the figure in the cash flow statement itself.

2 *Reconciliation of net cash flow to movement in net debt*

|  | £'000 |
|---|---:|
| Net cash inflow for the period | 21 |
| Cash received from debenture issue | (30) |
| Change in net debt | (9) |
| Net debt at 1 January 20X8 | (64) |
| Net debt at 31 December 20X8 | (73) |

> **Helping hand**
>
> You should have set out the proforma for this note, then slot in the figures from note 3.

## Questions and answers

3   Analysis of changes in net debt

|  | At 1 January 20X8 £'000 | Cash flows £'000 | At 31 December 20X8 £'000 |
|---|---|---|---|
| Cash at bank | - | 7 | 7 |
| Overdrafts | (14) | 14 | - |
|  |  | 21 |  |
| Debt due after 1 year | (50) | (30) | (80) |
| Total | (64) | (9) | (73) |

> **Helping hand**
>
> There is no short cut that will enable you to avoid learning this format by heart.

*Workings*

1   *Cash received from customers*

DEBTORS CONTROL ACCOUNT

|  | £'000 |  | £'000 |
|---|---|---|---|
| B/f | 147 | Cash received (bal) | 579 |
| Sales | 600 | C/f | 168 |
|  | 747 |  | 747 |

2   *Cash paid to suppliers*

CREDITORS CONTROL ACCOUNT

|  | £'000 |  | £'000 |
|---|---|---|---|
| Cash paid (bal) | 366 | B/f | 121 |
| C/f | 136 | Purchases (W3) | 381 |
|  | 502 |  | 502 |

3   *Purchases*

|  | £'000 |
|---|---|
| Cost of sales | 319 |
| Opening stock | (210) |
| Closing stock | 214 |
| Expenses (194 – 42 – 86 – 8 debenture interest) | 58 |
|  | 381 |

4   *Dividends*

DIVIDENDS

|  | £'000 |  | £'000 |
|---|---|---|---|
| ∴ Dividends paid | 22 | Balance b/f | 16 |
| Balance c/f | 18 | Dividend for year | 24 |
|  | 40 |  | 40 |

5   *Taxation*

TAXATION

|  | £'000 |  | £'000 |
|---|---|---|---|
| ∴ Tax paid | 20 | Balance b/f | 28 |
| Balance c/f | 39 | Charge for year | 31 |
|  | 59 |  | 59 |

6   *Purchase of fixed assets*

|  | £'000 |
|---|---|
| Opening fixed assets | 514 |
| Less depreciation | (42) |
| Add revaluation (110 – 100) | 10 |
|  | 482 |
| Closing fixed assets | 628 |
| Difference = additions | 146 |

## 30  NEWTON (6/00)

You are presented with Newton Ltd's summary profit and loss account for the year ended 31 December 20X9 and the balance sheet at the beginning and end of the year.

NEWTON LIMITED
PROFIT AND LOSS ACCOUNT FOR THE YEAR ENDED 31 DECEMBER 20X9

|  | £'000 |
|---|---|
| Profit on ordinary activities before taxation | 2,440 |
| Tax on profit on ordinary activities | 895 |
| Profit on ordinary activities after taxation | 1,545 |
| Less proposed dividends | 80 |
| Retained profit for the financial year | 1,465 |
| Profit and loss account at 1 January 20X9 | 1,090 |
| Profit and loss account at 31 December 20X9 | 2,555 |

NEWTON LIMITED
BALANCE SHEETS AS AT

|  | 1 January 20X9 |  | 31 December 20X9 |  |
|---|---|---|---|---|
|  | £'000 | £'000 | £'000 | £'000 |
| *Fixed assets* |  |  |  |  |
| Cost |  | 6,545 |  | 9,563 |
| Depreciation |  | 5,120 |  | 6,010 |
|  |  | 1,425 |  | 3,553 |
| *Current assets* |  |  |  |  |
| Stock | 2,695 |  | 4,217 |  |
| Debtors | 1,740 |  | 2,500 |  |
|  | 4,435 |  | 6,717 |  |
| *Current liabilities* |  |  |  |  |
| Creditors | 2,065 |  | 3,290 |  |
| Bank overdraft | 110 |  | 420 |  |
| Taxation | 400 |  | 895 |  |
| Proposed dividends | 30 |  | 80 |  |
|  | 2,605 |  | 4,685 |  |
| Net current assets |  | 1,830 |  | 2,032 |
|  |  | 3,255 |  | 5,585 |
| Long-term loans |  | 875 |  | 1,145 |
|  |  | 2,380 |  | 4,440 |
| *Capital and reserves* |  |  |  |  |
| Ordinary share capital |  | 795 |  | 1,235 |
| Share premium |  | 495 |  | 650 |
| Profit and loss account |  | 1,090 |  | 2,555 |
|  |  | 2,380 |  | 4,440 |

*Notes*

(a) During the year fixed assets were sold for £500,000. They cost £2,500,000 and had a net book value of £750,000.

(b) Interest paid during the year was £235,000.

(c) There was no under or over provision for corporation tax in the previous year.

*Required*

(a) Prepare a cash flow statement for Newton Ltd for the year ended 31 December 20X9 in accordance with recognised accounting standards. Present any additional notes or reconciliations required by the accounting standard adopted. **(24 marks)**

(b) Comment on the cash flows of Newton Ltd. **(6 marks)**

**(30 marks)**

## Questions and answers

> **Helping hand.**
> 
> 1  The key to this question is to know and set out the required format.
> 
> 2  Most workings are simple and can be shown on the face of the cash flow statement, but some aspects may need a more complicated working.

# 30 ANSWER: NEWTON

> **Examiner's comment.** Answers were better than in previous years, although not all candidates included the FRS 1 notes and reconciliations specifically asked for in the question.

(a) NEWTON LIMITED
CASH FLOW STATEMENT
FOR THE YEAR ENDED 31 DECEMBER 20X9

*Reconciliation of operating profit to net cash flows from operating activities*

|  | £'000 |
|---|---:|
| Profit before interest and tax (2,440 + 235) | 2,675 |
| Depreciation (W1) | 2,640 |
| Loss on disposal | 250 |
| Increase in stock (4,217 – 2,695) | (1,522) |
| Increase in debtors (2,500 – 1,740) | (760) |
| Increase in creditors (3,290 – 2,065) | 1,225 |
| Net cash inflow from operating activities | 4,508 |

*Cash flow statement*

|  | £'000 | £'000 |
|---|---:|---:|
| Net cash inflow from operating activities |  | 4,508 |
| *Returns on investments and servicing of finance* |  |  |
| Interest paid |  | (235) |
| *Taxation* |  |  |
| Corporation tax paid |  | (400) |
| *Capital expenditure* |  |  |
| Payments to acquire fixed assets (W) | (5,518) |  |
| Proceeds from sale of fixed assets | 500 |  |
|  |  | (5,018) |
|  |  | (1,145) |
| Equity dividends paid |  | (30) |
| *Financing* |  |  |
| Issue of share capital (1,235 – 795) | 440 |  |
| Share premium (650 – 495) | 155 |  |
| Long term loans (1,145 – 875) | 270 |  |
|  |  | 865 |
| Decrease in cash |  | (310) |

*Notes to the cash flow statement*

1   *Reconciliation of net cash flow to movement in net debt*

|  | £'000 |
|---|---:|
| Net cash outflow for the period | (310) |
| Increase in long term loans | (270) |
| Change in net debt | (580) |
| Net debt at 1 January 20X9 | (985) |
| Net debt at 31 December 20X9 | (1,565) |

2   *Analysis of changes in net debt*

|  | At 1 Jan 20X9 £'000 | Cash flows £'000 | At 31 Dec 20X9 £'000 |
|---|---:|---:|---:|
| Bank overdraft | (110) | (310) | (420) |
| Debt due after 1 year | (875) | (270) | (1,145) |
|  | (985) | (580) | (1,565) |

## Questions and answers

*Working: fixed assets and depreciation*

### FIXED ASSETS: COST

|  | £'000 |  | £'000 |
|---|---|---|---|
| Balance b/f | 6,545 | Disposals | 2,500 |
| Additions | 5,518 | Balance c/f | 9,563 |
|  | 12,063 |  | 12,063 |

### FIXED ASSETS: ACCUMULATED DEPRECIATION

|  | £'000 |  | £'000 |
|---|---|---|---|
| Disposals | 1,750 | Balance b/f | 5,120 |
| Balance c/f | 6,010 | P & L a/c (bal. fig.) | 2,640 |
|  | 7,760 |  | 7,760 |

### FIXED ASSETS: DISPOSALS

|  | £'000 |  | £'000 |
|---|---|---|---|
| Disposals | 2,500 | Accumulated depn. | 1,750 |
|  |  | Sale proceeds | 500 |
|  |  | Loss on disposal | 250 |
|  | 2,500 |  | 2,500 |

> **Helping hand.** It's best to show this working separately as you have a fixed asset disposal which makes it more complicated.

(b) Newton Ltd is showing a **net decrease in cash** for the year ended 31 December 20X9 of £310,000. This is not good news. The net cash inflow from operating activities is impressive at £4,508,000, but this is offset by the factors that are putting the company's working capital under strain.

The main cash outflow is the **purchase of fixed assets** for £5,518,000. This suggests that the company is **expanding, perhaps too rapidly,** although it is to be hoped that the fixed assets would generate profits in future years.

Newton Ltd has **borrowed heavily** to finance this expansion - the overdraft has increased and there are new long-term loans of £270,000. These incurred high interest costs. The company's gearing will be prevented from going too high by the issue of ordinary share capital of £595,000.

Stocks, debtors and creditors have all increased, again showing that the company's **working capital is under strain**.

## 31 EVANS (12/01)

You are presented with the following information for Evans Ltd.

EVANS LIMITED
PROFIT AND LOSS ACCOUNT FOR THE YEAR ENDED 31 OCTOBER 20X1

|  | £'000 |
|---|---:|
| Sales | 2,000 |
| Cost of goods sold | (1,350) |
| Gross profit | 650 |
| Distribution costs | (99) |
| Administrative expenses | (120) |
| Operating profit | 431 |
| Gain on disposal of fixed assets | 10 |
| Dividend received | 12 |
| Interest paid | (35) |
| Profit before taxation | 418 |
| Tax on profit on ordinary activities | (125) |
| Net profit on ordinary activities after taxation | 293 |
| *Less* proposed dividends | (90) |
| Retained profit for the financial year | 203 |
| Profit and loss account at 31 October 20X0 | 70 |
| Profit and loss account at 31 October 20X1 | 273 |

EVANS LIMITED
BALANCE SHEETS AS AT 31 OCTOBER

|  | 20X0 | | 20X1 | |
|---|---:|---:|---:|---:|
|  | £'000 | £'000 | £'000 | £'000 |
| *Fixed assets* | | | | |
| Furniture at cost | 700 | | 900 | |
| Less depreciation | 200 | | 270 | |
|  | | 500 | | 630 |
| Vehicles at cost | 820 | | 890 | |
| Less depreciation | 310 | | 340 | |
|  | | 510 | | 550 |
| Investments, at cost | | 80 | | 155 |
|  | | 1,090 | | 1,335 |
| *Current assets* | | | | |
| Stock | 505 | | 486 | |
| Debtors | 577 | | 790 | |
| Cash and bank | 10 | | 2 | |
|  | 1,092 | | 1,278 | |
| *Current liabilities* | | | | |
| Creditors | 546 | | 560 | |
| Taxation | 106 | | 125 | |
| Proposed dividends | 40 | | 90 | |
|  | 692 | | 775 | |
| Net current assets | | 400 | | 503 |
|  | | 1,490 | | 1,838 |
| *12% debentures* | | 150 | | 50 |
|  | | 1,340 | | 1,788 |
| *Capital and reserves* | | | | |
| Ordinary share capital | | 1,000 | | 1,200 |
| Share premium | | 270 | | 315 |
| Profit and loss account | | 70 | | 273 |
|  | | 1,340 | | 1,788 |

## Questions and answers

*Additional information for the year ended 31 October 20X1*

(a) Vehicles which had cost £155,000 were sold during the year when their net book value was £65,000.

(b) There were no prepaid or accrued expenses at the beginning or end of the year.

*Required*

(a) Prepare a cash flow statement for Evans Ltd for the year ended 31 October 20X1. State the accounting standard you have applied, and show any additional notes and reconciliations required. (24 marks)

(b) Briefly explain why cash flow statements are useful to external users. (6 marks)

**(30 marks)**

---

**Helping hand**

1. With the fixed asset working it's best to set up 'T' accounts for cost, accumulated depreciation and disposals.

2. Part (b) comes up very regularly in one form or another.

# 31 ANSWER: EVANS

> **Examiner's comment**
> In Part (a) candidates were well prepared. However, some were confused about movements in working capital (increase or decrease). Part (b) answers were mixed.

(a) EVANS LIMITED
CASH FLOW STATEMENT FOR THE YEAR ENDED 31 OCTOBER 20X1

*Reconciliation of operating profit to net cash inflow from operating activities*

|  | £'000 | £'000 |
|---|---|---|
| Operating profit (418 + 35 – 12) |  | 441 |
| Depreciation |  |  |
|     Vehicles (W) | 120 |  |
|     Furniture (270 – 200) | 70 |  |
|  |  | 190 |
| Gain on disposal |  | (10) |
| Decrease in stock (505 – 486) |  | 19 |
| Increase in debtors (790 – 577) |  | (213) |
| Increase in creditors (560 – 46) |  | 14 |
| Net cash inflow from operating activities |  | 441 |

*Cash flow statement*

|  | £'000 | £'000 |
|---|---|---|
| Net cash inflow from operating activities |  | 441 |
| *Returns on investments and servicing of finance* |  |  |
| Dividend received | 12 |  |
| Interest paid | (35) |  |
|  |  | (23) |
| *Taxation* |  |  |
| Corporation tax paid |  | (106) |
| *Capital expenditure* |  |  |
| Payments to acquire fixed assets (W) | (425) |  |
| Payments to acquire investments (155 – 80) | (75) |  |
| Proceeds from sale of fixed assets | 75 |  |
|  |  | (425) |
|  |  | (113) |
| Equity dividends paid |  | (40) |
|  |  | (153) |
| *Financing* |  |  |
| Issue of share capital (1,200 – 1,000) | 200 |  |
| Share premium (315 – 270) | 45 |  |
| Repayment of debentures (150 – 50) | (100) |  |
|  |  | 145 |
| Decrease in cash |  | (8) |

*Notes to the cash flow statement*

1 *Reconciliation of net cash flow to movement in net debt*

|  | £'000 |
|---|---|
| Net cash outflow for the period | (8) |
| Decrease in long-term loan | 100 |
| Change in net debt | 92 |
| Net debt at 1 November 20X0 | (140) |
| Net debt at 31 October 20X1 | (48) |

## Questions and answers

2     Analysis of changes in net debt

|  | At 1 November 20X0 £'000 | Cash flows £'000 | At 31 October 20X1 £'000 |
|---|---|---|---|
| Cash at bank | 10 | (8) | 2 |
| Debt due after one year | (150) | 100 | (50) |
|  | (140) | 92 | (48) |

*Working: fixed assets and depreciation*

### VEHICLES: COST

|  | £'000 |  | £'000 |
|---|---|---|---|
| Balance b/f | 820 | Disposals | 155 |
| Additions (bal fig) | 225 | Balance c/f | 890 |
|  | 1,045 |  | 1,045 |

### VEHICLES: ACCUMULATED DEPRECIATION

|  | £'000 |  | £'000 |
|---|---|---|---|
| Disposals (155 – 65) | 90 | Balance b/f | 310 |
| Balance c/f | 340 | P&L charge (bal fig) | 120 |
|  | 430 |  | 430 |

> **Helping hand.** Accumulated depreciation on disposals is cost less NBV of disposed of vehicles.

### VEHICLES: DISPOSALS

|  | £'000 |  | £'000 |
|---|---|---|---|
| Fixed assets | 155 | Accumulated depn | 90 |
| Gain on disposal | 10 | Sale proceeds (bal fig) | 75 |
|  | 165 |  | 165 |

Additions to fixed assets:

|  | £'000 |
|---|---|
| Vehicles | 225 |
| Furniture (900 – 700) | 200 |
|  | 425 |

> **Helping hand.** There are no disposals of furniture, so the additions figure is the difference between the two figures at cost.

(b) While the profit and loss account and balance sheet provide useful information to outside users, it could be argued that the profit figure in the accounts does not always give a meaningful picture of the company's operations. A company's performance and prospects depend not so much on the 'profits' earned in the period, but, more realistically on **liquidity** or cash flows.

Cash flow statements have the **following advantages**.

(i)     They are **easier to understand** than profit statements.

(ii)    They draw attention to **cash flow** which is **crucial to a business's survival**.

(iii)   **Creditors** are more interested in a company's **ability to pay** the debt than in profitability.

(iv)   **Profit** depends on **accounting conventions** and concepts and is thus easy to manipulate.

(v)    **Management decision making** is based on future cash flows.

(vi)   Cash flow is easier to audit than profit.

> **Helping hand.** Learn our answer for use in your exam!

## 32  DAWSON (6/01)

You are presented with the following information for Dawson Ltd.

DAWSON LIMITED
BALANCE SHEET AS AT

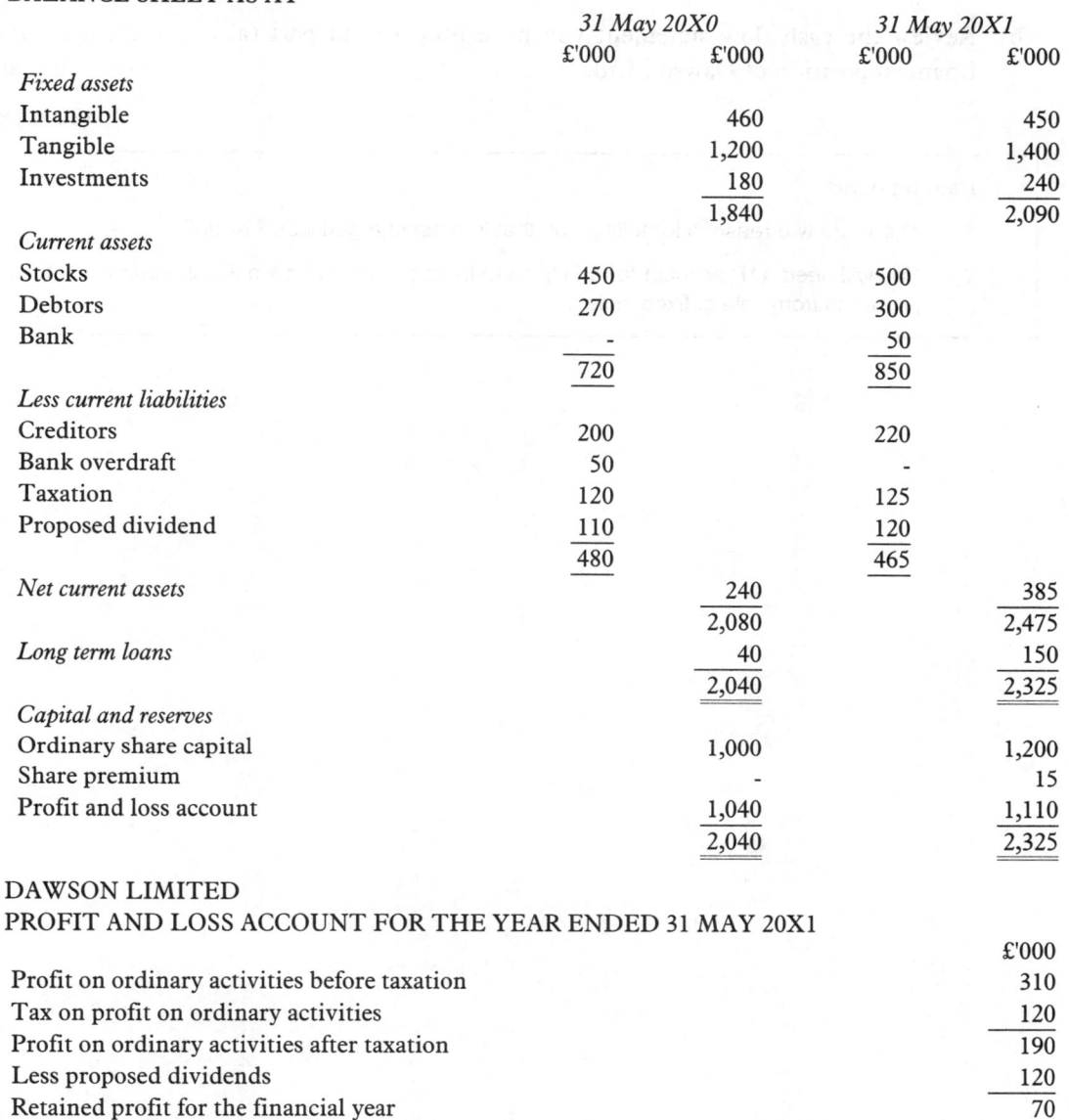

|  | 31 May 20X0 |  | 31 May 20X1 |  |
|---|---:|---:|---:|---:|
|  | £'000 | £'000 | £'000 | £'000 |
| *Fixed assets* |  |  |  |  |
| Intangible |  | 460 |  | 450 |
| Tangible |  | 1,200 |  | 1,400 |
| Investments |  | 180 |  | 240 |
|  |  | 1,840 |  | 2,090 |
| *Current assets* |  |  |  |  |
| Stocks | 450 |  | 500 |  |
| Debtors | 270 |  | 300 |  |
| Bank | - |  | 50 |  |
|  | 720 |  | 850 |  |
| *Less current liabilities* |  |  |  |  |
| Creditors | 200 |  | 220 |  |
| Bank overdraft | 50 |  | - |  |
| Taxation | 120 |  | 125 |  |
| Proposed dividend | 110 |  | 120 |  |
|  | 480 |  | 465 |  |
| Net current assets |  | 240 |  | 385 |
|  |  | 2,080 |  | 2,475 |
| Long term loans |  | 40 |  | 150 |
|  |  | 2,040 |  | 2,325 |
| *Capital and reserves* |  |  |  |  |
| Ordinary share capital |  | 1,000 |  | 1,200 |
| Share premium |  | - |  | 15 |
| Profit and loss account |  | 1,040 |  | 1,110 |
|  |  | 2,040 |  | 2,325 |

DAWSON LIMITED
PROFIT AND LOSS ACCOUNT FOR THE YEAR ENDED 31 MAY 20X1

|  | £'000 |
|---|---:|
| Profit on ordinary activities before taxation | 310 |
| Tax on profit on ordinary activities | 120 |
| Profit on ordinary activities after taxation | 190 |
| Less proposed dividends | 120 |
| Retained profit for the financial year | 70 |
| Profit and loss account at 31 May 20X0 | 1,040 |
| Profit and loss account at 31 May 20X1 | 1,110 |

*Additional information for the year ended 31 May 20X1*

(a)  No intangible fixed assets were acquired or sold.

(b)  Fixed assets with a net book value of £160,000 were sold for a profit of £85,000.

(c)  Depreciation charged on tangible fixed assets was £305,000.

(d)  Interest charged in the profit and loss account was £24,000.

(e)  There were no prepaid or accrued expenses at the beginning or end of the year.

## Questions and answers

*Required*

(a) Prepare a cash flow statement for Dawson Ltd for the year ended 31 May 20X1 in accordance with recognised accounting standards. Present any additional notes or reconciliations required by the accounting standard adopted. (24 marks)

(b) Review the cash flow statement you have prepared in part (a) and comment on the financial position of Dawson Ltd. (6 marks)

**(30 marks)**

> **Helping hand**
>
> 1 There are two reasons for telling you that interest charged was £24,000.
>
> 2 You will need a 'T' account for additions to fixed assets and a small columnar working for proceeds from sale of fixed assets.

# 32 ANSWER: DAWSON

> **Examiner's comment.** This question was answered fairly well in comparison to similar questions in previous years. However, once again not all candidates included the necessary notes and reconciliations as specifically asked for in the question. Also, those candidates who did not use a recognised format for a cash flow statement did not obtain all the marks available.

(a) DAWSON LIMITED
CASH FLOW STATEMENT FOR THE YEAR ENDED 31 MAY 20X1

*Reconciliation of operating profit to net cash inflow from operating activities*

|  | £'000 |
|---|---:|
| Profit before interest and tax (310 + 24) | 334 |
| Depreciation | 305 |
| Amortisation of intangible fixed assets (460 – 450) | 10 |
| Profit on disposal of fixed assets | (85) |
| Increase in stock (500 – 450) | (50) |
| Increase in debtors (300 – 270) | (30) |
| Increase in creditors (220 – 200) | 20 |
|  | 504 |

> **Helping hand.** You have to add back interest, to get 'profit before interest and tax'. Interest also appears in the main cash flow statement.

CASH FLOW STATEMENT

|  | £'000 | £'000 |
|---|---:|---:|
| *Net cash inflow from operating activities* |  | 504 |
| *Returns on investments and servicing of finance* |  |  |
| Interest paid |  | (24) |
| *Taxation* |  |  |
| Corporation in tax paid (W1) |  | (115) |
| *Capital expenditure* |  |  |
| Payments to acquire tangible fixed assets (W2) | (665) |  |
| Proceeds from sale of tangible fixed assets (W3) | 245 |  |
| Payments to acquire investments (240 – 180) | (60) |  |
|  |  | (480) |
|  |  | (115) |
| *Equity dividends paid* (W4) |  | (110) |
| *Net cash outflow before financing* |  | (225) |
| *Financing* |  |  |
| Issue of share capital (1,200 – 1,000) | 200 |  |
| Share premium | 15 |  |
| Increase in loans (150 – 40) | 110 |  |
| *Net cash inflow from financing* |  | 325 |
| *Increase in cash* |  | 100 |

## Questions and answers

*Notes to the cash flow statement*

1     Reconciliation of net cash flow to movement in net debt

|  | £'000 |
|---|---:|
| Net cash inflow | 100 |
| Increase in long term loans | (110) |
| Change in net debt | (10) |
| Net debt as at 31 May 20X0 | (90) |
| Net debt as at 31 May 20X1 | (100) |

2     Analysis of change in net debt

|  | At 31 May 20X0 £'000 | Cash flows £'000 | At 31 May 20X1 £'000 |
|---|---:|---:|---:|
| Cash at bank | (50) | 100 | 50 |
| Debt due after more than one year | (40) | (110) | (150) |
|  | (90) | (10) | (100) |

*Workings*

1     Corporation tax paid

**TAXATION**

| | £'000 | | £'000 |
|---|---:|---|---:|
| ∴ Tax paid (bal fig) | 115 | Bal b/d 1 June 20X0 | 120 |
| Bal c/d 31 May 20X1 | 125 | P&L charge | 120 |
|  | 240 |  | 240 |

2     Payments to acquire tangible fixed assets

**FIXED ASSETS**

| | £'000 | | £'000 |
|---|---:|---|---:|
| Bal b/d 1 June 20X0 | 1,200 | Disposals | 160 |
|  |  | Depreciation | 305 |
| ∴ Additions (bal fig) | 665 | Bal c/d 31 May 20X1 | 1,400 |
|  | 1,865 |  | 1,865 |

3     Proceeds from sale of tangible fixed assets

|  | £'000 |
|---|---:|
| Net book value | 160 |
| Profit | 85 |
| ∴ Proceeds | 245 |

> **Helping hand.** These workings (2 and 3) come up very often so make sure you understand them.

4     Equity dividends paid

**DIVIDENDS**

| | £'000 | | £'000 |
|---|---:|---|---:|
| ∴ Cash paid | 110 | Bal b/d 1 June 20X1 | 110 |
| Bal c/d 31 May 20X1 | 120 | Profit and loss account | 120 |
|  | 230 |  | 230 |

(b)     At first sight Dawson Ltd's cash flow appears healthy; the company has gone from a £50,000 overdraft to a £50,000 positive bank balance. However, most of this **inflow** can be accounted for by a **long term loan** of £110,000. In other words, the company has merely rescheduled its debt from short to long term. The reconciliation of net cash flow to movement in net debt shows an **increase in overall debt** of £10,000.

Much of the cash paid has been **invested in new fixed assets**, costing £665,000. This has been financed partly by the loan, and partly by the issue of new shares. The aim of this investment will be to **generate future profits,** and to enable the company to operate more efficiently.

The company generated enough cash from operating activities to **meet payments of interest, tax and dividends.** It also made a **large profit on disposal** of fixed assets. However, this is a bookkeeping adjustment and suggests that depreciation was underprovided in previous years.

## 33 PAPER (6/00)

Paper Ltd trades in the distribution of paper products. You have been given the following balance sheet as at 31 December and some other additional information.

|  | 20X8 £'000 | 20X9 £'000 |
|---|---|---|
| Fixed assets at cost | 850 | 1,272 |
| Less depreciation | 400 | 550 |
|  | 450 | 722 |
| Stock | 75 | 130 |
| Debtors | 98 | 150 |
| Bank | 75 | 0 |
|  | 698 | 1,002 |
| Trade creditors | (80) | (130) |
| Taxation | (30) | (55) |
| Dividend | (20) | (20) |
| Overdraft | 0 | (50) |
|  | 568 | 747 |
| Debentures | (70) | (190) |
|  | 498 | 557 |
| Issued share capital (5p shares) | 200 | 200 |
| Profit and loss account | 298 | 357 |
|  | 498 | 557 |

EXTRACTS FROM THE PROFIT AND LOSS ACCOUNTS FOR THE YEAR ENDED

|  | 20X8 £'000 | 20X9 £'000 |
|---|---|---|
| Sales (all on credit) | 880 | 1,200 |
| Gross profit | 380 | 532 |
| Overheads | 300 | 370 |
| Net profit | 80 | 162 |
| Interest | 10 | 38 |
| Profit before tax | 70 | 124 |
| Tax | 30 | 45 |
|  | 40 | 79 |
| Dividends | 20 | 20 |
|  | 20 | 59 |

*Required*

(a) Your manager has asked you to calculate and comment on the following ratios, for both years, for Paper Ltd.

   (i) Gearing ratio
   (ii) Interest cover
   (iii) Stock turnover
   (iv) Return on capital employed
   (v) Debtors payment period
   (vi) Quick/acid test ratio

   Give your workings and clearly state the definition used for each ratio. **(9 marks)**

(b) Prepare for your manager a memorandum that explains the limitations of ratio analysis. **(6 marks)**

**(15 marks)**

## Questions and answers

**Helping hand.**
1. Allow plenty of time for your comments, don't spend all the time on the calculations.
2. Make sure the comments relate to the company in question and don't just describe a ratio in general terms.

## 33 ANSWER: PAPER

> **Examiner's comment.** Comments on the ratios were a little disappointing. Many candidates ignored part (b) altogether or answered it incorrectly.

(a) (i) **Gearing ratio**

The gearing ratio is an effective measure of risk. It is the ratio of the long-term borrowing of the business to the total capital. In general, a high geared company faces a greater risk than a low-geared company.

Paper Ltd's gearing ratio has risen significantly, from 14% to 33%. This is because additional debentures of £120,000 have been issued. There may be an impact on dividends if profits fall – interest still has to be paid. However, the ratio is well below 50%, the threshold at which alarm bells would ring.

> **Helping hand.** It is a good idea, for each ratio to have one paragraph explaining the ratio in general terms and a longer paragraph talking specifically about Paper Ltd.

(ii) **Interest cover**

This ratio shows whether a company is earning enough profits before interest and tax to pay its interest costs comfortably, or whether its interest costs are high in relation to the size of its profits so that a fall in profit before interest and tax would have a significant effect on profits available for ordinary shareholders.

The interest cover for Paper Ltd has halved, from 8 times to 4 times. The main reason for this is that interest costs have risen because of the new bank overdraft and the additional debentures. Profits still cover interest comfortably, but the situation may have to be monitored in the future.

(iii) **Stock turnover**

This is an indication of how vigorously a business is trading. Paper Ltd's stock turnover has increased from 55 days to 71 days. This indicates a slowdown in trading or a build-up in stock levels, perhaps suggesting that investment in stocks is becoming excessive.

(iv) **Return on capital employed**

This ratio relates the profit to the amount of capital employed in making that profit. It is thus a measure of the efficiency and effectiveness with which the managers have made use of the resources available to them.

Paper Ltd's return on capital employed has nearly doubled (from 16% to 29%). This is a good sign and reflects the fact that the company has managed to increase sales without a proportionate increase in costs. Overheads have remained more or less constant. In absolute terms, net profit has more than doubled.

(v) **Debtors payment period**

This is an approximate measure of the length of time it takes for a company's debtors to pay what they owe. There has been an increase from 41 days in 20X8 to 46 days in 20X9. This suggest that management, keen to increase sales, has paid less attention to credit control. However, the increase is not large.

(vi) **Quick/acid test ratio**

The idea behind this ratio is that a company should have enough current assets that give a promise of 'cash to come' to meet its future commitments. Stock is

## Questions and answers

excluded from the ratio because, when stock turnover is slow, as here, stock is not a very liquid current asset.

Paper's liquidity as measured by this ratio has fallen to less than half, from 1.3 to 0.6. This suggests that the company may run into cash flow problems. Although the company is profitable and turnover has increased, the management need to pay more attention to working capital before the situation gets worse.

### APPENDIX: CALCULATION OF RATIOS

|      |                                                                                          | 20X8                                   |          | 20X9                                       |          |
|------|------------------------------------------------------------------------------------------|----------------------------------------|----------|--------------------------------------------|----------|
| (i)  | *Gearing ratio*                                                                          |                                        |          |                                            |          |
|      | $\dfrac{\text{Prior charge capital}}{\text{Total capital}}$                              | $\dfrac{70}{498} \times 100$           | 14%      | $\dfrac{190}{557} \times 100$              | 34%      |
| (ii) | *Interest cover*                                                                         |                                        |          |                                            |          |
|      | $\dfrac{\text{Profit before interest and taxation}}{\text{Interest payable}}$            | $\dfrac{80}{10}$                       | 8 times  | $\dfrac{162}{38}$                          | 4 times  |
| (iii)| *Stock turnover*                                                                         |                                        |          |                                            |          |
|      | $\dfrac{\text{Stock}}{\text{Cost of sales}}$                                             | $\dfrac{75}{(880-380)} \times 365$     | 55 days  | $\dfrac{130}{(1,200-532)} \times 365$      | 71 days  |
| (iv) | *Return on capital employed*                                                             |                                        |          |                                            |          |
|      | $\dfrac{\text{Profit before interest and taxation}}{\text{Capital + debentures}}$        | $\dfrac{80}{568} \times 100$           | 14%      | $\dfrac{162}{747} \times 100$              | 22%      |
| (v)  | *Debtors payment period*                                                                 |                                        |          |                                            |          |
|      | $\dfrac{\text{Debtors}}{\text{Sales}}$                                                   | $\dfrac{98}{880} \times 365$           | 41 days  | $\dfrac{150}{1,200} \times 365$            | 46 days  |
| (vi) | *Quick/acid test ratio*                                                                  |                                        |          |                                            |          |
|      | $\dfrac{\text{Current assets} - \text{stock}}{\text{Current liabilities}}$               | $\dfrac{173}{80+30+20}$                | 1.3:1    | $\dfrac{150}{130+55+20+50}$                | 0.6:1    |

> **Helping hand.** As you can see, our comments take up much more room that the calculations.

(b)

### MEMORANDUM

To: M Manager
From: C A Technician
Date: December 20X9

*Limitations of ratio analysis*

Ratio analysis is not foolproof. There are many problems in trying to identify trends and make comparisons. Below are just a few.

(i) **Information problems**

(1) The base information is often out of date, so timeliness of information leads to problems of interpretation.

(2) Historical cost information may not be the most appropriate information for the decision for which the analysis is being undertaken

(3) Information in published accounts is generally summarised information and detailed information may be needed.

(4) Analysis of accounting information only identifies symptoms not causes and thus is of limited use.

(ii) **Comparison problems: inter-temporal**

(1) Effects of price changes make comparisons difficult unless adjustments are made

(2) Impacts of changes in technology on the price of assets, the likely return and the future markets

(3) Impacts of a changing environment on the results reflected in the accounting information

(4) Potential effects of changes in accounting policies on the reported results

(5) Problems associated with establishing a normal base year to compare other years with

(iii) **Comparison problems: inter-firm**

(1) Selection of industry norms and the usefulness of norms based on averages

(2) Different firms having different financial and business risk profiles and the impact on analysis

(3) Different firms using different accounting policies

(4) Impacts of different environments on results, eg different countries or home-based versus multinational firms

## 34 PEANUT (12/98)

You are a Certified Accounting Technician in the Business Development Department of a large organisation. The development manager has presented you with the following financial statements for Peanut Ltd and some additional information.

PEANUT LIMITED
TRADING AND PROFIT AND LOSS ACCOUNT
FOR THE YEAR ENDED 30 SEPTEMBER 20X8

|  | £'000 | £'000 |
|---|---:|---:|
| Sales |  | 1,500 |
| Opening stock | 170 |  |
| Purchases | 1,105 |  |
|  | 1,275 |  |
| Less closing stock | 150 |  |
| Cost of goods sold |  | 1,125 |
| Gross profit |  | 375 |
| Selling expenses | 45 |  |
| General and administration | 135 |  |
|  |  | 180 |
| Operating profit |  | 195 |
| Interest |  | 30 |
| Profit on ordinary activities before taxation |  | 165 |
| Tax on profit on ordinary activities |  | 55 |
| Profit on ordinary activities after taxation |  | 110 |
| Less proposed dividends |  | 65 |
| Retained profit for the year |  | 45 |

PEANUT LIMITED
BALANCE SHEET AS AT 30 SEPTEMBER 20X8

|  | £'000 | £'000 | £'000 |
|---|---:|---:|---:|
| Fixed assets, at cost |  |  | 1,800 |
| Less accumulated depreciation |  |  | 450 |
|  |  |  | 1,350 |
| *Current assets* |  |  |  |
| Stock | 150 |  |  |
| Debtors | 120 |  |  |
| Cash | 155 |  |  |
|  |  | 425 |  |
| *Current liabilities* |  |  |  |
| Creditors | 135 |  |  |
| Accruals | 15 |  |  |
| Proposed dividend | 65 |  |  |
| Overdraft | 30 |  |  |
|  |  | 245 |  |
|  |  |  | 180 |
|  |  |  | 1,530 |
| *Capital and reserves* |  |  |  |
| £1 Ordinary Share Capital |  |  | 1,400 |
| Profit and loss account |  |  | 130 |
|  |  |  | 1,530 |

## Questions and answers

*Additional information*

|  | *Previous years' ratios* |  | *Industry average* |
|---|---|---|---|
|  | *20X5/X6* | *20X6/X7* | *20X7/X8* |
| Gross profit percentage | 24% | 25% | 27% |
| Net profit (before tax) percentage | 14% | 13% | 15% |
| Current ratio (ie working capital ratio) | 1.9 | 1.8 | 2.0 |
| Acid test ratio (ie liquidity ratio) | 1.5 | 1.3 | 1.2 |
| Stock turnover (No of times per annum) | 9.7 | 8.6 | 8.6 |
| Creditors payment period (days) | 58.2 | 51.3 | 44 |
| Debtors collection period (days) | 14.6 | 22.4 | 25 |
| Earnings per share (pence) | 6 | 7 | 8 |

*Required*

(a) Calculate each of the ratios in the table above for Peanut Ltd for the financial year 20X7/X8. **(8 marks)**

(b) Prepare a brief report for the development manager which comments on the ratios you have calculated and compares them with the previous years and the industry averages. Suggest reasons for the changes. (You are not required to reproduce the table in your report.) **(7 marks)**

**(15 marks)**

---

**Helping hand**

1  There are nearly as many marks for the discussion part of this question as for the calculations, so make sure you allocate sufficient time to this part of the question.

2  Make sure you can distinguish the current ratio and the acid test ratio.

3  You will come across as professional if you end your report with a conclusion.

# 34 ANSWER: PEANUT

> **Examiner's comment.** Most could calculate the ratios but the reports were often poor, with some candidates just describing the figures they calculated with no explanation.

(a) *Calculation of ratios for the financial year 20X7/X8*

$$\text{Gross profit percentage} = \frac{\text{Gross profit}}{\text{Turnover}} \times 100 = \frac{375}{1,500} = 25\%$$

$$\text{Net profit (before tax) percentage} = \frac{\text{NPBT}}{\text{Turnover}} \times 100 = \frac{165}{1,500} = 11\%$$

$$\text{Current ratio} = \frac{\text{Current assets}}{\text{Current liabilities}} = \frac{425}{245} = 1.7:1$$

$$\text{Acid test ratio} = \frac{\text{Current assets} - \text{stock}}{\text{Current liabilities}} = \frac{425 - 150}{245} = 1.1:1$$

> **Helping hand**
> The acid test excludes stock as this is less liquid than cash and debtors.

$$\text{Stock turnover} = \frac{\text{Cost of sales}}{\text{Average stock}} = \frac{1,125}{(170 + 150)/2} = 7 \text{ times}$$

$$\text{Creditors payment period (days)} = \frac{\text{Creditors}}{\text{Purchases}} \times 365 = \frac{135 \times 365}{1,105} = 44.6 \text{ days}$$

$$\text{Debtors collection period (days)} = \frac{\text{Debtors}}{\text{Sales}} \times 365 = \frac{120 \times 365}{1,500} = 29.2 \text{ days}$$

$$\text{Earnings per share} = \frac{\text{Profit after tax}}{\text{No of shares}} = \frac{110}{1,400} = 8p$$

(b) REPORT

To:     Development Manager, Peanut Ltd
From:   Chartered Accounting Technician
Date:   October 20X8

*Subject: Performance of Peanut Ltd*

This report analyses the performance and financial position of Peanut Ltd. The basis of the analysis is as follows.

- The financial statements for the year ended 30 September 20X8.
- Ratios calculated thereon.
- Ratios from two previous years and the industry average for purposes of comparison.

*Profitability*

The gross profit percentage has remained more or less constant. At 25% it is slightly below industry average - perhaps the mark up is not as high as it might be. The net profit percentage has fallen, however, and is more significantly below the industry average. It is possible that **costs are not being adequately controlled**.

Earnings per share is healthy and has increased to the industry average of 8p.

# Questions and answers

*Liquidity*

The **current ratio** has been **falling steadily** over the three year period and is below the industry average. It is still healthy, as is the acid test ratio, but the trend needs to be monitored, as there may be weaknesses in the management of working capital.

Stock levels have been kept under control, having reduced by £20,000 over the year. However, **stock turnover has slowed down** over the last few years to below the industry average.

There may be **problems with credit control** as the debtors collection period has doubled from 14.6 days in 20X6 to 29.2 days in 20X8. Either credit customers are insisting on longer payment periods or credit control has slackened. The company is paying its creditors earlier, as the creditors payment period has reduced from 58.2 to 44.6, which is nearly the industry average.

*Conclusion*

Overall the company is **performing reasonably** well, but there may be cash flow problems with **pressure on working** capital. More information on, for example, previous years' sales would be needed for a fuller explanation.

---

**Helping hand**

It is often a good idea, in a conclusion, to say what additional information you might need to amplify your answer. It shows you're thinking!

## 35 HESTER (6/99)

A business associate has invited you to invest in Hester Ltd. He has watched the company steadily grow over the last three years and considers it a good investment. You have requested the following financial information so that you can draw your own conclusions.

HESTER LIMITED
BALANCES AS AT THE END OF

|  | 20X7 £'000 | 20X8 £'000 | 20X9 £'000 |
|---|---|---|---|
| Sales | 1,000 | 1,250 | 1,500 |
| Cost of sales | 700 | 850 | 975 |
| Gross profit | 300 | 400 | 525 |
| Distribution costs | 55 | 75 | 100 |
| Administration expenses | 100 | 200 | 300 |
| Profit on ordinary activities before interest | 145 | 125 | 125 |
| Interest payable | 10 | 15 | 30 |
| Profit on ordinary activities before taxation | 135 | 110 | 95 |
| Taxation on profit on ordinary activities | 30 | 25 | 25 |
| Profits on ordinary activities after taxation | 105 | 85 | 70 |
| Less proposed dividends | 50 | 35 | 35 |
| Retained profit for the year | 55 | 50 | 35 |
|  |  |  |  |
| Debentures | 100 | 150 | 300 |
| Share capital: 500,000 ordinary shares of £1 each | 500 | 500 | 500 |
| Share premium account | 20 | 20 | 20 |
| Profit and loss account | 250 | 300 | 335 |
|  | 870 | 970 | 1,155 |

*Financial performance ratios*

| Gross profit percentage | 30.0% | 32.0% | 35.0% |
|---|---|---|---|
| Operating profit percentage | 14.5% | 10.0% | 8.3% |
| Return on capital employed | 16.7% | 12.9% | 10.8% |

*Required*

(a) Identify and comment on the key financial trends as indicated by the above information. *(7 marks)*

(b) Calculate the following ratios for Hester Ltd for 20X9 only and explain the purpose of the ratio.

   (i) Return on shareholders' capital
   (ii) Capital gearing ratio
   (iii) Earnings per share
   (iv) Dividend cover *(8 marks)*

**(15 marks)**

---

**Helping hand**

1  In part (a), do not waste time calculating gross profit percentage, operating profit percentage and return on capital employed, as these ratios are given to you.

2  In part (b), don't neglect the explanations.

## 35 ANSWER: HESTER

> **Examiner's comment.**
>
> In part (a), the majority of the candidates were able to identify the trends but not all could comment on them. In part (b), many candidates could not explain the purpose of their ratios.

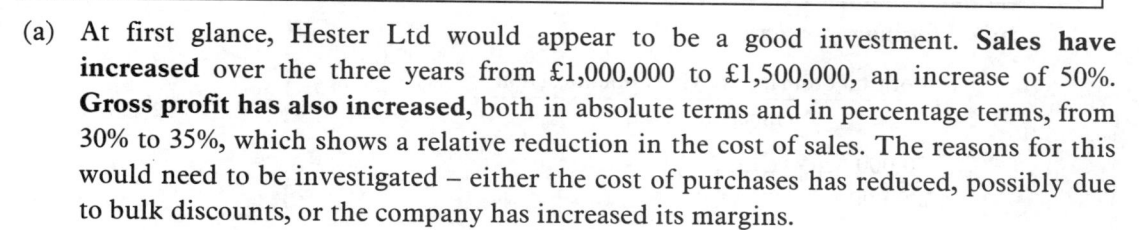

(a) At first glance, Hester Ltd would appear to be a good investment. **Sales have increased** over the three years from £1,000,000 to £1,500,000, an increase of 50%. **Gross profit has also increased**, both in absolute terms and in percentage terms, from 30% to 35%, which shows a relative reduction in the cost of sales. The reasons for this would need to be investigated – either the cost of purchases has reduced, possibly due to bulk discounts, or the company has increased its margins.

However, a closer look at the trends and percentages reveals that not all is well. The profit on ordinary activities before interest as a percentage of sales has actually fallen from 14.5% to = 8.3%. This may be because **administration costs** as a percentage of sales has **risen** from 100/1,000 = 10% to 300/1,500 = 20%. Perhaps more money has been spent on salaries, or on advertising to increase growth, but the trend needs to be carefully monitored.

Additional debentures have been issued during the three-year period to finance the company's expansion. This has meant that **interest payable has tripled**, with a consequent **fall in profit before tax** as a percentage of sales from 13.5/1,000 = to 95/1,500 = 6.3%.

**Return on capital employed has fallen** from 16.7% to 10.8%, which, together with the decline in retained profit from £55,000 to £35,000 suggests that there is a **problem with control of costs**. The **level of dividends** has also **fallen**, which casts doubt on Hester Ltd as an investment opportunity.

> **Helping hand**
>
> There is plenty of information in this question and any sensible comments will gain marks.

(b) *Return on shareholders' capital*

(i) $\dfrac{\text{Profit on ordinary activities before tax}}{\text{Share capital and reserves}} \times 100\%$

$\dfrac{95}{855} \times 100\% = 11.1\%$

This ratio measures profitability, concentrating on the return to **shareholders**. It differs from return on capital employed as the profit is after interest.

(ii) *Capital gearing ratio*

$\dfrac{\text{Prior charge capital}}{\text{Total capital}} \times 100\%$

$\dfrac{300}{1,155} \times 100 = 26\%$

Prior charge capital is capital with a fixed rate of return, such as preference shares or, in the case of Hester Ltd, debentures. The capital gearing ratio measures the proportion of a company's capital that is prior charge capital. Hester Ltd is not highly geared. In a highly geared company there is the **risk**

## Questions and answers

that, if profits are insufficient to pay the holders of prior charge capital, returns to shareholders will fall.

> **Helping hand**
> As well as showing how to calculate the ratio, we explain its significance.

(iii) *Earnings per share*

$$\frac{\text{Profit on ordinary activities after taxation}}{\text{Number of shares}}$$

$$\frac{70,000}{500,000} = 14 \text{ pence}$$

This ratio is useful for year-on-year comparisons and also for comparisons with other firms in the same industry. It shows the **earnings achieved** for each **ordinary share**.

(iv) *Dividend cover*

$$\frac{\text{Earnings per share}}{\text{Dividend per share}}$$

Dividend per share is $\frac{35}{500} = 7$ pence

$\therefore$ Dividend cover $= \frac{14}{7} = 2$ times

By comparing the amount of profit earned per ordinary share with the amount of dividend paid, this ratio shows the **proportion of profit** that the **company can retain** for future investment. The higher the dividend cover, the more confident the investor should be of future growth and dividends.

## 36 LEWIS AND GORDON (6/01)

You have been provided with the following information for Lewis Ltd and Gordon Ltd which are retail companies selling similar products in a similar market.

| Ratio | Lewis Ltd | Gordon Ltd |
|---|---|---|
| Gross profit percentage | 18% | 30% |
| Net profit percentage | 10% | 10% |
| Return on capital employed (ROCE) | 16% | 19% |
| Stock turnover | 21 days | 40 days |
| Average settlement period for debtors | 23 days | 67 days |
| Average settlement period for creditors | 39 days | 44 days |

*Required*

(a) State how each ratio is calculated. (3 marks)

(b) Comment on the performance of the two companies as indicated by the ratios. (8 marks)

(c) Briefly explain what further information about the companies would be helpful in assessing their performance. (4 marks)

**(15 marks)**

---

**Helping hand**

1 Part (a) should cause no problems.

2 Don't just state the difference. Try to think of reasons. Credit will be given for sensible comments.

3 In Part (c), don't forget to mention accounting policies.

## 36 ANSWER: LEWIS AND GORDON

> **Examiner's comment.** In Part (a), with the exception of the stock turnover ratio, most candidates were able to correctly answer this part of the question. In Part (b) comments on the ratios were generally lengthy and merely described the figures given. To gain the maximum marks candidates needed to interpret the ratios before they could comment on the performance of the companies. For example Gordon Ltd's stock turnover ratio and the length of the settlement periods for debtors and creditors indicated it had cash flow problems. Part (c) was poorly answered. Most candidates did not state some of the more obvious answers like the financial statements for the current and previous year, comparative industry ratios and activity information. A number of candidates just listed all the other ratios they had memorised for the exam.

(a) Gross profit percentage $\quad \dfrac{\text{Gross profit}}{\text{Sales}} \times 100$

Net profit percentage $\quad \dfrac{\text{Net profit}}{\text{Sales}} \times 100$

Return on capital employed $\quad \dfrac{\text{Net profit}}{\text{Capital employed}} \times 100$

Stock turnover $\quad \dfrac{\text{Average stock}}{\text{Cost of sales}} \times 365$

Average settlement period for debtors $\quad \dfrac{\text{Debtors}}{\text{Credit sales}} \times 365$

Average settlement period for creditors $\quad \dfrac{\text{Creditors}}{\text{Credit purchases}} \times 365$

(b) The **gross profit percentage of Gordon Ltd** at 30% is significantly higher than that of Lewis Ltd (18%). There may be a number of reasons for this. Gordon Ltd may be a larger company using its size to obtain discounts from suppliers, or it may be a more established company, able to charge higher prices for the same product.

The **net profit percentage** is the same for both companies at 10%. Given the disparity in gross profit percentage, **Lewis Ltd appears to be better at controlling expenses** than Gordon Ltd. Possibly Gordon Ltd is spending a lot of money on advertising or marketing or on a comprehensive aftersales service.

> **Helping hand.** Obviously these comments are speculative, but they are logical. Credit will be given for **reasonable** answers.

At 19%, Gordon Ltd's **return on capital employed** is slightly higher than Lewis Ltd's. Both returns are **reasonable**, however. One would need further information about how the assets are valued to make sure one was comparing like with like.

Gordon Ltd's stock turnover is high, and about twice as high as that of Lewis Ltd. As both companies are selling similar products, **Gordon Ltd's stockholding strategy is clearly less efficient** and needs to be reviewed. It is **risky** to have a high proportion of working capital tied up in stock, the least liquid of the current assets.

The debtor settlement period for Gordon is high, around three times that for Lewis. This suggests that **Gordon** is having **credit control problems**, which need to be addressed. The settlement period for creditors is similar for both companies. Of particular concern is the fact that Gordon Ltd pays its creditors 23 days before it receives income from debtors. This suggests **deficient controls over cash flow**. By contrast, Lewis Ltd pays creditors 16 days after it receives the cash from debtors, suggesting that it is much more in control in this area.

## Questions and answers

Overall, it would appear that **Lewis Ltd is the more efficiently managed** company.

(c) **Other useful information**

(i) **Financial statements** for the current and previous year. This would enable us to see the actual figures for turnover and so on to see which company is bigger. Forecast financial statements would also be useful.

(ii) **Ratios for the previous year,** so a trend could be observed.

(iii) **Relevant information on the industry** in which the companies operate, including industry average ratios, number and size of competitors, whether or not it is a growth industry.

(iv) In order to compare return on capital employed more meaningfully, **details about asset valuation** would be useful.

(v) Details of other accounting policies, for example, depreciation or capitalisation of research and development costs would enable a comparison to be made.

---

**Helping hand.** Accounting policies can make a considerable difference – not all candidates will think to mention them.

## 37 GILSON AND WARDNER (12/99)

You have been asked to analyse the performance of two sole traders who run similar businesses. Their financial statements for the year ending 31 October 20X9 are given below.

|  | *John Gilson* £'000 | £'000 | *David Wardner* £'000 | £'000 |
|---|---|---|---|---|
| **TRADING AND PROFIT AND LOSS ACCOUNT** | | | | |
| Sales | | 140 | | 200 |
| Less cost of goods sold | | | | |
| Opening stock | 36 | | 40 | |
| Purchases | 85 | | 137 | |
|  | 121 | | 177 | |
| Less closing stock | 18 | | 45 | |
|  | | 103 | | 132 |
| Gross profit | | 37 | | 68 |
| Less depreciation | 3 | | 5 | |
| Other expenses | 16 | | 11 | |
|  | | 19 | | 16 |
| Net profit | | 18 | | 52 |
| **BALANCE SHEET** | | | | |
| *Fixed assets* | | | | |
| Fixtures and fittings | 18 | | 35 | |
| *Less* depreciation | 14 | | 11 | |
|  | | 4 | | 24 |
| *Current assets* | | | | |
| Stock | 18 | | 45 | |
| Debtors | 44 | | 35 | |
| Bank | 9 | | 4 | |
|  | 71 | | 84 | |
| *Current liabilities* | | | | |
| Creditors | 19 | | 50 | |
| Net current assets | | 52 | | 34 |
|  | | 56 | | 58 |
| *Capital* | | | | |
| Balance at start of year | | 53 | | 70 |
| Add net profit | | 18 | | 52 |
|  | | 71 | | 122 |
| Less drawings | | 15 | | 64 |
|  | | 56 | | 58 |

*Required*

Your manager has asked you to prepare two things.

(a) A table of accounting ratios (with supporting workings) which compares the profitability, liquidity and efficiency of the two businesses (6 marks)

(b) A brief report which comments on the accounting ratios you have calculated (9 marks)

**(15 marks)**

> **Helping hand**
>
> In this kind of question, you will not be penalised too heavily for arithmetical mistakes.

## 37 ANSWER: GILSON AND WARDNER

> **Examiner's comment**
>
> In part (a) a significant number of candidates gained full marks. In part (b) the weaker candidates just described the figures they had calculated and did not demonstrate any understanding of them.

(a) *Profitability*

| Ratio | Formula | John Gibson | David Wardner |
|---|---|---|---|
| Return on capital employed | $\dfrac{\text{Profit before interest and tax}}{\text{Capital employed}}$ | $\dfrac{18}{56} = 32\%$ | $\dfrac{52}{58} = 90\%$ |
| Gross profit margin | $\dfrac{\text{Gross profit}}{\text{Sales}}$ | $\dfrac{37}{140} = 26\%$ | $\dfrac{68}{200} = 34\%$ |

*Liquidity*

| Ratio | Formula | John Gibson | David Wardner |
|---|---|---|---|
| Current ratio | $\dfrac{\text{Current assets}}{\text{Current liabilities}}$ | $\dfrac{71}{19} = 3.74$ | $\dfrac{84}{50} = 1.68$ |
| Acid test ratio | $\dfrac{\text{Current assets less stock}}{\text{Current liabilities}}$ | $\dfrac{71-18}{19} = 2.79$ | $\dfrac{84-45}{50} = 0.78$ |

*Efficiency*

| Ratio | Formula | John Gibson | David Wardner |
|---|---|---|---|
| Asset turnover | $\dfrac{\text{Sales}}{\text{Total assets less current liabilities}}$ | $\dfrac{140}{56} = 2.5$ | $\dfrac{200}{58} = 3.45$ |
| Expenses to sales | $\dfrac{\text{Expenses (other than depreciation)}}{\text{Sales}}$ | $\dfrac{16}{140} = 11\%$ | $\dfrac{11}{200} = 6\%$ |

> **Helping hand**
>
> If you got the formula right but the numbers wrong, you would probably get around half the marks.

(b)

REPORT

To: The Manager, XYZ Limited
From: A Technician
Date: 20 January 20Y0

*Performance of John Gilson and David Wardner*

As you are aware, the two sole traders John Gilson and David Wardner both operate in the same industry, so a comparison of accounting ratios is appropriate.

At first sight it appears that David **Wardner** is the more successful of the two businesses. Not only are sales and profits higher in absolute terms, but the **profitability ratios are better.** Wardner's return on capital employed is a massive 90%, as against Gilson's – still healthy – 32%, and Wardner's gross profit ratio, at 34% is higher than Gilson's 26%.

## Questions and answers

Similarly, **Wardner** seems to have made **more efficient use of the assets employed**. A good indication of this is the asset turnover ratio of 3.45, as against Gilson's 2.5. Efficiency can be measured in a number of ways, but controlling costs is a good measure. Wardner's expenses are a mere 6% of sales, while Gilson's ratio is nearly twice as high at 11%.

> **Helping hand**
>
> If you had calculated these ratios incorrectly in part (a) but your comments were consistent with your numbers and sensible, you would get credit for your answer.

Bear in mind, however, that **differing accounting policies** can make a difference to how the figure for capital employed is calculated. More information would be needed on this point.

It is the **liquidity ratios that let Wardner down**. Its current ratio of 1.68 compares unfavourably with that of Gilson which is a healthy 3.74. When you strip out stock to give the quick ratio, the figures are 0.78 and 2.79 respectively, showing that Wardner has **a lot of working capital tied up in stock** and may encounter liquidity problems.

Overall, Wardner's looks the more successful business, but is perhaps **overstretching itself**, as shown by the liquidity ratios.

Signed: A Technician

# DO YOU KNOW? - SIMPLE CONSOLIDATED ACCOUNTS

- *Check that you can fill in the blanks in the statements below before you attempt any questions. If in doubt, you should go back to your BPP Interactive Text and revise first.*

- Relevant standards:
    - *FRS 2* ..............................
    - *SSAP 20* ..............................
    - *FRS 6* ..............................
    - *FRS 7* ..............................
    - *FRS 9* ..............................
    - *FRS 10* ..............................

- Learn by heart the format and the working schedules for the consolidated balance sheet and the consolidated profit and loss account.

- Learn how to calculate the balance sheet figure for interest in associated companies and the results of associated companies which are brought into and disclosed in the consolidated P & L account.

- .............................. determines the treatment of different holdings in companies.

    - An investment in under 20% of a company's shares, where the investing company has no significant influence over the other company, is a .............................. and is .............................. or treated in any way differently from any other investment.

    - A 20% + investment (or a smaller one where there is significant influence) is treated as an investment in an .............................. . (A 20%+ investment is presumed to give significant influence but if it can be shown that this does not exist then the investment is a trade investment).

    - An investment in over 50% of another company's shares usually results in .............................. of that company, which makes it a .............................. . The CA 1989 introduced the idea of a controlled non-subsidiary, requiring such subsidiaries to be consolidated. This description of 'dominant influence' effectively outlawed off balance sheet finance involving such arrangements.

    - Associated companies are not consolidated. The investment is shown in the balance sheet at .............................. plus the investing company's share of .............................., called equity accounting.

    - Subsidiaries are consolidated. There are two ways of doing this, the .............................. method (more common) and the .................... method (restricted).

- FRS 6 places severe restrictions on the use of .............................. .

- FRS 7 reflects the perceived need for a standard to govern the .............................. exercise undertaken under acquisition accounting.

- The complexities of consolidation which you must be able to explain include .............................., at the year end or during the year.

    *Such questions, are likely to be fairly straightforward, dealing only with simple groups.*

    YOU SHOULD ATTEMPT **ALL** THE QUESTIONS IN THIS SECTION AS THIS TOPIC IS COMPLETELY NEW TO YOU AND REQUIRES A GREAT DEAL OF PRACTICE.

- *Possible pitfalls*

    *Write down the mistakes you know you should avoid.*

## Questions and answers

### DID YOU KNOW? - SIMPLE CONSOLIDATED ACCOUNTS

- *Could you fill in the blanks? The answers are in bold. Use this page for revision purposes as you approach the exam.*

- Relevant standards:
    - FRS 2     **Accounting for subsidiary undertakings**
    - FRS 6     **Acquisitions and mergers**
    - FRS 7     **Fair values in acquisition accounting**
    - FRS 9     **Associates and joint ventures (not joint ventures)**
    - FRS 10    **Goodwill and intangible assets**

- Learn by heart the format and the working schedules for the consolidated balance sheet and the consolidated P & L account.

- Learn how to calculate the balance sheet figure for 'interests in associated companies' and the results of associated companies which are brought into and disclosed in the consolidated P & L account.

- **FRS 2** determines the treatment of different holdings in companies.

    - An investment in under 20% of a company's shares, where the investing company has no significant influence over the other company, is a trade investment and is not consolidated or treated in any way differently from any other investment.

    - A 20%+ investment (or a smaller one where there is significant influence) is treated as an investment in an associated company. (A 20%+ investment is presumed to give significant influence but if it can be shown that this does not exist then the investment is a trade investment).

    - An investment in >50% of another company's shares usually results in control of that company, which makes it a subsidiary. The CA 1989 introduced the idea of a controlled non-subsidiary, requiring such subsidiaries to be consolidated. This description of 'dominant influence' effectively outlawed off balance sheet finance involving such arrangements.

    - Associated companies are not consolidated. The investment is shown in the balance sheet at cost plus the investing company's share of **post-acquisition retained profit**, called equity accounting.

    - Subsidiaries are consolidated. There are two ways of doing this, the **acquisition** method (more common) and the **merger** method (restricted).

- FRS 6 places severe restrictions on the use of **merger accounting**.

- FRS 7 reflects the perceived need for a standard to govern the **fair value** exercise undertaken under acquisition accounting.

- The complexities of consolidation which you must be able to explain include **acquisition of subsidiaries**, at the year end or during the year.

    *Such questions, are likely to be fairly straightforward, dealing only with simple groups.*

    YOU SHOULD ATTEMPT **ALL** THE QUESTIONS IN THIS SECTION AS THIS TOPIC IS COMPLETELY NEW TO YOU AND REQUIRES A GREAT DEAL OF PRACTICE.

- *Possible pitfalls*
    - **Confusing the status of an investment. In particular, the status is now determined by control rather than mere share ownership.**
    - **Confusing merger accounting and merger relief.**
    - **Treatment of joint ventures - this is the subject of a relatively recent standard, FRS 9.**

# 38 QUESTION WITH HELP: BOO AND GOOSE

Boo plc has owned 80% of Goose Ltd's equity since its incorporation. On 31 December 20X8 it despatched goods which cost £80,000 to Goose, at an invoiced cost of £100,000. Goose received the goods on 2 January 20X9 and recorded the transaction then. The two companies' draft accounts as at 31 December 20X8 are shown below.

PROFIT AND LOSS ACCOUNTS FOR THE YEAR ENDED 31 DECEMBER 20X8

|  | Boo plc £'000 | Goose Limited £'000 |
|---|---|---|
| Sales | 5,000 | 1,000 |
| Cost of sales | 2,900 | 600 |
| Gross profit | 2,100 | 400 |
| Other expenses | 1,700 | 320 |
| Net profit | 400 | 80 |
| Tax | 130 | 25 |
| Profit after tax | 270 | 55 |
| Dividends proposed | 130 | 40 |
| Retained profit for the year | 140 | 15 |
| Retained profit brought forward | 260 | 185 |
| Retained profit carried forward | 400 | 200 |

BALANCE SHEETS AT 31 DECEMBER 20X8

|  | £'000 | £'000 |
|---|---|---|
| *Fixed assets* | 2,000 | 200 |
| *Current assets* |  |  |
| Stock | 500 | 120 |
| Trade debtors | 650 | 40 |
| Bank and cash | 390 | 35 |
|  | 1,540 | 195 |
| *Current liabilities* |  |  |
| Trade creditors | 910 | 30 |
| Dividend payable | 100 | 40 |
| Tax | 130 | 25 |
|  | 1,140 | 95 |
| *Net current assets* | 400 | 100 |
| *Total assets less current liabilities* | 2,400 | 300 |
| *Capital and reserves* |  |  |
| Share capital | 2,000 | 100 |
| Profit and loss account | 400 | 200 |
|  | 2,400 | 300 |

*Required*

Prepare draft consolidated financial statements.

> *If you are stuck, look at the next page for detailed help as to how you should tackle this question.*

## Questions and answers

**APPROACHING THE ANSWER**

**Step 1** Set out the pro forma financial statements. Note that the only difference between the pro forma consolidated financial statements and the individual company financial statements is the line minority interest, which appears in the profit and loss account and the balance sheet. The important parts are illustrated below.

**Step 2** CONSOLIDATED PROFIT AND LOSS ACCOUNT (EXTRACT)

| | |
|---|---|
| Profit after tax | X |
| Minority interest (20% × Goose's PAT) | (X) |
| Group profit for the year | X |
| Dividend proposed (Boo only) | (X) |
| Retained profit for the year | X |
| Retained profit brought forward | X |
| Retained profit carried forward | X |

CONSOLIDATED BALANCE SHEET (EXTRACT)

*Capital and reserves*

| | |
|---|---|
| Share capital (Boo only) | X |
| Minority interests (20% × Goose's share capital and reserves) | X |
| Profit and loss account | X |

**Step 2** Include stock in transit in the balance sheet and deduct from cost of sales at cost to the group.

**Step 3** Similarly, the intra-group debtor and sale should be eliminated as a consolidation adjustment.

**Step 4** The minority interest in the P&L account is easily calculated as 20% of post-tax profit for the year as shown in Goose's accounts. However, in the balance sheet, the minority interest represents the minority interest in retained profits and share capital only. The proposed dividend payable to the minority is a current liability.

**Step 5** Don't forget that Boo's accounts must somewhere contain a balance for its investment in Goose Ltd (its holding of shares in Goose, at cost since no share premium is shown in Goose's books). Fixed assets must therefore be reduced by this amount to correspond to the cancellation of Goose's share capital. A valid (although less likely) alternative would be to assume that Boo had provided against the cost of the investment in full, thus reducing the value of the investment in its books to nil. This provision would be reversed as a consolidation adjustment, thus increasing group reserves by the amount of the provision.

## 38 ANSWER TO QUESTION WITH HELP: BOO AND GOOSE

BOO GROUP
CONSOLIDATED PROFIT AND LOSS ACCOUNT
FOR THE YEAR ENDED 31 DECEMBER 20X8

|  | £'000 |
|---|---|
| Sales (5,000 + 1,000 − 100) | 5,900 |
| Cost of sales (2,900 + 600 − 80) | 3,420 |
| Gross profit | 2,480 |
| Other expenses (1,700 + 320) | 2,020 |
| Net profit | 460 |
| Tax (130 + 25) | 155 |
| Profit after tax | 305 |
| Minority interest (20% × £55,000) | 11 |
| Group profit for the year | 294 |
| Dividend proposed (Boo only) | 130 |
| Retained profit for the year | 164 |
| Retained profit brought forward | 408 |
| Retained profit carried forward | 572 |

CONSOLIDATED BALANCE SHEET AS AT 31 DECEMBER 20X8

|  | £'000 | £'000 |
|---|---|---|
| *Fixed assets* (2,000 + 200 − 80) |  | 2,120 |
| *Current assets* |  |  |
| Stock (500 + 120 + 80) | 700 |  |
| Trade debtors (650 − 100 + 40) | 590 |  |
| Bank and cash (390 + 35) | 425 |  |
|  | 1,715 |  |
| *Current liabilities* |  |  |
| Trade creditors (910 + 30) | 940 |  |
| Dividend payable: Boo plc | 100 |  |
| to minority in Goose Ltd | 8 |  |
| Tax (130 + 25) | 155 |  |
|  | 1,203 |  |
| *Net current assets* |  | 512 |
| *Total assets less current liabilities* |  | 2,632 |
|  |  | 2,632 |
| *Capital and reserves* |  |  |
| Share capital (Boo only) |  | 2,000 |
| Minority interest (20% × 300) |  | 60 |
| Profit and loss account (W) |  | 572 |
|  |  | 2,632 |

*Working*

GROUP RESERVES

|  | £'000 |  | £'000 |
|---|---|---|---|
| Inter company sale | 100 | Boo | 400 |
| Minority interest in Goose's |  | Goose | 200 |
| retained profits (20% × 200) | 40 | Dividend from Goose to Boo |  |
| CBS | 572 | (80% × 40) | 32 |
|  |  | Closing stock in transit (at cost) | 80 |
|  | 712 |  | 712 |

This working is, of course, only necessary when you are not required to prepare the consolidated P&L account. Here, it serves as a proof of the consolidated P&L account as well as of the reserves figure in the balance sheet.

## 39 CONSOLIDATED FINANCIAL STATEMENTS

'The consolidation of financial statements hides rather than provides information.'

You are required to discuss this statement.

(20 marks)

**Helping hand**

1   A perusal of real financial statements should come in useful here.
2   Construct a plan and a coherent argument around the topic.
3   Watch your grammar, spelling and handwriting.

## 39 ANSWER: CONSOLIDATED FINANCIAL STATEMENTS

> **Helping hand**
>
> This question is basically asking you to state the arguments for and against group accounts. If you really couldn't think of any, learn the points we have made in our answer.

The **individual** accounts of a parent company are **inadequate** by themselves for the information needs of shareholders and other interested parties.

(a) The parent company accounts **do not reveal the true size and importance** of the economic entity in which shareholders have invested.

(b) They show investments in subsidiaries at **historical cost**, which may be a very poor indication of the resources actually controlled by the group.

(c) Parent company profit will consist only of its **own operating profit**, other investment income and so on and dividends received from subsidiaries. Shareholders will not know the amount of profits retained by subsidiaries.

(d) Creditors cannot assess, from the parent company accounts alone, the **liquidity and solvency** of the group as a whole.

The preparation of group accounts helps to overcome these difficulties and therefore provides fuller information than would be available from the parent company accounts. The statement in the question cannot be strictly justified: since individual accounts must still be prepared for each group company, the consolidated accounts are an **additional** source of information which can only be helpful to accounts users.

> **Helping hand**
>
> The above is a very important point to make. Any user determined to find out about about an individual company can do so by reference to its own accounts.

However, it is true that group accounts taken by themselves suffer from serious **shortcomings**.

(a) They conceal the liquidity and solvency position of individual group companies. Similarly, the losses of some group companies may be concealed by the overall profitability of the group.

(b) They **aggregate assets** which may be very **disparate** in nature.

(c) The do **not** reveal the extent of **intra-group trading** and intra-group indebtedness.

(d) They are **unsuitable** for detailed **ratio analysis** because they do not indicate which sectors of the group's activities are generating a high level of return and which are less satisfactory.

Some of these objections have been reduced in recent years by statutory provisions on the disclosure of segmental information, but the Companies Act 1985 does not go very far in this direction. SSAP 25 *Segmental reporting* has increased the amount of information to be disclosed in this way although the basis of inter-segmental pricing need not be disclosed.

# Questions and answers

## 40 SHARK AND MINNOW (12/00)

You are provided with the following balance sheets for Shark plc and Minnow Ltd.

BALANCE SHEETS AS AT 31 OCTOBER 20X0

|  | Shark plc £'000 | Shark plc £'000 | Minnow Limited £'000 | Minnow Limited £'000 |
|---|---|---|---|---|
| *Fixed assets, at net book value* |  |  |  |  |
| Plant |  | 325 |  | 70 |
| Fixtures |  | 200 |  | 50 |
|  |  | 525 |  | 120 |
| *Investment* |  |  |  |  |
| Shares in Minnow Ltd at cost |  | 200 |  |  |
| *Current assets* |  |  |  |  |
| Stock at cost | 220 |  | 70 |  |
| Debtors | 145 |  | 105 |  |
| Bank | 100 |  | 0 |  |
|  | 465 |  | 175 |  |
| *Creditors: amounts falling due within one year* |  |  |  |  |
| Creditors | 275 |  | 55 |  |
| Bank overdraft | 0 |  | 20 |  |
|  | 275 |  | 75 |  |
| *Net current assets* |  | 190 |  | 100 |
|  |  | 915 |  | 220 |
| *Capital and Reserves* |  |  |  |  |
| £1 Ordinary shares |  | 700 |  | 170 |
| Reserves |  | 215 |  | 50 |
|  |  | 915 |  | 220 |

The following information is also available.

(a) Shark plc purchased 70% of the issued ordinary share capital of Minnow Ltd on 1 November 20W0 when the reserves of Minnow Ltd were £20,000. Goodwill was fully amortised through the profit and loss account by 31 October 20W9.

(b) For the purposes of the acquisition, plant in Minnow Ltd with a book value of £50,000 was revalued to its fair value of £60,000. The revaluation was not recorded in the accounts of Minnow Ltd. Depreciation is charged at 20% using the straight-line method.

(c) Shark plc sells goods to Minnow Ltd at a mark up of 25%. At 31 October 20X0, the stocks of Minnow Ltd included £45,000 of goods purchased from Shark plc.

(d) Minnow Ltd owes Shark plc £35,000 for goods purchased and Shark Ltd owes Minnow Ltd £15,000.

*Required*

(a) Prepare the consolidated balance sheet of Shark plc as at 31 October 20X0. (22 marks)

(b) Explain briefly why adjustments need to be made in group accounts for:

    (i) Inter-company trading (4 marks)
    (ii) Inter-company transfers of fixed assets (4 marks)

**(30 marks)**

## Questions and answers

**Helping hand**

1. Set out the proforma and produce the standard workings.
2. There are a lot of easy marks to be gained for just adding across.
3. In part (b), think about what consolidation is for.

# 40 ANSWER: SHARK AND MINNOW

> **Examiner's comment.** Part (a) was not tackled quite as well as previous consolidated balance sheet questions. In particular, the adjustments required by some of the notes caused some difficulties. Most candidates were able to deal with the inter-company trading aspects of the question. However, the weaker students demonstrated their lack of preparation and were unable to calculate the goodwill on acquisition, the consolidated reserves or the minority interest. Once again, the importance of using the correct format for a consolidated balance sheet cannot be over emphasised. In part (b), those candidates who had thoroughly revised were able to give clear, concise explanations and consequently gained most marks.

(a) SHARK PLC
CONSOLIDATED BALANCE SHEET AS AT 31 OCTOBER 20X0

|  | £'000 | £'000 |
|---|---|---|
| *Fixed assets* |  |  |
| Plant (W2) |  | 397 |
| Fixtures (200 + 50) |  | 250 |
|  |  | 647 |
| *Current assets* |  |  |
| Stock (W3) | 281 |  |
| Debtors (W4) | 200 |  |
| Bank | 100 |  |
|  | 581 |  |
| *Creditors: amounts falling due within one year* |  |  |
| Creditors (W5) | 280 |  |
| Bank overdraft | 20 |  |
|  | 300 |  |
| *Net current assets* |  | 281 |
|  |  | 928 |
| *Capital and reserves* |  |  |
| Share capital |  | 700 |
| Reserves (W6) |  | 161 |
|  |  | 861 |
| Minority interests (W7) |  | 67 |
|  |  | 928 |

*Workings*

1   Goodwill

|  | £'000 | £'000 |
|---|---|---|
| Cost of investment |  | 200 |
| Net assets acquired |  |  |
|    Share capital | 170 |  |
|    Reserves | 20 |  |
|    Revaluation reserve (60 – 50) | 10 |  |
|  | 200 |  |
| Group share: 70% |  | 140 |
| Goodwill |  | 60 |

## Questions and answers

**2  Plant**

|  | £'000 | £'000 |
|---|---|---|
| Shark |  | 325 |
| Minnow |  |  |
|    Per question | 70 |  |
|    Revalued (60 – 50) | 10 |  |
|    Depreciation on revalued plant (10 × 20% × 4) | (8) |  |
|  |  | 72 |
|  |  | 397 |

**3  Stock**

|  | £'000 | £'000 |
|---|---|---|
| Shark |  | 220 |
| Minnow | 70 |  |
| Less PUP (45 × 20/100) | (9) |  |
|  |  | 61 |
|  |  | 281 |

**4  Debtors**

|  | £'000 | £'000 |
|---|---|---|
| Shark |  | 145 |
| Less intercompany |  | 35 |
|  |  | 110 |
| Minnow | 105 |  |
| Less intercompany | 15 |  |
|  |  | 90 |
|  |  | 200 |

**5  Creditors**

|  | £'000 | £'000 |
|---|---|---|
| Shark |  | 275 |
| Less intercompany |  | 15 |
|  |  | 260 |
| Minnow | 55 |  |
| Less intercompany | 35 |  |
|  |  | 20 |
|  |  | 280 |

**6  Reserves**

|  | £'000 | £'000 |
|---|---|---|
| Shark |  | 215 |
| Less goodwill fully amortised (W1) | 60.0 |  |
| PUP (W3) | 9.0 |  |
| Excess depn on plant (8 (W2) × 70%) | 5.6 |  |
|  |  | 74.6 |
|  |  | 140.4 |
| Minnow: 70% × (50 – 20) |  | 21.0 |
|  |  | 161.4 |

**7  Minority interests**

|  | £'000 | £'000 |
|---|---|---|
| Share capital |  | 170 |
| Revaluation | 10 |  |
| Less excess depreciation | (8) |  |
|  |  | 2 |
| Reserves |  | 50 |
|  |  | 222 |

∴ Minority interests: 30% × £222,000 = £66,600.

> **Helping hand.** Goodwill, reserves and minority interests are standard workings in any consolidation.

(b) (i) **Intercompany trading**

The purpose of consolidated accounts is to present the financial position of connected companies as that of a single entity, the group. This means that **in the consolidated balance sheet the only profits recognised should be those earned by the group** in providing goods or services **to outsiders**; similarly, stock in the consolidated balance sheet should be valued at cost to the group.

When a company sells goods to another company in the same group, it will recognise the turnover and profit in its own books. However, from the point of view of the group, no sale has taken place, because the goods have not been sold outside the group. The sale must therefore be **eliminated** from turnover and from cost of sales and the unrealised profit eliminated from stock.

(ii) **Intercompany transfers of fixed assets**

Companies within a group may occasionally transfer fixed assets to each other. In their individual accounts, the companies will treat the transfer just like a sale between unconnected parties. The selling company will record a profit or loss on sale, while the purchasing company will record the asset at the amount paid to acquire it, and will use that amount as the basis for calculating depreciation.

On consolidation the **group; entity principle** applies. The consolidated balance sheet must show assets at their **cost to the group**, and any depreciation charged must be based on that cost. Accordingly, reserves and fixed asset cost are adjusted to **remove any element of unrealised profit** or loss, as for stock. Additionally, an adjustment is made to alter reserves and accumulated depreciation, so that **consolidated depreciation is based on the asset's cost to the group**.

> **Helping hand.** If you realise that the purpose of consolidation is to present the financial position of group companies as that of a single entity, it becomes clear why intragroup transactions need to be eliminated.

## 41 OAK (12/98)

The draft balance sheets of Oak plc and its subsidiary Chestnut Ltd at 30 September 20X8 are as follows.

|  | Oak plc £ | Oak plc £ | Chestnut Ltd £ | Chestnut Ltd £ |
|---|---|---|---|---|
| *Fixed assets* | | | | |
| Tangible assets, net book value | | | | |
| Land and buildings | | 225,000 | | 270,000 |
| Plant | | 202,500 | | 157,500 |
| | | 427,500 | | 427,500 |
| *Investment* | | | | |
| Shares in Chestnut Ltd at cost | | 562,500 | | |
| *Current assets* | | | | |
| Stock | 255,000 | | 180,000 | |
| Debtors | 375,000 | | 90,000 | |
| Bank | 112,500 | | 22,500 | |
| | 742,500 | | 292,500 | |
| *Creditors: amounts falling due within one year* | 157,500 | | 67,500 | |
| Net current assets | | 585,000 | | 225,000 |
| | | 1,575,000 | | 652,500 |
| *Capital and reserves* | | | | |
| Called up share capital - issued and fully paid | | | | |
| £1 ordinary shares | | 1,125,000 | | 450,000 |
| Reserves | | 450,000 | | 202,500 |
| | | 1,575,000 | | 652,500 |

The following information is also available.

(a) Oak plc purchased 360,000 shares in Chestnut Ltd some years ago when that company had a credit balance of £105,000 in reserves. The goodwill was fully amortised through the profit and loss account by 30 September 20X7.

(b) For the purpose of the takeover, the land of Chestnut Ltd was revalued at £120,000 in excess of its book value. This was not reflected in the accounts of Chestnut Ltd. Land is not depreciated.

(c) At 30 September 20X8 Chestnut Ltd owed Oak plc £15,000 for goods purchased.

(d) The stock of Chestnut Ltd includes goods purchased from Oak plc at a price which includes a profit to Oak plc of £10,500.

*Required*

(a) Prepare the consolidated balance sheet for Oak plc as at 30 September 20X8. (22 marks)

(b) Explain the accounting treatment of inter-company trading transactions and balances when consolidating accounts. Use the data for the companies in this question to illustrate your answer. (8 marks)

**(30 marks)**

---

**Helping hand**

1 The key with consolidation questions is to think of the group as an entity. Thus group transactions cancel each other out.

2 Set out the pro forma first and do the standard workings (goodwill, minority interests, reserves).

3 When dealing with the unrealised profit in stock, think about who sold the goods to who.

# 41 ANSWER: OAK

> **Examiner's comment.**
> 
> Most candidates made a 'brave attempt' at part (a), but in part (b) some candidates incorrectly produced a list of detailed instructions on how to consolidate two balance sheets.

(a) OAK PLC
CONSOLIDATED BALANCE SHEET AS AT 30 SEPTEMBER 20X8

|  | £ | £ |
|---|---|---|
| *Fixed assets* | | |
| Land and buildings (W3) | | 615,000 |
| Plant | | 360,000 |
| | | 975,000 |
| *Current assets* | | |
| Stock (W6) | 424,500 | |
| Debtors (W7) | 450,000 | |
| Bank | 135,000 | |
| | 1,009,500 | |
| | (210,000) | |
| *Creditors: amounts falling due within one year* (W8) | | 799,500 |
| | | 1,774,500 |
| *Capital and reserves* | | |
| Ordinary £1 shares | | 1,125,000 |
| Reserves (W5) | | 495,000 |
| | | 1,620,000 |
| Minority interest (W4) | | 154,500 |
| | | 1,774,500 |

*Workings*

1. Group structure: $\frac{360,000}{450,000} = 80\%$

2. *Goodwill*

|  | £ | £ |
|---|---|---|
| Cost of investment | | 562,500 |
| Net assets acquired | | |
|   Share capital | 450,000 | |
|   Reserves | 105,000 | |
|   Revaluation reserve | 120,000 | |
| | 675,000 | |
| × 80% | | 540,000 |
| Goodwill | | 22,500 |

3. *Land and buildings*

|  | £ | £ |
|---|---|---|
| Oak plc | | 225,000 |
| Chestnut Ltd: | | |
|   Net book value | 270,000 | |
|   Revaluation | 120,000 | |
| | | 390,000 |
| | | 615,000 |

4. *Minority interests*

|  | £ |
|---|---|
| Share capital | 450,000 |
| Revaluation | 120,000 |
| Reserves | 202,500 |
| | 772,500 |
| 20% × £772,500 = | £154,500 |

## Questions and answers

5   *Reserves*

|   | £ |
|---|---|
| Oak plc | 450,000 |
| Chestnut Ltd (202,500 − 105,000) × 80% | 78,000 |
| Goodwill | (22,500) |
| Unrealised profit | (10,500) |
|   | 495,000 |

> **Helping hand**
>
> Because the sale is made by the holding company, the **whole** of the unrealised profit is deducted, not just the group's share.

6   *Stock*

|   | £ |
|---|---|
| Oak | 225,000 |
| Chestnut | 180,000 |
| Less unrealised profit | 10,500 |
|   | 424,500 |

7   *Debtors*

|   | £ |
|---|---|
| Oak | 375,000 |
| Chestnut | 90,000 |
| Less intercompany | (15,000) |
|   | 450,000 |

> **Helping hand**
>
> The intercompany balance is eliminated from debtors and from creditors.

8   *Creditors: amounts falling due within one year*

|   | £ |
|---|---|
| Oak | 157,500 |
| Chestnut | 67,500 |
| Less intercompany | (15,000) |
|   | 210,000 |

(b) We prepare group accounts to reflect the group's trading as if it were a **single** entity. Companies within a group may trade with each other, and any profit made on such trading must be shown in the individual company accounts.

For example, Oak plc has sold goods to Chestnut plc at a profit. The individual accounts of Oak plc rightly show this profit. However, the group does not make a sale or achieve a profit until the goods are sold outside the group. Similarly, any goods that Chestnut Ltd has not sold by the end of the year will be included in Chestnut Ltd's stock at cost plus profit. In terms of the group's position, stock could be overvalued, because the actual cost to the group at the start will be what it cost Oak plc.

This anomaly is dealt with by **eliminating the unrealised profit** from stock in the consolidated balance sheet and from consolidated reserves.

The same reasoning can be applied to intercompany debtors and creditors. Chestnut Ltd owes £15,000 to Oak plc which is included in the creditors of Chestnut Ltd and the debtors of Oak plc. However, the group does not owe this amount to any outsiders and is not owed the money by outsiders. The balances should therefore be eliminated on consolidation.

## 42 BAMBER (12/99)

You are provided with the following summarised financial information for Bamber Ltd and Renshaw Ltd.

PROFIT AND LOSS ACCOUNT FOR THE YEAR ENDED 31 OCTOBER 20X9

|  | Bamber Limited £'000 | Renshaw Limited £'000 |
|---|---|---|
| Turnover | 1,000 | 250 |
| Cost of sales | 650 | 180 |
| Gross profit | 350 | 70 |
| Distribution costs | 75 | 15 |
| Administrative expenses | 60 | 20 |
| Operating profit | 215 | 35 |
| Investment income | 14 | 0 |
| Profit on ordinary activities before tax | 229 | 35 |
| Tax on profit on ordinary activities | 70 | 10 |
| Profit on ordinary activities after taxation | 159 | 25 |
| Proposed ordinary dividends | 80 | 15 |
| Retained profit for the year | 79 | 10 |

BALANCE SHEET AS AT 31 OCTOBER 20X9

|  | Bamber Limited £'000 | £'000 | Renshaw Limited £'000 | £'000 |
|---|---|---|---|---|
| *Fixed assets* |  |  |  |  |
| Tangible assets at net book value |  | 350 |  | 75 |
| *Investment* |  |  |  |  |
| Shares in Renshaw Ltd at cost |  | 100 |  |  |
| *Current assets* |  |  |  |  |
| Stock at cost | 180 |  | 45 |  |
| Debtors | 145 |  | 55 |  |
| Bank | 70 |  | 20 |  |
|  | 395 |  | 120 |  |
| *Creditors: amounts falling due within one year* |  |  |  |  |
| Creditors | 50 |  | 30 |  |
| Proposed dividends | 80 |  | 15 |  |
| Corporation tax | 70 |  | 10 |  |
|  | 200 |  | 55 |  |
| Net current assets |  | 195 |  | 65 |
|  |  | 645 |  | 140 |
| *Capital and reserves* |  |  |  |  |
| Called up share capital - issued and fully paid |  |  |  |  |
| £1 ordinary shares |  | 500 |  | 100 |
| Profit and loss account |  | 145 |  | 40 |
|  |  | 645 |  | 140 |

The following information is also available.

(a) Bamber Ltd purchased 80% of the issued ordinary share capital of Renshaw Ltd on 1 November 20X7 when the profit and loss account of Renshaw Ltd was £20,000. Goodwill is amortised over its estimated useful life of four years.

(b) Bamber Ltd sold goods costing £100,000 to Renshaw Ltd for £160,000 during the year ended 31 October 20X9. At 31 October 20X9, 25% of these goods remained in Renshaw Ltd's stocks.

## Questions and answers

(c) Bamber Ltd has recognised the dividends proposed by Renshaw Ltd in its profit and loss account.

*Required*

(a) Prepare the following statements for Bamber Ltd.

    (i) The consolidated profit and loss account for the year ended 31 October 20X9. Disclosure notes are not required. (12 marks)

    (ii) The consolidated balance sheet as at 31 October 20X9. (10 marks)

(b) Explain the circumstances in which the accounts of a subsidiary company need not be consolidated into the group accounts. (8 marks)

**(30 marks)**

---

**Helping hand**

1. Some workings can be done on the face of the profit and loss account/balance sheet to save time.
2. Take care with the intercompany adjustment.
3. In part (b), there are easy marks to be gained for knowledge. Distinguish 'must be' and 'may be'.

# 42 ANSWER: BAMBER

> **Examiner's comment**
>
> Most candidates made a reasonable attempt at this question, but the inter-company adjustments caused problems.

(a) (i) BAMBER LIMITED
CONSOLIDATED PROFIT AND LOSS ACCOUNT
FOR THE YEAR ENDED 31 OCTOBER 20X9

|  | £'000 |
|---|---:|
| Turnover (1,000 + 250 − 160) | 1,090 |
| Cost of sales (bal. fig.) | 685 |
| Gross profit (350 + 70 − 15 (W3)) | 405 |
| Distribution costs (75 + 15) | 90 |
| Administrative expenses (W5) | 81 |
| Operating profit | 234 |
| Investment income (W4) | 2 |
| Profit on ordinary attributes before tax | 236 |
| Tax on profit on ordinary activities (70 + 10) | 80 |
| Profit on ordinary activities after tax | 156 |
| Minority interests (25 × 20%) | 5 |
| Group profit for the year | 151 |
| Dividends | 80 |
| Group retained profit for the year | 71 |

> **Helping hand**
>
> Use a separate working for the unrealised profit, then put in your turnover/gross profit figure, leaving cost of sales as the balancing figure.

(ii) BAMBER LIMITED
CONSOLIDATED BALANCE SHEET AS AT 31 OCTOBER 20X9

|  | £'000 | £'000 |
|---|---:|---:|
| *Fixed assets* |  |  |
| Goodwill (W2) 4 − 2 |  | 2 |
| Tangible fixed assets (350+75) |  | 425 |
|  |  |  |
| *Current assets* |  |  |
| Stock (180 + 45 − 15(W3)) | 210 |  |
| Debtors (145 + 55 − 12*) | 188 |  |
| Bank (70 + 20) | 90 |  |
|  | 488 |  |
| *Creditors: amounts falling due within one year* |  |  |
| Creditors (50 + 30 + 3**) | 83 |  |
| Proposed dividends (80 + 15) | 80 |  |
| Corporation tax (70 + 10) | 80 |  |
|  | 243 |  |
|  |  |  |
| *Net current assets* |  | 245 |
|  |  | 672 |
|  |  |  |
| *Capital and reserves* |  |  |
| £1 ordinary shares |  | 500 |
| Profit and loss account |  | 144 |
|  |  | 644 |
| Minority interests (W6) |  | 28 |
|  |  | 672 |

## Questions and answers

*Exclusion of intragroup dividends from debtors
**Dividends to minority included in creditors

*Workings*

1 *Group structure*

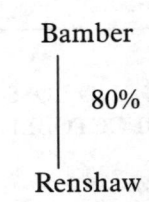

```
            Bamber
              |
             80%
              |
            Renshaw
```

2 *Goodwill*

|  | £'000 | £'000 |
|---|---|---|
| Cost of acquisition |  | 100 |
| Share of net assets acquired |  |  |
|     Share capital | 100 |  |
|     Profit and loss account | 20 |  |
|  | 120 |  |
| Group share: 80% |  | 96 |
| Goodwill |  | 4 |

Amortised over 4 years = £1,000 per year

3 *Provision for unrealised profit*

$(160,000 - 100,000) \times 25\% = £15,000$

Because the sale was made by the holding company, the whole of this unrealised profit must be eliminated.

4 *Investment income*

Dividends receivable from Renshaw Ltd = £15,000 × 80% = £12,000

These will cancel on consolidation, leaving £14,000 − £12,000 = £2,000 investment income due to the group.

> **Helping hand**
> Remember, it is the income due to the group we are interested in, ie from outside the group.

5 *Administrative expenses*

|  | £'000 |
|---|---|
| Bamber | 60 |
| Renshaw | 20 |
| Goodwill amortised | 1 |
|  | 81 |

6 *Minority interest (b/s)*

Net assets of Renshaw at 31 October 20X9 = £140,000
∴ Minority interest = 20% × £140,000 = £28,000

7   Group reserves at 31 October 20X9

|  | £ | £ |
|---|---|---|
| Bamber Ltd |  | 145 |
| Less goodwill amortisation |  | (2) |
| £4,000 × 2/4 |  | 143 |
| Less PUP (W3) |  | (15) |
|  |  | 128 |
| Renshaw Ltd |  |  |
| Per 31.10.X9 b/s | 40 |  |
| Less pre-acquisition | (20) |  |
|  | 20 |  |
| Group share: 80% |  | 16 |
|  |  | 144 |

(b) The circumstances under which a subsidiary *may be* excluded from consolidation are set out in the **Companies Act 1985**. They should be distinguished from those circumstances under which a subsidiary *must be* excluded, which are set out in FRS **2**.

(i) In the opinion of the directors it is **not material** for the purpose of giving a true and fair view, but two or more undertakings may be excluded only if they are not material taken together.

(ii) There are **severe long-term restrictions** in exercising the parent company's rights, eg civil war in the country of an overseas subsidiary.

(iii) The holding is **exclusively for resale**.

(iv) The information cannot be obtained without **disproportionate expense or undue delay**.

FRS 2 states that a subsidiary **must** be excluded from consolidation in the following cases.

(i) Severe long term restrictions are **substantially hindering the exercise of the parent's rights** over the subsidiary's assets or management.

(ii) The interest in the subsidiary undertaking is held **exclusively with a right to subsequent resale** and has not been previously consolidated.

(iii) The activities of the subsidiary undertaking are so **different** from those of other undertakings to be consolidated that its inclusion should **not give a true and fair view**.

> **Helping hand**
>
> FRS 2 is more prescriptive than the Companies Act, as it says when a subsidiary must be excluded.

## 43 ADDLEY (6/01)

The summarised profit and loss accounts for the companies that comprise the Addley Group for the year ended 31 May 20X1 are as follows.

|  | Addley plc £'000 | O'Brien Ltd £'000 | Quirke Ltd £'000 |
|---|---|---|---|
| Turnover | 1,800 | 700 | 300 |
| Cost of sales | 760 | 375 | 140 |
| Gross profit | 1,040 | 325 | 160 |
| Distribution costs | 370 | 160 | 75 |
| Administrative expenses | 230 | 110 | 50 |
| Operating profit | 440 | 55 | 35 |
| Dividend from O'Brien Ltd | 15 |  |  |
| Dividend from Quirke Ltd | 13 |  |  |
| Profit on ordinary activities before tax | 468 | 55 | 35 |
| Tax on profit on ordinary activities | 100 | 18 | 10 |
| Profit on ordinary activities after taxation | 368 | 37 | 25 |
| Proposed ordinary dividends | 160 | 20 | 20 |
| Retained profit for the year | 208 | 17 | 5 |
| Retained profit brought forward | 400 | 120 | 20 |
| Retained profit carried forward | 608 | 137 | 25 |

The following information is also available.

(a) The issued share capital of the three companies was as follows.

Addley plc 5,000,000 ordinary shares of £1 each
O'Brien Ltd 1,000,000 ordinary shares of £1 each
Quirke Ltd 500,000 ordinary shares of £1 each

(b) Addley plc purchased 75% of the issued ordinary share capital of O'Brien Ltd for £850,000 on 1 June 20W9. At that time the retained profits of O'Brien Ltd were £80,000.

(c) Addley plc purchased 65% of the issued ordinary share capital of Quirke Ltd for £346,000 on 1 June 20X0. At that time the retained profits of Quirke Ltd were £60,000.

(d) Goodwill is amortised over four years.

(e) Addley plc sold goods costing £80,000 to Quirke Ltd for £100,000 during the year ended 31 May 20X1. At 31 May 20X1, 50% of these goods remained in Quirke Ltd's stocks.

*Required*

Prepare the consolidated profit and loss account for Addley plc for the year ended 31 May 20X1. Your consolidated profit and loss account should include group retained profit brought forward and carried forward. Disclosure notes are not required.

**(15 marks)**

---

**Helping hand**

1 This question is unusual in that there are two subsidiaries. This generally means more to add together, but don't forget that you've got two lots of goodwill.

2 There is intercompany trading with an unrealised profit to eliminate.

# 43 ANSWER: ADDLEY

> **Examiner's comment.** Many candidates seemed to be ill prepared for this question. Candidates either ignored the intercompany trading adjustment or they were unaware of how to deal with it. In addition, a significant number of candidates were not able to calculate the goodwill and the minority interest figures. Those candidates who provided workings were at least able to obtain some marks.

ADDLEY PLC
CONSOLIDATED PROFIT AND LOSS ACCOUNT
FOR THE YEAR ENDED 31 MAY 20X1

|  | £'000 |
|---|---|
| Turnover (W1) | 2,700 |
| Cost of sales (W2) | 1,185 |
| Gross profit | 1,515 |
| Distribution costs (370 + 160 + 75) | 605 |
| Administrative expenses (W4) | 402 |
| Profit on ordinary activities before taxation | 508 |
| Tax on profit on ordinary activities (100 + 18 + 10) | 128 |
| Profit on ordinary activities after tax | 380 |
| Minority interests (W5) | 18 |
| Group profit for the year | 362 |
| Proposed dividends | 160 |
| Retained profit for the year | 202 |
| Retained profit brought forward (W6) | 420 |
| Retained profit carried forward | 622 |

*Workings*

1 *Turnover*

|  | £'000 | £'000 |
|---|---|---|
| Addley | 1,800 |  |
| Less intercompany | (100) |  |
|  |  | 1,700 |
| O'Brien |  | 700 |
| Quirke |  | 300 |
|  |  | 2,700 |

2 *Cost of sales*

|  | £'000 | £'000 |
|---|---|---|
| Addley |  | 760 |
| O'Brien |  | 375 |
| Quirke | 140 |  |
| Less intercompany | (100) |  |
|  |  | 40 |
| Unrealised profit in closing stock (100 − 80) × 50% |  | 10 |
|  |  | 1,185 |

> **Helping hand**
>
> You can also eliminate the URP in closing stock from gross profit and have cost of sales as the balancing figure.

## Questions and answers

### 3 Goodwill

|  | £'000 | £'000 |
|---|---|---|
| *O'Brien* |  |  |
| Cost of investment |  | 850 |
| Net assets acquired |  |  |
|   Share capital | 1,000 |  |
|   Retained profits | 80 |  |
|  | 1,080 |  |
| Group share: 75% |  | 810 |
| Goodwill |  | 40 |

Amortisation: £40,000/4 = £10,000

|  | £'000 | £'000 |
|---|---|---|
| *Quirke* |  |  |
| Cost of investment |  | 346 |
| Net assets acquired |  |  |
|   Share capital | 500 |  |
|   Retained profits | 20 |  |
|  | 520 |  |
| Group share: 65% |  | 338 |
| Goodwill |  | 8 |

Amortisation: £8,000/4 = £2,000

Total goodwill amortisation: £(10,000 + 2,000) = £12,000

> **Helping hand.** The goodwill calculation is not more complicated – it's just that there are two lots.

### 4 Administrative expenses

|  | £'000 |
|---|---|
| Addley | 230 |
| O'Brien | 110 |
| Quirke | 50 |
|  | 390 |
| Goodwill amortisation | 12 |
|  | 402 |

### 5 Minority interests

|  |  | £'000 |
|---|---|---|
| O'Brien: | 25% × 37 | 9.25 |
| Quirke: | 35% × 25 | 8.75 |
|  |  | 18.00 |

### 6 Revised profit brought forward

|  | £'000 | £'000 |
|---|---|---|
| Addley |  | 400 |
| O'Brien |  |  |
|   Retained profits at 1 June 20X0 | 120 |  |
|   Less pre-acquisition | 80 |  |
|  | 40 |  |
| Group share: 75% | 30 |  |
| Less goodwill amortised at 1 June 20X0 | 10 |  |
|  |  | 20 |
| Quirke |  |  |
|   Retained profits at 1 June 20X0 | 20 |  |
|   Less pre-acquisition | (20) |  |
|  | 0 |  |
| Group share: 65% |  | 0 |
|  |  | 420 |

## 44 SAND (12/01)

The following balance sheets have been prepared as at 31 October 20X1.

|  | Sand plc £'000 | Sand plc £'000 | Lind Limited £'000 | Lind Limited £'000 | Gard Limited £'000 | Gard Limited £'000 |
|---|---|---|---|---|---|---|
| *Fixed assets* | | | | | | |
| Tangible, at net book value | | 280 | | 120 | | 220 |
| Investments | | | | | | |
|   100,000 shares in Lind Ltd at cost | | 250 | | | | |
|   160,000 shares in Gard Ltd at cost | | 300 | | | | |
| *Current assets* | | | | | | |
| Stock, at cost | 100 | | 70 | | 90 | |
| Debtors | 70 | | 40 | | 70 | |
| Bank | 40 | | 30 | | 50 | |
| | 210 | | 140 | | 210 | |
| *Creditors: amounts falling due within one year* | | | | | | |
| Creditors | 170 | | 30 | | 80 | |
| Net current assets | | 40 | | 110 | | 130 |
| | | 870 | | 230 | | 350 |
| *Capital and reserves* | | | | | | |
| £1 ordinary shares | | 500 | | 100 | | 200 |
| General reserve | | 140 | | 60 | | 60 |
| Profit and loss account | | 230 | | 70 | | 90 |
| | | 870 | | 230 | | 350 |

*Additional information*

(a) There was no inter-company trading during the year.

(b) The subsidiaries had the following balances on their reserve accounts at their dates of acquisition.

|  | Lind Ltd as at 31 Oct 20W9 £'000 | Gard Ltd as at 31 Oct 20W6 £'000 |
|---|---|---|
| General reserve | 30 | 50 |
| Profit and loss account | 60 | 80 |

(c) The goodwill arising from the acquisitions is to be written off over 10 years.

*Required*

Prepare the consolidated balance sheet of Sand plc as at 31 October 20X1.

**(15 marks)**

**Helping hand**

1. A straightforward question, but remember to calculate two lots of goodwill and amortisation.
2. Any reasonable layout will do for your reserve workings.

# 44 ANSWER: SAND

> **Examiner's comment.** The question was designed to be fairly straightforward with the marks mainly weighted toward the calculation of the goodwill. Candidates either gained maximum marks for this question or had little understanding of how to calculate goodwill. The calculation of goodwill is an important aspect of preparing group accounts and there was evidence to suggest that some candidates had not covered this area of the syllabus in their studies. Those candidates who had stated the goodwill figure incorrectly in the consolidated balance sheet, but had provided workings, were awarded marks as appropriate.

SAND PLC
CONSOLIDATED BALANCE SHEET AS AT 31 OCTOBER 20X1

|  | £'000 | £'000 |
|---|---|---|
| *Fixed assets* |  |  |
| Intangible: goodwill (W2) |  | 66 |
| Tangible (280 + 120 + 220) |  | 620 |
|  |  | 686 |
| *Current assets* |  |  |
| Stock (100 + 70 + 90) | 260 |  |
| Debtors (70 + 40 + 70) | 180 |  |
| Bank (40 + 30 + 50) | 120 |  |
|  | 560 |  |
| *Creditors: amounts falling due within one year* (170 + 30 + 80) | (280) |  |
| Net current assets |  | 280 |
|  |  | 966 |
| *Capital and reserves* |  |  |
| Share capital |  | 500 |
| General reserve (W4) |  | 178 |
| Profit and loss account (W5) |  | 218 |
|  |  | 896 |
| Minority interests (W3) |  | 70 |
|  |  | 966 |

*Workings*

1  Group structure

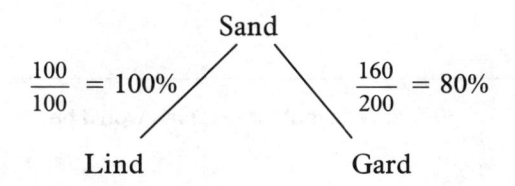

$$\frac{100}{100} = 100\% \qquad \text{Sand} \qquad \frac{160}{200} = 80\%$$

Lind           Gard

2  Goodwill

|  | £'000 | £'000 |
|---|---|---|
| *Lind* |  |  |
| Cost of investment |  | 250 |
| Net assets acquired |  |  |
|   Share capital | 100 |  |
|   General reserve | 30 |  |
|   Profit and loss account | 60 |  |
|  | 190 |  |
| Group share: 100% |  | 190 |
| Goodwill |  | 60 |
| Amortisation $\frac{60}{10} \times 2$ |  | (12) |
|  |  | 48 |

## Questions and answers

|  | £'000 | £'000 |
|---|---|---|
| *Gard* | | |
| Cost of investment | | 300 |
| Net assets acquired | | |
|   Share capital | 200 | |
|   General reserve | 50 | |
|   Profit and loss account | 80 | |
| | 330 | |
| Group share: 80% | | 264 |
| Goodwill | | 36 |
| Amortisation $\frac{36}{10} \times 5$ | | (18) |
| | | 18 |

Total goodwill: £48,000 + £18,000 = £66,000

> **Helping hand.** Total goodwill amortisation will go into the reserve working (W5).

3 *Minority interests*

Net assets of Gard Ltd at 31 October 20X1 = £350,000

∴ Minority interest = £350,000 × 20% = £70,000

4 *General reserve*

|  | £'000 |
|---|---|
| Sand | 140 |
| Find 100% (60 – 30) | 30 |
| Gard 80% (60 – 50) | 8 |
| | 178 |

5 *Profit and loss account*

|  | £'000 |
|---|---|
| Sand | 230 |
| Less goodwill amortised (W2): 12 + 18 | (30) |
| | 200 |
| Find: 100% (70 – 60) | 10 |
| Gard: 80% (90 – 80) | 8 |
| | 218 |

> **Helping hand.** An alternative layout for reserves would be:
>
> |  | Sand | Find | Gard |
> |---|---|---|---|
> | Per question | 230 | 70 | 90 |
> | Less pre acqn | | (60) | (80) |
> | | | 10 | 10 |
> | Share of Find: 100% × 10 | 10 | | |
> | Share of Gard: 80% × 10 | 8 | | |
> | Less goodwill amortised (W2): 12 + 18 | (30) | | |
> | | 218 | | |

# Mock exam 1

# Drafting Financial Statements
- Industry and Commerce

## June 2002

| Question Paper: | |
|---|---|
| Time allowed | 3 hours |
| All FOUR questions are compulsory and MUST be answered. | |

# Level C
# Paper 1

DO NOT OPEN THIS PAPER UNTIL YOU ARE READY TO START UNDER EXAMINATION CONDITIONS

*Mock exam 1*

# ALL FOUR questions are compulsory and MUST be attempted.

**1** Until January 20X2, Jack and Jill were business partners, sharing profits in the ratio 2:1 respectively, after allowing for interest on capital of 6%. On 1 February 20X2 Jean was admitted to the partnership. She is to receive a one-sixth share of the profits for introducing £40,000 capital and £30,000 as her share of goodwill.

The trial balance extracted from the partnership books on 31 May 20X2, the end of the financial year, is as follows.

JACK, JILL AND JEAN PARTNERSHIP
TRIAL BALANCE AS AT 31 MAY 20X2

|  | Dr £'000 | Cr £'000 |
|---|---|---|
| Fittings at cost | 210 | |
| Vehicles at cost | 180 | |
| Stock as at 1 June 20X1 | 190 | |
| Purchases | 725 | |
| Sales | | 979 |
| Rent and insurance | 33 | |
| Sales commission | 18 | |
| Debtors | 140 | |
| Creditors | | 154 |
| Cash and bank | 33 | |
| Advertising and other expenses | 52 | |
| Discounts allowed | 25 | |
| Bad debts | 7 | |
| Fittings depreciation to 31 May 20X1 | | 60 |
| Vehicle depreciation to 31 May 20X1 | | 40 |
| Drawings: Jack | 25 | |
| Jill | 10 | |
| Jean | 2 | |
| Capital: Jack | | 250 |
| Jill | | 100 |
| Current accounts: Jack | | 12 |
| Jill | 15 | |
| Suspense account | | 70 |
| | 1,665 | 1,665 |

*Additional notes*

(a) Stock on 31 May 20X2 was £214,000.

(b) There is outstanding sales commission of £2,000 for the year.

(c) Insurance of £1,000 has been paid in advance.

(d) The partnership depreciates fittings and vehicles at 10% and 20% respectively using the reducing balance method.

(e) Goodwill is to be adjusted for, but is not to be maintained in the books of account.

(f) Assume that income and expenditure has accrued evenly throughout the year.

(g) The suspense account represents the investment made by Jean.

**Required:**

(a) **Calculate the new profit sharing ratio as from 1 February 20X2.** (3 marks)

(b) **Calculate the new balances on the partners' capital accounts as at 1 February 20X2.** (5 marks)

(c) **Prepare the trading, profit and loss and appropriation accounts for the year ended 31 May 20X2.** (16 marks)

(d) **Prepare the partners' current accounts for the year ended 31 May 20X2** (7 marks)

# Mock exam 1

(e) **Prepare the balance sheet as at 31 May 20X2.** (9 marks)

(Calculations and workings may be rounded to the nearest £'000)

**(40 marks)**

2 Lawton Ltd paid £500,000 to acquire 300,000 ordinary shares in Doig Ltd on 1 May 20X0 when the profit and loss account of Doig Ltd was £140,000. The following are the summarised financial statements of the two companies for the financial year ended 30 April 20X3

PROFIT AND LOSS ACCOUNTS FOR THE YEAR ENDED 30 APRIL 20X3

|  | Lawton Limited £'000 | Doig Limited £'000 |
|---|---|---|
| Turnover | 3,400 | 1,200 |
| Cost of sales | 2,300 | 820 |
| Gross profit | 1,100 | 380 |
| Distribution costs | 260 | 80 |
| Administrative expenses | 200 | 60 |
| Operating profit | 640 | 240 |
| Investment income | 64 | 0 |
| Profit on ordinary activities before taxation | 704 | 240 |
| Taxation on profit on ordinary activities | 200 | 60 |
| Profit on ordinary activities after taxation | 504 | 180 |
| Proposed ordinary dividends | 280 | 80 |
| Retained profit for the year | 224 | 100 |

BALANCE SHEETS AS AT 30 APRIL 20X3

|  | Lawton Limited £'000 | Lawton Limited £'000 | Doig Limited £'000 | Doig Limited £'000 |
|---|---|---|---|---|
| *Fixed assets* | | | | |
| Total assets at net book value | | 1,300 | | 360 |
| *Investment* | | | | |
| Shares in Doig Ltd at cost | | 500 | | |
| *Current assets* | | | | |
| Stock, at cost | 660 | | 220 | |
| Debtors | 540 | | 280 | |
| Bank | 240 | | 140 | |
|  | 1,440 | | 640 | |
| *Creditors: amounts falling due within one year* | | | | |
| Creditors | 180 | | 140 | |
| Proposed dividends | 280 | | 80 | |
| Corporation tax | 220 | | 60 | |
|  | 680 | | 280 | |
| Net current assets | | 760 | | 360 |
|  | | 2,560 | | 720 |
| *Capital and reserves* | | | | |
| £1 Ordinary shares | | 1,800 | | 400 |
| Profit and loss account | | 760 | | 320 |
|  | | 2,560 | | 720 |

The following information is also available.

(a) During the year Lawton Ltd sold goods which originally cost £300,000 to Doig Ltd. Lawton Ltd invoiced Doig Ltd at cost plus 20%. These goods had all been sold by Doig Ltd by 30 April 20X3.

(b) Doig Ltd's creditors includes £40,000 owing to Lawton Ltd.

(c) Lawton Ltd has recognised the dividends proposed by Doig Ltd in its profit and loss account.

(d) Lawton Ltd's policy is to amortise goodwill equally over five years. The goodwill on acquisition of Doig Ltd was £95,000.

*Mock exam 1*

Required:

(a) Prepare the following for Lawton Ltd.

(i) The consolidated profit and loss account for the year ended 30 April 20X3 (10 marks)
(ii) The consolidated balance sheet as at 30 April 20X3 (14 marks)

Disclosure notes are not required.

(b) Define an associated company and briefly explain how its results would be reported by the investing company in its consolidated accounts. (6 marks)

**(30 marks)**

3  Your manager has asked you to analyse the financial performance of Moran Ltd. You have been given the following summarised financial information.

MORAN LIMITED
FINANCIAL YEAR ENDED 30 APRIL

|  | 20X0 £'000 | 20X1 £'000 | 20X2 £'000 |
|---|---|---|---|
| Sales | 75 | 120 | 200 |
| Cost of sales | 40 | 70 | 130 |
| Gross profit | 35 | 50 | 70 |
| Distribution and administration expenses | 6 | 20 | 38 |
| Profit before taxation | 29 | 30 | 32 |
| Taxation on profit | 5 | 6 | 7 |
| Profit after taxation | 24 | 24 | 25 |
| Dividends | 4 | 4 | 5 |
| Retained profit | 20 | 20 | 20 |
| Fixed assets | 30 | 60 | 100 |
| *Current assets* |  |  |  |
| Stock | 15 | 20 | 50 |
| Debtors | 10 | 40 | 45 |
| Cash and bank | 70 | 30 | 5 |
|  | 95 | 90 | 100 |
| *Current liabilities* |  |  |  |
| Creditors | (5) | (10) | (40) |
| Net current assets | 90 | 80 | 60 |
| Net assets | 120 | 140 | 160 |
| *Capital and reserves* |  |  |  |
| £1 ordinary shares | 100 | 100 | 100 |
| Reserves | 20 | 40 | 60 |
|  | 120 | 140 | 160 |

Required:

(a) Identify and comment on the main trends as shown by the above financial information. (5 marks)

(Use the figures provided above – do not calculate ratios to answer this part of the question.)

(b) State the further information that would be useful to help interpret Moran Ltd's financial position. (3 marks)

(c) Calculate the following ratios for Moran Ltd for the year ended 30 April 20X2 *only*. Clearly state the definitions used for each ratio.

(i) Return on capital employed
(ii) Quick/acid test ratio
(iii) Stock turnover (days)
(iv) Debtors collection period
(v) Earnings per share

(7 marks)

**(15 marks)**

*Mock exam 1*

4 Required:

(a) Briefly explain the objective of financial statements (2 marks)

(b) State the main financial information requirements of existing and potential investors in a business. (3 marks)

(c) Identify and explain four qualitative characteristics that make financial information useful. (10 marks)

**(15 marks)**

# ANSWERS TO MOCK EXAM 1

DO NOT TURN THIS PAGE UNTIL YOU
HAVE COMPLETED MOCK EXAM 1

# WARNING! APPLYING THE ACCA MARKING SCHEME

If you decide to mark your paper using the ACCA marking scheme you should bear in mind the following points.

1. The BPP answers are not definitive: you will see that we have applied our own interpretation of the marking scheme to our solutions to show how good answers should gain marks, but there may be more than one way to answer the question. You must try to judge fairly whether different points made in your answers are correct and relevant and therefore worth marks according to the ACCA marking scheme.

2. In numerical answers, do not penalise yourself too much for minor arithmetical errors: if you have followed the correct principles you should gain most of the marks. This emphasises the importance of including workings, which show the marker which principles you were following.

3. If you have a friend or colleague who is studying or has studied this paper, you might ask him or her to mark your paper for you, thus gaining a more objective assessment. Remember you and your friend are not trained or objective markers, so try to avoid complacency or pessimism if you appear to have done very well or very badly.

# Mock exam 1: answers

## 1

> **Helping hand.** The question concerned a partnership which had admitted a new partner during the year. Candidates were given the trial balance of the Jack, Jill and Jean partnership as at 31 May 20X2 and some additional information. The question stated that Jean had only been admitted to the partnership on 1 February 20X2 and that she was to receive a one-sixth share of the profits for introducing £40,000 capital and £30,000 as her share of goodwill. In Part (a) candidates were required to calculate the new profit-sharing ratio for the partnership as from the 1 February 20X2. The main difficulty in Part (c), the preparation of the trading, profit and loss account was in calculating the interest on capital and the share of profit for each partner. In Part (d) candidates were required to calculate the partners' current accounts, and Part (e) was a straightforward balance sheet.
>
> **Examiner's comment.** It would appear that candidates found this the most difficult question on the paper. In Part (a), surprisingly few candidates were able to calculate correctly the correct profit sharing ratio. Candidates also showed a lack of understanding in constructing the partners' capital accounts required in Part (b). Only a few candidates were able to deal correctly with the admission of Jean to the partnership and adjust the goodwill figures. Most candidates did well on Parts (c) to (e). Candidates who calculated the profit sharing ratio wrongly in Part (a), but followed their answer through consistently, were given credit.

(a) Jack and Jill will keep their profit sharing ratio with respect to each other, but their combined share of the profits is reduced by 1/6.

| Partners | Original ratio | Adjustment | New ratio | |
|---|---|---|---|---|
| Jack | 2/3 | Less $2/3 \times 1/6 = 12/18 - 2/18$ | = 10/18 | 1 mark |
| Jill | 1/3 | Less $1/3 \times 1/6 = 6/18 - 1/18$ | = 5/18 | 1 mark |
| Jean | - | | 3/18 | 1 mark |

Total marks = 3

(b) Jean's goodwill is 1/6 of the total in the new profit sharing ratio.

∴ Total goodwill is £180,000

The partners' shares may be calculated as follows.

| Partner | Share of goodwill | Amount £'000 |
|---|---|---|
| Jean | 3/18 | 30 |
| Jill | 5/18 | 50 |
| Jack | 10/18 | 100 |
| | | 180 |

In the old profit sharing ratios, the goodwill would be split 2:1, ie Jack: £120,000, Jean: £60,000. This is not to remain in the books. The capital account is thus as follows.

### CAPITAL ACCOUNTS

| | Jack £'000 | Jill £'000 | Jean £'000 | | Jack £'000 | Jill £'000 | Jean £'000 | |
|---|---|---|---|---|---|---|---|---|
| Goodwill: new ratio | 100 | 50 | 30 | Balance b/fwd | 250 | 100 | - | 2 marks |
| Balance c/fwd | 270 | 110 | 40 | Cash introduced | - | - | 70 | 2 marks |
| | | | | Goodwill: old ratio | 120 | 60 | - | 1 mark |
| | 370 | 160 | 70 | | 370 | 160 | 70 | |

Total marks = 5

229

## Mock exam 1: answers

(c) JACK, JILL AND JEAN
TRADING AND PROFIT AND LOSS ACCOUNT
FOR THE YEAR ENDED 31 MAY 20X2

|  | £'000 | £'000 |
|---|---|---|
| Sales |  | 979 |
| Cost of goods sold |  |  |
|   Opening stock | 190 |  |
|   Purchases | 725 |  |
|  | 915 |  |
| Closing stock | (214) |  |
|  |  | 701 |
| Gross profit |  | 278 |
| Expenses |  |  |
|   Deprecation (W1) | 43 |  |
|   Rent and insurance (33 – 1) | 32 |  |
|   Sales commission (18 + 2) | 20 |  |
|   Advertising and other expenses | 52 |  |
|   Discounts allowed | 25 |  |
|   Bad debts | 7 |  |
|  |  | 179 |
| Net profit before appropriation |  | 99 |
| Interest on capital:   Jack | 15 |  |
|                                 Jill | 6 |  |
|                                 Jean | 1 |  |
|  |  | (22) |
|  |  | 77 |
| Share of profit:   Jack |  | 49 |
|                             Jill |  | 24 |
|                             Jean |  | 4 |
|  |  | 77 |

(d)

CURRENT ACCOUNTS
FOR THE YEAR ENDED 31 MAY 20X2

|  |  | *Jack* £'000 | *Jill* £'000 | *Jean* £'000 |  | *Jack* £'000 | *Jill* £'000 | *Jean* £'000 |
|---|---|---|---|---|---|---|---|---|
| 0.5 marks | Balance b/fwd | - | 15 | - | Balance b/fwd | 12 | - | - |
| 4 marks | Drawings | 25 | 10 | 2 | Interest on capital |  |  |  |
| 2.5 marks | Balance c/fwd | 51 | 5 | 3 | (W2) | 15 | 6 | 1 |
|  |  |  |  |  | Share of profit (W2) | 49 | 24 | 4 |
| Total marks = 7 |  | 76 | 30 | 5 |  | 76 | 30 | 5 |

## Mock exam 1: answers

(e) JACK, JILL AND JEAN
BALANCE SHEET AS AT 31 MAY 20X2

|  | Cost £'000 | Acc den £'000 | NBV £'000 | |
|---|---|---|---|---|
| *Fixed assets* | | | | |
| Fittings (W1) | 210 | 75 | 135 | 1 mark |
| Vehicles (W1) | 180 | 68 | 112 | 1 mark |
| | 390 | 143 | 247 | |
| *Current assets* | | | | |
| Stock | | 214 | | 0.5 marks |
| Debtors | | 140 | | 0.5 marks |
| Prepayment: insurance | | 1 | | 1 mark |
| Bank | | 33 | | 0.5 marks |
| | | 388 | | |
| *Current liabilities* | | | | |
| Creditors | 154 | | | 0.5 marks |
| Accruals: sales commission | 2 | | | 1 mark |
| | | 156 | | |
| *Net current assets* | | | 232 | |
| | | | 429 | |
| *Capital accounts* | | | | |
| Jack | | 270 | | 0.5 marks |
| Jill | | 110 | | 0.5 marks |
| Jean | | 40 | | 0.5 marks |
| | | | 420 | |
| *Current accounts* | | | | |
| Jack | | 51 | | 0.5 marks |
| Jill | | 5 | | 0.5 marks |
| Jean | | 3 | | 0.5 marks |
| | | | 59 | |
| | | | 479 | Total marks = 9 |

*Workings*

1 Fixed assets and depreciation

|  | Fittings £'000 | Vehicle £'000 | Total £'000 |
|---|---|---|---|
| Cost | 210 | 180 | 390 |
| *Accumulated depreciation* | | | |
| At 31.5.X1 | 60 | 40 | 100 |
| Charge for year* | 15 | 28 | 43 |
| At 31.5.X2 | 75 | 68 | 143 |
| NBV at 31.5.X2 | 135 | 112 | 247 |

* Charge for year:

Fittings: $(210 - 60) \times 10\% = 15$
Vehicles: $(180 - 40) \times 20\% = 28$

## Mock exam 1: answers

2  Appropriation of profit for the year ended 31 May 20X2

|  | 8 months to 1.2.X2 £'000 | 4 months to 31.5.X2 £'000 | Total for year £'000 |
|---|---|---|---|
| Profit apportioned: 8/12:4/12 | 66 | 33 | 99 |
| Interest on capital: Jack | 10 | 5 | 15 |
| Jill | 4 | 2 | 6 |
| Jean | - | 1 | 1 |
| Available profit | 52 | 25 | 77 |
| Profit share: Jack | 35 | 14 | 49 |
| Jill | 17 | 7 | 24 |
| Jean | 0 | 4 | 4 |
|  | 52 | 25 | 77 |

## 2

**Helping hand.** Part (a) of this question required candidates to prepare a consolidated profit and loss account and balance sheet for Lawton Ltd. Adjustments were required for inter-company trading, dividends and inter-company indebtedness. Part (b) required candidates to define an associated company and briefly explain how its results would be reported in the investing company accounts.

**Examiner's comment.** This question was answered either very well or very poorly. Those candidates who had prepared well and practised previous exam questions scored well. The weaker candidates merely added the figures for Lawton Ltd and Doig Ltd together. Unlike previous examination questions, the figure for goodwill on acquisition was given in the question. However, some candidates still decided to calculate it for themselves. Unfortunately, no additional marks were awarded for undertaking this unnecessary calculation. Part (b) was not particularly well answered. Candidates who stated an associated company is one where the investing company can 'exercise significant influence but not control' and then referred to 'equity accounting' scored well.

(a) (i)

**BPP Note.** All figures are the aggregate of the two profit and loss account or balance sheet figures unless other wise indicated.

LAWTON LIMITED
CONSOLIDATED PROFIT AND LOSS ACCOUNT
FOR THE YEAR ENDED 30 APRIL 20X3

| | | £'000 |
|---|---|---|
| Heading: 0.5 marks | | |
| 1.5 marks | Turnover (W2) | 4,240 |
| 1.5 marks | Cost of sales (W2) | 2,760 |
| | Gross profit | 1,480 |
| 0.5 marks | Distribution costs | 340 |
| 0.5 marks | Administration expenses | 260 |
| | | 880 |
| 1 mark | Amortisation of goodwill: 95/5 | 19 |
| 1 mark | Operating profit | 861 |
| | Investment income (W3) | 4 |
| | Profit on ordinary activities before taxation | 865 |
| 0.5 marks | Tax on profit on ordinary activities | 260 |
| | Profit on ordinary activities after taxation | 605 |
| 2 marks | Minority interests: 180 × 25% | 45 |
| | Group profit for the year | 560 |
| 1 mark | Proposed dividends | 280 |
| | Retained profit for the year | 280 |

Total marks = 10

**Mock exam 1: answers**

(ii) LAWTON LIMITED
CONSOLIDATED BALANCE SHEET
AS AT 30 APRIL 20X3

|  | £'000 | £'000 | |
|---|---|---|---|
| *Fixed assets* | | | Heading: 0.5 marks |
| Intangible: goodwill (W4) | | 38 | 1.5 marks |
| Tangible assets at net book value | | 1,660 | 0.5 marks |
| | | 1,698 | |
| *Current assets* | | | |
| Stock at cost | 880 | | 0.5 marks |
| Debtors (W5) | 720 | | 2.5 marks |
| Bank | 380 | | 0.5 marks |
| | 1,980 | | |
| *Current liabilities* | | | |
| Creditors (W5) | 280 | | 1.5 marks |
| Dividend to minority interest: 80 × 25% | 20 | | 1 mark |
| Proposed dividend | 280 | | 0.5 marks |
| Corporation tax | 280 | | 0.5 marks |
| | 860 | | |
| *Net current assets* | | 1,120 | 0.5 marks |
| | | 2,818 | |
| *Capital and reserves* | | | |
| Share capital: £1 ordinary shares | | 1,800 | 0.5 marks |
| Profit and loss account (W7) | | 838 | 2.5 marks |
| | | 2,638 | |
| Minority interest (W6) | | 180 | 1 mark |
| | | 2,818 | |

Total marks = 14

*Workings*

1  *Group structure*

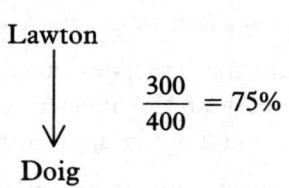

Lawton
↓   $\frac{300}{400} = 75\%$
Doig

2  *Turnover and cost of sales*

| | Turnover | | Cost of sales | |
|---|---|---|---|---|
| | £'000 | £'000 | £'000 | £'000 |
| Lawton per question | 3,400 | | | 2,300 |
| Less intercompany | | | | |
| (300 × 120/100) | 360 | | | |
| | | 3,040 | | 2,300 |
| Doig per question | | 1,200 | 820 | |
| Less intercompany | | | (360) | |
| | | | | 460 |
| | | 4,240 | | 2,760 |

3  *Investment income*

| | £'000 |
|---|---|
| Lawton per question | 64 |
| Less dividend from Doig: 75% × 80 | 60 |
| | 4 |

4  *Unamortised goodwill*

| | £'000 |
|---|---|
| Goodwill per question | 95 |
| Less 3 years' amortisation: 95 × 3/5 | 57 |
| Unamortised goodwill | 38 |

233

## Mock exam 1: answers

### 5 Debtors and creditors

|  | Debtors £'000 | Creditors £'000 |
|---|---|---|
| Lawton | 540 | 180 |
| Doig | 280 | 140 |
| Less intercompany sale | (40) | (40) |
| Intercompany dividends (W3) | (60) | - |
|  | 720 | 280 |

### 6 Minority interest

Doig: net assets at balance sheet date

|  | £'000 |
|---|---|
| Share capital | 400 |
| Profit and loss account | 320 |
|  | 720 |

∴ Minority interest: £720,000 × 25% = £180,000

### 7 Profit and loss account

|  | Lawton £'000 | Doig £'000 |
|---|---|---|
| Per question | 760 | 320 |
| Pre-acquisition |  | 140 |
|  |  | 180 |
| Share of Doig: 75% × 180 | 135 |  |
| Goodwill amortised (W4) | (57) |  |
|  | 838 |  |

(b) An associate (associated company) is an investment held for the long term where the investing company exercises **significant influence** over the financial and operating policies of the company invested in, but **no control**. The position is different from a subsidiary, where control is exercised, and is in fact more important than ownership.

It would not be realistic to account for associates merely in terms of the dividends received, or simply to show the cost of the investment. On the other hand, full consolidation, as with a subsidiary, would not be appropriate either.

To reflect the investment's intermediate status, company law and accounting standards require the use of **equity accounting**. This method operates as follows.

(i) **Investing company's consolidated profit and loss account**

Income credited to the profit and loss account (or debited) is the investing company's share of the profit (loss) of the associated company, regardless of the dividend received or receivable.

(ii) **Investing company's balance sheet**

|  | $ |
|---|---|
| Share of associate's net assets | X |
| Premium on acquisition not written off | X |
| Investment in associate | X |

# 3

> **Helping hand.** In Part (a) candidates were required to identify and comment on the main trends as shown by the three years of financial information of Moran Ltd. In Part (b) candidates were asked to state what further information would be useful in interpreting Moran Ltd's financial position.
>
> **Examiner's comment.** In Part (a) candidates were rather better at identifying the trends than commenting on them. Those candidates who used bullet points for their answers were able to gain marks more efficiently than those that chose to write long, rambling answers. In Part (b) most candidates gave the obvious answer of accounting ratios and listed them.

(a) The company has clearly been **expanding rapidly** over the three-year period. **Sales have increased by 167%, (£125,000). Gross profit** has also **increased, but the increase is not proportionally as great as that in sales (100%).**

There could be a number of reasons for this. Perhaps **margins have been cut to generate more sales.** Alternatively, perhaps **costs have risen** and it is suppliers that are putting pressure on margins. Interestingly, the creditors figure has increased substantially.

The **increase in profit before tax is only marginal** compared to the increase in turnover (profit after tax even more so). This appears to be because **distribution and administrative expenses have increased by more than six times.** This may indicate **lack of control over costs,** but it could also mean that, because the market is competitive, **more money is being spent on advertising.**

**Dividends have remained constant,** which is prudent as **retained earnings have not increased in line with sales.**

The company's **liquidity position** gives some cause for concern. **Cash and bank** have **declined substantially, and creditors have increased,** as already mentioned. There are no long-term loans, so **the increase in fixed assets may have been paid for in cash,** that is out of working capital.

**Debtors** have also **risen substantially.** The company needs to **pay attention to credit control,** otherwise there may be cash flow problems.

*1 mark per valid point*

*Total marks = 5*

(b) **Further useful information** would include the following.

  (i) A **cash flow statement** would shed light on some of the liquidity problems identified above.

  (ii) Details of **the nature of the business** and the market it is in would make the figures more meaningful.

  (iii) **Comparisons with an industrial average** would put this company's results in perspective.

  (iv) **Forecasts and budgets,** together with justifications for the forecast figures, would indicate whether the trend is set to continue.

  (v) Details of the **accounting policies** used by the company would be useful in supplementing traditional ratio analysis, particularly as regards depreciation of fixed assets.

*1 mark per item*

*Total marks = 3*

## Mock exam 1: answers

(c) **Accounting ratios**

| Marks | | | Formula | Calculation | Result |
|---|---|---|---|---|---|
| 1.5 marks | (i) | Return on capital employed | $\dfrac{\text{Net profit after tax}}{\text{Capital and reserves}} \times 100$ | $\dfrac{25}{160} \times 100$ | = 15.6% |
| 1 mark | (ii) | Quick/acid test ratio | $\dfrac{\text{Current assets} - \text{Stock}}{\text{Current liabilities}} :1$ | $\dfrac{100-50}{40} :1$ | = 1.25:1 |
| 2 marks | (iii) | Stock turnover period (days) | $\dfrac{\text{Average stock}}{\text{Cost of sales}} \times 365$ | $\dfrac{(20+50)/2}{130} \times 365$ | = 98.3 days |
| 1.5 marks | (iv) | Debtors collection period | $\dfrac{\text{Debtors}}{\text{Sales}} \times 365$ | $\dfrac{45}{200} \times 365$ | = 82.1 days |
| 1 mark | (v) | Earnings per share | $\dfrac{\text{Profits on ordinary activities after tax}}{\text{Ordinary share capital}}$ | $\dfrac{25}{100}$ | = 25 pence |

Total = 7

## 4

> **Helping hand.** This question was split into three parts. In Part (a) candidates were asked to briefly explain the objective of financial statements. In Part (b) candidates were asked to state the main financial information requirements of existing and potential investors, and in Part (c) to identify and explain four qualitative characteristics that make financial information useful.
>
> **Examiner's comment.** Although not specifically stated, this question was focussed around the ASB *Statement of Principles*. The answers on the whole were of a good standard. However, several candidates described the qualities of good internal management information, but credit was given provided it related to financial information.

(a) **Objectives of financial statements**

2 marks

The objective of producing financial statements is explained in the *Statement of Principles*, a document published by the Accounting Standards Board in December 1999. It is 'to provide information about the reporting entity's **financial performance and financial position** that is **useful** to a wide range of users for assessing the **stewardship** of the entity's management for making **economic decisions**'.

(b) **Requirements of existing and potential investors in a business**

The *Statement* goes on to state that **investors**, ie shareholders are the **most important class of user**, and that the information they need must enable them to assess the entity's ability to generate cash and to assess its **financial adaptability**.

The main financial statements aim to achieve these objectives as follows.

(i) The **performance statements**, that is the profit and loss account and the statement of total recognised gains and losses show the **return on the resources** that the entity controls.

(ii) The **balance sheet** provides information on the **financial position** of the company by identifying the economic resources it controls and its liquidity and solvency.

3 marks

(iii) The **cash flow statement** specifies the principle sources of the company's cash inflows and outflows, thereby showing the company's **ability to generate cash** in accordance with the objective.

> **Helping hand**
> This material is from the *Statement of Principles*.

(c) **Qualitative characteristics of financial statements**

Below are some features that accounting information should have if it is to be useful.

(i) **Relevance.** The information provided should satisfy the needs of information users. In the case of company accounts, clearly a wide range of information will be needed to satisfy a wide range of users.

(ii) **Comprehensibility.** Information may be difficult to understand because it is skimpy or incomplete; but too much detail is also a defect which can cause difficulties of understanding.

(iii) **Reliability.** Information will be more reliable if it is independently verified. The law requires that the accounts published by limited companies should be verified by auditors, who must be independent of the company and must hold an approved qualification.

(iv) **Completeness.** A company's accounts should present a rounded picture of its economic activities.

(v) **Objectivity.** Information should be as objective as possible. This is particularly the case where conflicting interests operate and an unbiased presentation of information is needed. In the context of preparing accounts, where many decisions must be based on judgement rather than objective facts, this problem often arises. Management are often inclined to paint a rosy picture of a company's profitability to make their own performance look impressive. By contrast, auditors responsible for verifying the accounts are inclined to take a more prudent view so that they cannot be held liable by, say, a supplier misled into granting credit to a shaky company.

(vi) **Timeliness.** The usefulness of information is reduced if it does not appear until long after the period to which it relates, or if it is produced at unreasonably long intervals. What constitutes a long interval depends on the circumstances: management of a company may need very frequent (perhaps daily) information on cash flows to run the business efficiently; but shareholders are normally content to see accounts produced annually.

½ mark for characteristic

(vii) **Comparability.** Information should be produced on a consistent basis so that valid comparisons can be made with information from previous periods and with information produced by other sources (for example the accounts of similar companies operating in the same line of business).

2 marks for explanation

Total marks = 10

**Helping hand**

Any four of these points would be sufficient.

# *Mock exam 2*

# Drafting Financial Statements
# - Industry and Commerce

## December 2002

| Question Paper: | |
|---|---|
| Time allowed | 3 hours |
| All FOUR questions are compulsory and MUST be answered. | |

# Level C
# Paper 1

DO NOT OPEN THIS PAPER UNTIL YOU ARE READY TO START UNDER EXAMINATION CONDITIONS

# Mock exam 2

**ALL FOUR questions are compulsory and MUST be attempted.**

1     L Thacker is a sole trader. She asks you to help her prepare the final accounts for her business for the year ended 31 October 20X2. She provides you with the following information for the financial year to 31 October 20X2.

(a) Cash drawings were £30,000.

(b) Payments to suppliers were £115,000.

(c) there was £18,000 owing to suppliers as at 31 October 20X2.

(d) Receipts from customers were £220,000.

(e) Trade debtors at 31 October 20X2 were £65,000.

(f) During the year bad debts of £10,000 were written off and settlement discounts given to customers were £9,000.

(g) Stock at 31 October 20X2 was £34,000.

(h) Rent of £3,000 and insurance of £1,000 were paid in advance at 31 October 20X2.

(i) A £2,000 electricity bill was unpaid at 31 October 20X2.

(j) Depreciation on equipment is provided at 20% of its written down value.

(k) Depreciation on vehicles is provided at 25% on their original cost.

(l) Carriage inwards on goods purchased by the business was £1,000 and was paid for in full.

(m) Total payments made for the following costs were:

|  | £'000 |
|---|---|
| Wages | 24 |
| Motor vehicle expenses | 8 |
| Insurance | 9 |
| Electricity | 7 |
| Telephone | 4 |
| Rates | 5 |
| Rent | 16 |
|  | 73 |

You are able to establish that at 1 November 20X1 the business had the following balances.

|  | £'000 |
|---|---|
| Cash at bank | 5 |
| Stock | 12 |
| Capital | 114 |
| Trade creditors | 40 |
| Trade debtors | 60 |
| Prepayments |  |
|    Rent | 10 |
|    Insurance | 8 |
| Accruals |  |
|    Telephone | 1 |
|    Electricity | 2 |
| Vehicles at cost | 20 |
| Equipment at cost | 75 |
| Provisions for depreciation |  |
|    Vehicles | 8 |
|    Equipment | 25 |

## Mock exam 2

**Required:**

(a) Prepare the following statements for L Thacker:

    (i) The trading and profit and loss account for the year ended 31 October 20X2

        (21 marks)

    (ii) The balance sheet as at 31 October 20X2     (13 marks)

    (You are advised to show any necessary supporting workings.)

(b) State six reasons why sole traders should maintain good accounting records     (6 marks)

**(40 marks)**

2    You are presented with the balance sheet of Sargant plc for the year ended 31 October 20X2, together with comparative figures for the previous year.

SARGANT PLC
BALANCE SHEET AS AT 31 OCTOBER

|  | 20X2 £'000 | 20X2 £'000 | 20X1 £'000 | 20X1 £'000 |
|---|---|---|---|---|
| *Fixed assets* | | | | |
| Tangible assets | | 2,900 | | 2,000 |
| Less depreciation | | 700 | | 470 |
| | | 2,200 | | 1,530 |
| *Current assets* | | | | |
| Stock | 1,000 | | 800 | |
| Trade debtors | 550 | | 440 | |
| Bank | 100 | | - | |
| | 1,650 | | 1,240 | |
| *Current liabilities* | | | | |
| Trade creditors | 400 | | 360 | |
| Taxation | 245 | | 200 | |
| Proposed dividend | 200 | | 120 | |
| Bank overdraft | 0 | | 30 | |
| | 845 | | 710 | |
| Net current assets | | 805 | | 530 |
| | | 3,005 | | 2,060 |
| Long-term loans | | 350 | | 100 |
| | | 2,655 | | 1,960 |
| *Capital and reserves* | | | | |
| Ordinary share capital | | 2,000 | | 1,500 |
| Share premium | | 250 | | - |
| Profit and loss account | | 405 | | 460 |
| | | 2,655 | | 1,960 |

*Additional information*

(a) Land which cost £130,000, and which was not depreciated, was sold for a profit of £55,000 during the year ended 31 October 20X2.

(b) Depreciation charged for the year ended 31 October 20X2 was £230,000.

(c) Interest paid was £33,000 during the year ended 31 October 20X2.

(d) There was no over or under provision of corporation tax in 20X1.

(e) There was no interim dividend paid during 20X2.

*Mock exam 2*

**Required:**

(a) Calculate the operating profit of Sargant plc for the year ended 31 October 20X2. (3 marks)

(b) Prepare a cash flow statement for Sargant plc for the year ended 31 October 20X2. Identify the accounting standard you have applied and show any additional notes and reconciliations required by that standard. (21 marks)

(c) State four advantages of cash flow accounting (6 marks)

**(30 marks)**

3    Spice Ltd's capital consists of 2,000,000 ordinary shares of £1 each. On 1 November 20X1 Sugar plc acquired 80% of the issued ordinary share capital of Spice Ltd for £2,100,000. At that time, the retained profits of Spice Ltd were £125,000. The summarised profit and loss accounts of the two companies for the year ended 31 October 20X2 are as follows.

|  | Sugar plc £'000 | Spice Ltd £'000 |
|---|---|---|
| Turnover | 2,800 | 1,000 |
| Cost of sales | 1,650 | 550 |
| Gross profit | 1,150 | 450 |
| Distribution costs | 500 | 190 |
| Administrative expenses | 300 | 120 |
| Operating profit | 350 | 140 |
| Dividend from Spice Ltd | 40 | - |
| Profit on ordinary activities before taxation | 390 | 140 |
| Tax on profit on ordinary activities | 175 | 35 |
| Profit on ordinary activities after taxation | 215 | 105 |
| Proposed ordinary dividends | 100 | 50 |
| Retained profit for the year | 115 | 55 |
| Retained profit brought forward | 275 | 150 |
| Retained profit carried forward | 390 | 205 |

The following information is also available.

(a) Goodwill is amortised over five years.

(b) Sugar plc sold goods costing £85,000 to Spice Ltd for £165,000 during the year ended 31 October 20X2. At 31 October 20X2, 40% of these goods remained in Spice Ltd's stocks.

**Required:**

Prepare the consolidated profit and loss account for Sugar plc for the year ended 31 October 20X2. Your consolidated profit and loss account should include the group's retained profit brought forward and carried forward. Disclosure notes are not required.

**(15 marks)**

## Mock exam 2

4   Bond Ltd and Fraser Ltd are companies operating in a similar market. Your manager has asked you to help her review the performance of both companies from their financial statements which are summarised below.

PROFIT AND LOSS ACCOUNTS
FOR THE YEAR ENDED 31 OCTOBER 20X2

|  | Bond Limited £'000 | Fraser Limited £'000 |
|---|---|---|
| Sales | 23,800 | 24,000 |
| Cost of sales | 17,850 | 16,800 |
| Gross profit | 5,950 | 7,200 |
| Expenses | 2,500 | 4,800 |
| Profit before tax | 3,450 | 2,400 |
| Tax on profit | 900 | 600 |
| Profit after tax | 2,550 | 1,800 |
| Dividends | 1,000 | 900 |
| Retained profit | 1,550 | 900 |

BALANCE SHEETS
AS AT 31 OCTOBER 20X2

|  | Bond Limited £'000 | Bond Limited £'000 | Fraser Limited £'000 | Fraser Limited £'000 |
|---|---|---|---|---|
| Fixed assets |  | 15,000 |  | 24,000 |
| Current assets |  |  |  |  |
| Stock | 500 |  | 1,200 |  |
| Debtors | 2,000 |  | 600 |  |
| Cash | 100 |  | - |  |
|  | 2,600 |  | 1,800 |  |
| Current liabilities |  |  |  |  |
| Creditors | 775 |  | 150 |  |
| Overdraft | - |  | 55 |  |
| Tax | 900 |  | 600 |  |
|  | 1,675 |  | 805 |  |
| Net current assets |  | 925 |  | 995 |
|  |  | 15,925 |  | 24,995 |
| Debentures |  | 300 |  | 1,000 |
|  |  | 15,625 |  | 23,995 |
| Capital and reserves |  |  |  |  |
| £1 ordinary shares |  | 12,000 |  | 20,000 |
| Reserves |  | 3,625 |  | 3,995 |
|  |  | 15,625 |  | 23,995 |

Required:

(a)   Calculate four profitability ratios and two liquidity ratios for Bond Ltd and Fraser Ltd. Show all workings (9 marks)

(b)   Comment briefly on the performance of the two companies as indicated by the ratios you have calculated in Part (a). (6 marks)

**(15 marks)**

# ANSWERS TO MOCK EXAM 2

DO NOT TURN THIS PAGE UNTIL YOU
HAVE COMPLETED MOCK EXAM 2

**Mock exam 2: answers**

**1 (a) (i)** L THACKER
TRADING, PROFIT AND LOSS ACCOUNT
FOR THE YEAR ENDED 31 OCTOBER 20X2

|  | £'000 | £'000 |  |
|---|---|---|---|
| Sales (W2) |  | 244 | 3 marks |
| Cost of goods sold |  |  |  |
|     Opening stock | 12 |  | 1 mark |
|     Purchases (W3) | 93 |  | 2 marks |
|     Carriage inwards | 1 |  | 0.5 marks |
|  | 106 |  |  |
|     Closing stock | 34 |  |  |
|  |  | 72 | 0.5 marks |
| Gross profit |  | 172 | 0.5 marks |
| Expenses |  |  |  |
|     Wages | 24 |  | 0.5 marks |
|     Depreciation (W4) | 15 |  | 2 marks |
|     Insurance (W5) | 16 |  | 2 marks |
|     Telephone (W6) | 3 |  | 2 marks |
|     Electricity (W7) | 7 |  | 2 marks |
|     Rent (W8) | 23 |  | 2 marks |
|     Rates | 5 |  | 0.5 marks |
|     Bad debts | 10 |  | 0.5 marks |
|     Discounts allowed | 9 |  | 0.5 marks |
|     Motor vehicle expenses | 8 |  | 0.5 marks |
|  |  | 120 | 0.5 marks |
| Net profit |  | 52 |  |

Total marks = 21

**(ii)** L THACKER
BALANCE SHEET AS AT 31 OCTOBER 20X2

|  | Cost £'000 | Accumulated depreciation £'000 | NBV £'000 |  |
|---|---|---|---|---|
| *Fixed assets* |  |  |  |  |
| Equipment (W4) | 75 | 35 | 40 | 1 mark |
| Vehicles (W4) | 20 | 13 | 7 | 1 mark |
|  | 95 | 48 | 47 |  |
| *Current assets* |  |  |  |  |
| Stock | 34 |  |  | 0.5 marks |
| Debtors | 65 |  |  | 0.5 marks |
| Prepayments (3,000 + 1,000) | 4 |  |  | 1 mark |
| Bank (W1) | 6 |  |  | 2 marks |
|  | 109 |  |  |  |
| *Current liabilities* |  |  |  |  |
| Creditors | 18 |  |  | 0.5 marks |
| Accruals (electricity) | 2 |  |  | 1 mark |
|  | 20 |  |  |  |
| Net current assets |  |  | 89 | 0.5 marks |
|  |  |  | 136 |  |
| *Proprietor's capital* |  |  |  |  |
| As at 1 November 20X1 |  |  | 114 |  |
| Profit for the year |  |  | 52 | 4 marks |
| Drawings |  |  | (30) |  |
|  |  |  | 136 |  |

Total marks = 13

## Mock exam 2: answers

*Workings*

1 *Bank account*

### BANK

| | £'000 | | £'000 |
|---|---|---|---|
| Balance b/fwd | 5 | Drawings | 30 |
| Debtors control | 220 | Creditors control | 115 |
| | | Carriage inwards | 1 |
| | | Wages | 24 |
| | | Motor vehicle expenses | 8 |
| | | Insurance | 9 |
| | | Electricity | 7 |
| | | Telephone | 4 |
| | | Rates | 5 |
| | | Rent | 16 |
| | | Balance c/fwd | 6 |
| | 225 | | 225 |

2 *Sales*

### DEBTORS CONTROL

| | £'000 | | £'000 |
|---|---|---|---|
| Balance b/fwd | 60 | Bank | 220 |
| Credit sales | 244 | Discounts allowed | 9 |
| | | Bad debts written off | 10 |
| | | Balance c/fwd | 65 |
| | 304 | | 304 |

3 *Purchases*

### CREDITORS CONTROL

| | £'000 | | £'000 |
|---|---|---|---|
| Bank | 115 | Balance b/fwd | 40 |
| Balance c/fwd | 18 | Purchases (bal fig) | 93 |
| | 133 | | 133 |

4 *Fixed assets and depreciation*

| | Vehicles £'000 | Equipment £'000 | Total £'000 |
|---|---|---|---|
| Cost | 20 | 75 | 95 |
| Accumulated depreciation | | | |
|   At 1.11.X1 | 8 | 25 | 33 |
|   Charge for year* | 5 | 10 | 15 |
|   At 31.10.X2 | 13 | 35 | 48 |
| NBV at 31.10.X2 | 7 | 40 | 47 |

* Charge for year:

| | £'000 |
|---|---|
| Vehicles: £20,000 × 25% = | 5 |
| Equipment: £(75,000 − £25,000) × 20% = | 10 |
| | 15 |

5 *Insurance*

### INSURANCE

| | £'000 | | £'000 |
|---|---|---|---|
| Balance b/fwd | 8 | Prepayment c/fwd | 1 |
| Bank | 9 | Profit & loss a/c (bal fig) | 16 |
| | 17 | | 17 |

## Mock exam 2: answers

**6** *Telephone*

### TELEPHONE

| | £'000 | | £'000 |
|---|---|---|---|
| Bank | 4 | Balance b/fwd | 1 |
| | | Profit & loss a/c | 3 |
| | 4 | | 4 |

**7** *Electricity*

### ELECTRICITY

| | £'000 | | £'000 |
|---|---|---|---|
| Bank | 7 | Balance b/fwd | 2 |
| Balance c/fwd | 2 | Profit & loss a/c | 7 |
| | 9 | | 9 |

**8** *Rent*

### RENT

| | £'000 | | £'000 |
|---|---|---|---|
| Balance b/fwd | 10 | Prepayment c/fwd | 3 |
| Bank | 16 | Profit & loss a/c | 23 |
| | 26 | | 26 |

(b) **Reasons why sole traders should maintain good accounting records**

(i) Proper accounting records **enable management to make decisions**. They cannot do this if they do not know how the business is doing.

(ii) With proper records, management can **budget** and plan ahead.

(iii) The **bank** will be interested in the **overall liquidity position**, ie the working capital, as well as just the bank balance or overdraft.

(iv) The Inland Revenue requires records to be kept for **tax** purposes.

(v) **Potential suppliers** need to know how easily they can get paid.

(vi) The owner may wish to **sell up**. A buyer is more likely to be interested in a business when he or she can see how it is doing.

(vii) Proper accounting records **save time** in the long run. For example, preparing accounts is a lot easier: you do not have to work out what amounts are as a balancing figure, as you so often need to where the records are incomplete.

*1 mark for each valid point*

*Total marks = 6*

**2** (a) **Calculation of operating profit**

### PROFIT AND LOSS ACCOUNT

| | £'000 | | £'000 | |
|---|---|---|---|---|
| Taxation* | 245 | Balance at 1 November 20X1 | 460 | 1 mark |
| Dividends* | 200 | Operating profit (bal fig) | 423 | 1 mark |
| Interest | 33 | | | 0.5 mark |
| Balance at 31 October 20X2 | 405 | | | 0.5 mark |
| | 883 | | 883 | |

*Because there is no over- or under- provision of corporation tax, the tax charge may be taken as the year end liability. Similarly there is no interim dividend, so the dividend in the profit and loss account is the proposed dividend.

*Total marks = 3*

## Mock exam 2: answers

Headings: 1 mark

(b) SARGANT PLC
CASH FLOW STATEMENT
FOR THE YEAR ENDED 31 OCTOBER 20X2

| | | £'000 |
|---|---|---:|
| | RECONCILIATION OF OPERATING PROFIT TO NET CASH INFLOW FROM OPERATING ACTIVITIES | |
| 1 mark | Operating profit | 423 |
| 1 mark | Depreciation | 230 |
| 1 mark | Profit on disposal | (55) |
| 1 mark | Increase in stock (1,000 – 800) | (200) |
| 1 mark | Increase in debtors (550 – 440) | (110) |
| 1 mark | Increase in creditors (400 – 360) | 40 |
| | Net cash inflow from operating activities | 328 |

CASH FLOW STATEMENT

| | | £'000 | £'000 |
|---|---|---:|---:|
| 1 mark | Net cash inflow from operating activities | | 328 |
| | *Returns on investments and servicing of finance* | | |
| 1 mark | Interest paid | | (33) |
| | *Taxation* | | |
| 1 mark | Corporation tax paid | | (200) |
| | *Capital expenditure* | | |
| 2 marks | Payment to acquire fixed assets (W) | (1,030) | |
| 1 mark | Proceeds from sale of fixed assets (W) | 185 | |
| | | | (845) |
| 1 mark | *Equity dividends paid* | | (120) |
| | *Financing* | | |
| 0.5 marks | Issue of share capital (2,000 – 1,500) | 500 | |
| 0.5 marks | Share premium (250 – nil) | 250 | |
| 1 mark | Long-term loans (350 – 100) | 250 | |
| | | | 1,000 |
| 1 mark | Increase in cash | | 130 |

*Notes to the cash flow statement*

1 Reconciliation of net cash flow to movement in net debt

| | | £'000 |
|---|---|---:|
| 0.5 marks | Net cash inflow for the period | 130 |
| 0.5 marks | Increase in long-term loans | (250) |
| 0.5 marks | Change in net debt | (120) |
| 0.5 marks | Net debt at 31 October 20X1 | (130) |
| | Net debt at 31 October 20X2 | (250) |

2 Analysis of changes in net debt

| | | At 31 October 20X1 £'000 | Cash flows £'000 | At 31 October 20X2 £'000 |
|---|---|---:|---:|---:|
| 1 mark | Cash at bank (overdraft) | (30) | 130 | 100 |
| 1 mark | Debt due after 1 year | (100) | (250) | (350) |
| | | (130) | (120) | (250) |

Total marks = 21

*Working: fixed assets*

FIXED ASSETS

| | £'000 | | £'000 |
|---|---:|---|---:|
| Balance b/fwd | 1,530 | Disposals | 130 |
| Additions (bal fig) | 1,030 | Depreciation | 230 |
| | | Balance c/fwd | 2,200 |
| | 2,560 | | 2,560 |

Disposal proceeds:

|  | £'000 |
|---|---|
| Cost | 130 |
| Profit | 55 |
| ∴ Proceeds | 185 |

(c) While the profit and loss account and balance sheet provide useful information to outside users, it could be argued that the profit figure in the accounts does not always give a meaningful picture of the company's operations. A company's performance and prospects depend not so much on the 'profits' earned in the period, but, more realistically on **liquidity** or cash flows.

Cash flow statements have the **following advantages**.

(i) They are **easier to understand** than profit statements.

(ii) They draw attention to **cash flow** which is **crucial to a business's survival**.

(iii) **Creditors** are more interested in a company's **ability to pay** the debt than in profitability.

(iv) **Profit** depends on **accounting conventions** and concepts and is thus easy to manipulate.

(v) **Management decision making** is based on future cash flows.

(vi) Cash flow is easier to audit than profit.

1.5 marks per relevant point

Total marks = 6

## 3 SUGAR PLC
### CONSOLIDATED PROFIT AND LOSS ACCOUNT
### FOR THE YEAR ENDED 31 OCTOBER 20X2

|  | £'000 |  |
|---|---|---|
| Turnover (W3) | 3,635 | 1.5 marks |
| Cost of sales (bal fig) | 2,067 | 2.5 marks |
| Gross profit (W4) | 1,568 |  |
| Distribution costs | 690 | 0.5 marks |
| Administrative expenses | 420 | 0.5 marks |
| Amortisation of goodwill (W1) | 80 | 3 marks |
| Profit on ordinary activities before taxation | 378 |  |
| Tax on profit on ordinary activities | 210 | 0.5 marks |
| Profit on ordinary activities after taxation | 168 |  |
| Minority interests (105 × 20%) | (21) | 2 marks |
| Group profit for the year | 147 | 0.5 marks |
| Proposed dividends | (100) | 1 mark |
| Retained profit for the year | 47 | 0.5 marks |
| Retained profits brought forward (W2) | 215 | 2.5 marks |
| Retained profits carried forward | 262 |  |

Total marks = 15

*Workings*

1 *Goodwill*

|  | £'000 | £'000 |
|---|---|---|
| Cost of investment |  | 2,100 |
| Share of net assets acquired |  |  |
|   Share capital | 2,000 |  |
|   Profit and loss account | 125 |  |
|  | 2,125 |  |
| Group share: 80% |  | 1,700 |
| Goodwill |  | 400 |

Annual charge to profit and loss account $\dfrac{£400,000}{5} = £80,000$

*Mock exam 2: answers*

2    Retained profits brought forward

|  | Sugar £'000 | Spice £'000 |
|---|---|---|
| Per question | 275 | 150 |
| Pre acquisition |  | 125 |
|  |  | 25 |
| Share of Spice: 25 × 80% | 20 |  |
| Goodwill amortised at 31 October 20X1 (1 year - see (W1)) | (80) |  |
|  | 215 |  |

3    Turnover

|  | £'000 |
|---|---|
| Sugar | 2,800 |
| Spice | 1,000 |
|  | 3,800 |
| Less intercompany | 165 |
|  | 3,635 |

4    Gross profit

|  | £'000 |
|---|---|
| Sugar | 1,150 |
| Spice | 450 |
| Less provision for unrealised profit: (165,000 – 85,000) × 40% | (32) |
|  | 1,568 |

*Note.* Because the intercompany sale was made by the parent company, the whole of the unrealised profit must be eliminated.

4    (a)

| Ratio | Formulae | Bond Limited | Fraser Limited |
|---|---|---|---|
| *Profitability ratios* |  |  |  |
| Gross profit percentage | $\dfrac{\text{Gross profit}}{\text{Sales}} \times 100$ | $\dfrac{5,950}{23,800} \times 100 = 25\%$ | $\dfrac{7,200}{24,000} \times 100 = 30\%$ |
| Net profit percentage | $\dfrac{\text{Net profit}}{\text{Sales}} \times 100$ | $\dfrac{3,450}{23.800} \times 100 = 14\%$ | $\dfrac{2,400}{24,000} \times 100 = 10\%$ |
| Earnings per share | $\dfrac{\text{Net profit after tax}}{\text{No of ordinary shares}}$ | $\dfrac{2,500}{12,000} = 21\text{p}$ | $\dfrac{1,800}{20,000} = 9\text{p}$ |
| Return on capital employed | $\dfrac{\text{Net profit}}{\text{Capital employed}}$ | $\dfrac{3,450}{15,625} \times 100 = 22\%$ | $\dfrac{2,400}{23,995} \times 100 = 10\%$ |
| *Liquidity ratios* |  |  |  |
| Current ratio | $\dfrac{\text{Current assets}}{\text{Current liabilities}} :1$ | $\dfrac{2,600}{1,675} :1 = 1.6:1$ | $\dfrac{1,800}{805} :1 = 2.2:1$ |
| Acid test ratio | $\dfrac{\text{Current assets – stock}}{\text{Current liabilities}} :1$ | $\dfrac{2,100}{1,675} :1 = 1.3:1$ | $\dfrac{600}{805} :1 = 0.7:1$ |

*0.5 marks for each formula/ratio*

*Total marks = 9*

(b) **Profitability ratios**

*Gross profit percentage*

Fraser Ltd has a higher gross profit percentage than Bond Ltd. The companies both operate in a similar market and have similar turnovers, so it is unclear why there is a difference. Possibly Fraser is better at keeping supplier costs down.

*Net profit percentage*

**Bond does better** than Fraser on net profit percentage, reversing the gross profit percentage finding. The company is obviously better at **controlling its expenses**, which are around half those of Fraser.

*Earnings per share*

**Bond Ltd's** EPS figure is twice that of Fraser Ltd, suggesting on the face of it that it is a **better investment**. The difference is mainly due to the number of shares by which the earnings figure is being divided. However, Bond Ltd's post tax profit is also higher than that of Fraser Ltd. We do not know the market value of the shares, which would be an important factor when deciding to invest.

*Return on capital employed*

Bond Ltd's return on capital employed is double that of Fraser Ltd. **Fraser** Ltd has more money invested, in both shares and loans, but is **not making as effective use of the capital employed.**

**Liquidity ratios**

*Current ratio*

Both companies have sufficient assets to cover their liabilities. The **current ratio of Bond Ltd is not as high as that of Fraser Ltd**. However, it is important to look at the individual components of working capital.

Bond Ltd's cash position (£100,000) is more favourable than Fraser Ltd's (£55,000 overdraft).

*Acid test ratio*

Much of **Fraser Ltd's working capital is tied up in stock**. When this is taken out to give the acid test ratio, Bond Ltd's is better. Fraser Ltd may be storing up liquidity or cash flow problems.

**Conclusion**

Overall, **Bond Ltd looks to be the better performer**, both in terms of liquidity and profitability. It would be helpful to have more background information about the market in which the companies operate, for example industry average ratios, and also to see the trend compared with previous years.

1 mark per relevant comment

**Total marks = 6**

# Topic index

# Topic index

This index is provided as a ready reference aid to your revision.

**A**ccounting Standards Board, 123
Accumulated fund, 29
Acid test ratio, 181, 185
Asset turnover, 185

**B**ad debt, 87
Balance sheet, 7, 41, 97, 103
Bank account, 41
Bonus share issues, 103

**C**apital gearing ratio, 175
Capital, 7
Cash flow statement, 156, 157, 163
Companies Act 1985, 115
Company accounts, 81ff
Conceptual framework, 111, 115
Consolidated balance sheet, 191
Consolidated financial statements, 187
Consolidated profit and loss account, 189
Consolidated reserves, 211, 215
Corporation tax, 85
Creditors, 83
Current assets, 7
Current cost accounting, 24
Current liabilities, 7
Current purchasing power, 24
Current ratio, 85, 188

**D**ebenture loan, 83
Debentures, 12
Debtors payment period, 167
Deferred income, 35
Depreciation, 81
Direct method, 145
Discount, 39
Dissolution of a partnership, 77
Dividend cover, 175
Drawings, 7, 50

**E**arnings per share, 175
EU Directives, 123
Excluded, 219
Expenses to sales, 185

**F**inancial Reporting Standards, 123
Fixed assets, 7
FRS 1 (revised) Cash flow statements, 139
FRS 2 Accounting for subsidiary undertakings, 191
FRS 7 Fair values in acquisition accounting, 191
FRS 9 Associates and joint ventures, 188

FRS 10 Goodwill and intangible assets, 130
FRS 12 Provisions, contingent liabilities and contingent assets, 129
FRS 15 Tangible fixed assests, 115

**G**arner v Murray, 67
Gearing ratios, 173, 177, 181
Goodwill, 133
Gross profit margin, 181
Gross profit percentage, 181
Group accounts, 189

**H**istorical cost basis, 23

**I**ncome and expenditure account, 29
Intangible fixed asset, 137
Inter company sale, 191
Intercompany trading, 205
Intercompany transfers of fixed assets, 205
Interest cover, 167
Investors' ratios, 139, 140

**L**edger accounts, 77
Liability, 35
Life membership fees, 27
Life membership fund, 29
Life subscriptions, 35
Limited liability, 11
Liquidity ratios, 181
Liquidity, 181
Listing Rules, 115

**M**inority interest, 195

**N**et current assets, 7

**O**bjectives of financial statements, 19
Opening balance sheet, 57
Ordinary shares, 87

**P**arent company, 195
Partnership agreement, 69
Partnership, 75
Preference shares, 87
Profit and loss account, 7, 41
Profitability ratios, 181
Profitability, 181
Provision for doubtful debts, 81, 97
Purchases, 7

## Topic index

**Q**ualitative characteristics of financial statements, 19
Quick/acid test ratio, 171

**R**atios, 181
Realisation account, 79
Realisation expenses, 77
Receipts and payments account, 53
Regulatory framework, 111
Return on capital employed, 181, 185
Return on shareholders' capital, 173
Revaluation account, 69

**S**ales, 7
Share capital, 11, 83
Share premium, 83
Sole trader, 67
Statement of Principles, 19, 111, 112
Statements of Standard Accounting Practice, 123
Stock Exchange, 115
Stock turnover, 181
Subscriptions received in advance, 35
Subsidiary, 189
Suspense account, 81

**T**rading account, 53
Trading, profit and loss account, 106
True and fair view, 111

**U**nrealised profit, 24, 215

**W**orking capital, 83, 169

See overleaf for information on other
BPP products and how to order

# CAT Order

To BPP Professional Education, Aldine Place, London W12 8AW
Tel: 020 8740 2211  Fax: 020 8740 1184
email: publishing@bpp.com  online: www.bpp.com

**Mr/Mrs/Ms (Full name)**

**Daytime delivery address**

Postcode

**Daytime Tel**  Email  Date of exam (month/year)

## POSTAGE & PACKING

**Texts**

| | Mail Order | | On-line |
|---|---|---|---|
| | First | Each extra | per item |
| UK | £5.00 | £2.00 | £2.00 |  £ ___
| Europe* | £6.00 | £4.00 | £4.00 | £ ___
| Rest of world | £20.00 | £10.00 | £10.00 | £ ___

**Kits**

| | Mail Order | | On-line |
|---|---|---|---|
| | First | Each extra | per item |
| UK | £2.00 | £1.00 | £1.00 | £ ___
| Europe* | £3.00 | £2.00 | £2.00 | £ ___
| Rest of world | £8.00 | £8.00 | £8.00 | £ ___

**CDs**

| | Mail Order | | On-line |
|---|---|---|---|
| | First | Each extra | per item |
| UK | £2.00 | £1.00 | £1.00 | £ ___
| Europe* | £3.00 | £2.00 | £2.00 | £ ___
| Rest of world | £8.00 | £8.00 | £8.00 | £ ___

**Grand Total** (incl. Postage)  £ ___

I enclose a cheque for
(Cheques to *BPP Professional Education*)

Or charge to Visa/Mastercard/Switch

Card Number _____

Expiry date _____  Start Date _____

Issue Number (Switch Only) _____

Signature _____

| | | 6/02 Texts | 2/03 Kits | 2/03 i-Learn CD* | 2/03 i-Pass CD | Virtual Campus enrolment |
|---|---|---|---|---|---|---|
| **LEVEL A** | | | | | | |
| Paper A1 | Transaction Accounting | £16.95 ☐ | £8.95 ☐ | £29.95 ☐ | | £80 ☐ |
| Paper A2 | Office Practice and Procedure | £16.95 ☐ | | £29.95 ☐ | £19.95 ☐ | £80 ☐ |
| **LEVEL B** | | | | | | |
| Paper B1 | Maintaining Financial Records and Accounts (UK) | £16.95 ☐ | £8.95 ☐ | £30.95 ☐ | £19.95 ☐ | £80 ☐ |
| Paper B2 | Cost Accounting Systems | £16.95 ☐ | £8.95 ☐ | £30.95 ☐ | £19.95 ☐ | £80 ☐ |
| Paper B3 | Information Technology Processes | £16.95 ☐ | £8.95 ☐ | £30.95 ☐ | £19.95 ☐ | £80 ☐ |
| **LEVEL C** | | | | | | |
| Paper C1 | Drafting Financial Statements (Industry and Commerce) (UK) | £16.95 ☐ | £8.95 ☐ | £30.95 ☐ | £21.95 ☐ | £80 ☐ |
| Paper C2 | Information for Management | £16.95 ☐ | £8.95 ☐ | £30.95 ☐ | £21.95 ☐ | £80 ☐ |
| Paper C3 | Auditing Practice and Procedure (UK) | £16.95 ☐ | £8.95 ☐ | £30.95 ☐ | £21.95 ☐ | £80 ☐ |
| Paper C4 | Preparing Taxation Computations and Returns FA2002 (10/02 Text, 2/03 Kit) | £16.95 ☐ | £8.95 ☐ | | | |
| Paper C5 | Managing Finances | £16.95 ☐ | £8.95 ☐ | £30.95 ☐ | £21.95 ☐ | £80 ☐ |
| Paper C6 | Managing People | £16.95 ☐ | £8.95 ☐ | £30.95 ☐ | £21.95 ☐ | £80 ☐ |
| **INTERNATIONAL STANDARDS** | | | | | | |
| Paper B1 | Maintaining Financial Records and Accounts | £16.95 ☐ | £8.95 ☐ | | | |
| Paper C1 | Drafting Financial Statements (Industry and Commerce) | £16.95 ☐ | £8.95 ☐ | | | |
| Paper C3 | Auditing Practice and Procedure | £16.95 ☐ | £8.95 ☐ | | | |

*Now incorporates i-Learn Workbook

SUBTOTAL £ ___

Register via our website, www.bpp.com/virtualcampus/cat and pay on-line

We aim to deliver to all UK addresses inside 5 working days; a signature will be required. Orders to all EU addresses should be delivered within 6 working days. All other orders to overseas addresses should be delivered within 8 working days.  * Europe includes the Republic of Ireland and the Channel Islands.

*CAT – C1 Drafting Financial Statements (02/03)*

# REVIEW FORM & FREE PRIZE DRAW

All original review forms from the entire BPP range, completed with genuine comments, will be entered into one of two draws on 31 July 2003 and 31 January 2004. The names on the first four forms picked out on each occasion will be sent a cheque for £50.

Name: _____   Address: _____

Date: _____

**How have you used this Practice & Revision Kit?**
*(Tick one box only)*
☐ Home study (book only)
☐ On a course: college _____
☐ With 'correspondence' package
☐ Other _____

**Why did you decide to purchase this Practice & Revision Kit?** *(Tick one box only)*
☐ Have used complementary Interactive Text
☐ Have used BPP Texts in the past
☐ Recommendation by friend/colleague
☐ Recommendation by a lecturer at college
☐ Saw advertising in journals
☐ Saw website
☐ Other _____

**During the past six months do you recall seeing/receiving any of the following?**
*(Tick as many boxes as are relevant)*
☐ Our advertisement in *ACCA Student Accountant*
☐ Other advertisement _____
☐ Our brochure with a letter through the post

**Which (if any) aspects of our advertising do you find useful?**
*(Tick as many boxes as are relevant)*
☐ Prices and publication dates of new editions
☐ Information on Practice & Revision Kit content
☐ Facility to order books off-the-page
☐ None of the above

Have you used the companion Interactive Text for this subject?   ☐ Yes   ☐ No

**Your ratings, comments and suggestions would be appreciated on the following areas**

|  | Very useful | Useful | Not useful |
|---|---|---|---|
| Introductory section (How to use this Practice & Revision Kit) | ☐ | ☐ | ☐ |
| 'Do You Know' checklists | ☐ | ☐ | ☐ |
| 'Did You Know' checklists | ☐ | ☐ | ☐ |
| Possible pitfalls | ☐ | ☐ | ☐ |
| Questions with help | ☐ | ☐ | ☐ |
| Helping hands | ☐ | ☐ | ☐ |
| Content of answers | ☐ | ☐ | ☐ |
| Mock exams | ☐ | ☐ | ☐ |
| Structure & presentation | ☐ | ☐ | ☐ |
| Icons | ☐ | ☐ | ☐ |

|  | Excellent | Good | Adequate | Poor |
|---|---|---|---|---|
| Overall opinion of this Kit | ☐ | ☐ | ☐ | ☐ |

Do you intend to continue using BPP Interactive Texts/Kits?   ☐ Yes   ☐ No

Please note any further comments and suggestions/errors on the reverse of this page. The BPP author of this edition can be emailed at katyhibbert@bpp.com

Please return to: Lynn Watkins, BPP Professional Education, FREEPOST, London, W12 8BR

## CAT – C1 Drafting Financial Statements (02/03)

### REVIEW FORM & FREE PRIZE DRAW (continued)
**Please note any further comments and suggestions/errors below**

**FREE PRIZE DRAW RULES**

1. Closing date for 31 July 2003 draw is 30 June 2003. Closing date for 31 January 2004 draw is 31 December 2003.
2. Restricted to entries with UK and Eire addresses only. BPP employees, their families and business associates are excluded.
3. No purchase necessary. Entry forms are available upon request from BPP Professional Education. No more than one entry per title, per person. Draw restricted to persons aged 16 and over.
4. Winners will be notified by post and receive their cheques not later than 6 weeks after the relevant draw date.
5. The decision of the promoter in all matters is final and binding. No correspondence will be entered into.